FOOTBALL
FACTS & TRIVIA

FOOTBALL
FACTS & TRIVIA

THOUSANDS OF FASCINATING FACTS
FOR EVERY FOOTBALL FAN

COMPILED BY CHRIS SWANN

SIENA

This edition published and distributed by Siena

This edition published 1999
Siena is an imprint of Parragon

Parragon
Queen Street House
4-5 Queen Street
Bath BA1 1HE

Printed and bound in the UK

© Dilemma Puzzles

ISBN 0 75252 974 9

CONTENTS

English League Sides   7
Scottish League Clubs   187
The International Teams   201
The Great Players   251
Club Cup Results   467

ENGLISH

LEAGUE

SIDES

Arsenal...

Were founded in 1886 at the government's Royal Arsenal arms factory at Woolwich Arsenal, south London.

Were originally called Dial Square, later becoming Royal Arsenal, then Woolwich Reds and finally Woolwich Arsenal.

Used a milk cart on which to wheel off their injured players for treatment at the side of the pitch during the very early days.

Used to wear an all red strip until 1933 as their very first kit had been donated by Nottingham.

Did the League and Cup 'double' in 1998 under former French coach, Arsene Wenger. He is the first foreign manager ever to win the English League Championship.

Became, in 1935, the first London Club to win the English League title.

Recorded only one home win during the season 1912-13, the year of their relegation. It is still an all-time record. ' The Gunners' won only three matches in total that season.

Most successful manager is George Graham having won six trophies in eight years.

Is haunted by one of the club's most famous former managers, Frank Chapman. His ghost is said to walk the corridors of Highbury Stadium.

Have a very unusual good luck mascot, a workman's horse, which died in an accident during the building of the Highbury Stadium, buried under what is now the North Bank stand.

Have occupied the top English League division every year since 1919, the longest unbroken run of any top flight English football team.

Arsenal...

Famous fans include the chat show host and sometime barrister, Clive James and Fever Pitch author, Nicky Hornby.

Unofficial historian is former _EastEnders'_ actor, Tom Watt, who played Lofty. He has penned a small volume about the club entitled 'the North Bank'.

Irish central defender, David O'Leary holds the record for the most appearances in an Arsenal shirt, 558 appearances between the years 1975-93.

Best win and worst defeat were, oddly enough, against the same club. Back in 1896 'The Gunners' were beaten 8-0 by Loughborough Town during a Division Two game; some four years later, in 1900, they blasted 12 goals past the shell-shocked Town goalkeeper, without reply.

Fullback and skipper, Kenny Sansom, has won more international caps than any other of his Arsenal team mates, 86 England appearances in all between 1979 and 1988.

Ian Wright was Arsenal's top scorer in every season he played for the club.

Aston Villa...

Can trace back its origins back to the cricket team attached to the Villa Cross Wesleyan Chapel in Aston, Birmingham. Having identified the need for an additional sport to occupy the winter months a football team was establish in 1873. Birmingham was not known as a footballing area and due to the lack of clubs the Villa Cross team was forced to play their first game against Aston Brook St Mary's Rugby team. The teams played rugby during the first half and soccer during the second.

Appointed a Scottish football fanatic named George Ramsey as captain in 1876.

The club played its first League game in 1888.

Was a founder member of the Football League in 1888.

First ground was Aston Park.

Moved to Perry Barr in 1876, then Villa Park in 1897.

Have spent the second highest number of seasons in the top flight, a total of 88 compared to Everton's 95.

Player Charlie Aitken scored 561 goals between 1961-1976.

Are nicknamed 'The Villans'.

Foreign import, Savo Milosevic joined Aston Villa in a club record transfer deal for £3.5 million in June 1995. Manager Brian Little had never seen Savo playing live, only on video.

Have won the League Championship an incredible seven times and the FA Cup seven times, as well.

Aston Villa...

Have scored more league goals than any other club in the history of the Football League, an amazing total of 6,549 goals.

Became only the second club, ever, to do the League and FA Cup 'double', in 1897.

Manager George Ramsay, is the most successful manager in the history of the FA Cup. He led 'The Villans' to six FA Cup Final wins.

Won a grand total of 12 major trophies under the self-same George Ramsay, a record second only to that of Liverpool's Bob Paisley.

George Ramsay also holds the record as the second-longest serving manager in the history of English Football. He managed Villa Park for a grand total of 42 years between 1884 and 1926.

Manager Ron Saunders used only 14 players when Villa won the League Championship in 1981.

Became, in 1982, only the fourth English team to win the European Cup.

Have had more sets of brothers on their books at the same time than any other British league club.

Was the first club to have won all three major English trophies when they beat Rotherham United 3-2, on aggregate, in the first ever League Cup in 1961.

Record score is 12-2 against Accrington Stanley, then in Division One, way back in 1892.

Aston Villa...

Have supplied more full England internationals than any other club, a total of 57.

Most capped player is former Republic of Ireland central defender, Paul McGrath with 45 appearances for his country.

Record signing was local boy Stan Collymore for £7 million from Liverpool in May 1997. However, he scored only six goals during his first season.

Received £5.5 million from Italian club, Bari, for England midfield dynamo David Platt in 1991.

Has the fourth highest capacity of any football ground in England, with room for 40,310 fans.

Famous Holte End has one of the highest capacities of any single stand in Europe, a total of 13,501 seats.

Most famous fan is punk violinist Nigel Kennedy.

Barnet...

Was founded in 1888, but disbanded in 1901. Alston Works FC rose from the ashes and became Barnet Alston FC in 1906. By 1912 the club had joined forces with The Avenue FC to become Barnet and Alston FC.

Underhill ground has the smallest capacity in the whole of the English League, accommodating a mere 3,924 fans.

First ground was at Queens Road. The club moved to Totteridge Lane in 1901, arriving at the Underhill Stadium in 1907.

Had no offices at their Underhill ground up until 1926. Prior to this date the club officials had to hold their committee meetings in the Red Lion pub on Barnet Hill.

Are nicknamed, 'The Bees' because of their amber and black strip.

Players escorted a streaker from the Underhill pitch during their club's 4-0 win over Torquay during the 1995-96 season.

Unbeaten 16 match run at home in the League was finally ended by Scarborough's first ever win at Underhill in October, 1996.

Manager, Barry Fry was found by police mowing the Underhill pitch by moonlight at 4.00am one Saturday morning. He explained that he had not been able to sleep because of the tension leading up to the afternoon match and decided to do something useful.

Barry Fry so loved the club that he once re-mortgaged his house to pay off its outstanding debts.

Barnet...

Lost 7-4 at home to Crewe in their first game of the season after having at long last won promotion to the Football League in 1991.

Included legendary England striker Jimmy Greaves in their line-up during the 1970s

Are one of only seven clubs who have never supplied a full international for any country.

Andy Clarke's transfer, £350,000, from Barnet (then a non-League club) to Wimbledon in 1991 is the record signing ever from the Vauxhall Conference to the Football League.

Are one of just four League clubs who have never finished top, or runners-up, in any Division.

Barnsley...

Were founded in 1887 by the Rev. TT Preedy, curate of Barnsley St Peter's. The club used the church name up until 1897. A year later the club turned professional and joined the Football League.

Are unusual in that the club has always played at their current Oakwell ground.

The club bought the Oakwell land as early as 1888. One condition of the sale was that the club could purchase the ground, "So long as you behave yourselves".

Oakwell ground had no changing rooms during the early years. Both teams changed at the nearby Dove Inn

Are nicknamed 'The Tykes'

Have spent more time in the old Division Two (now Division One) than any other club, a grand total of 65 years.

Were Division Three (North) champions in 1934, 1939, and 1955.

Were known as 'Battling Barnsley' because it took the club 12 games to reach the FA Cup final of 1912; their campaign included six 0-0 draws. They overcame Birmingham City at Bramall Lane, Sheffield, 3-1 in the Final. This was 'The Tykes' only FA Cup success.

First, and only, stay in the Premiership lasted for just one short season.

Won 1-0 at Oldham on the 13th January, 1996. It was 'The Tykes' first, ever, victory away against Oldham for 61 years.

Appointed Viv Anderson as the first black player/manager in the history of English football.

Birmingham City...

Were founded in 1875 by members of a cricket team attached to Trinity Church, Bordesley. Initially all their home games were played on waste ground in Arthur Street.

Played at Muntz Street, Small Heath from 1877 until 1906 when the club moved to their present-day St Andrew's ground.

Used to be called Small Heath Alliance, then just Small Heath.

Changed the club name from Small Heath to Birmingham in 1905. The addition of 'City' happened in 1945.

Are nicknamed 'The Blues'.

Main domestic honour is winning the League Cup in 1963.

One time manager, Barry Fry signed no fewer than 41 new players for the club.

Barry Fry also holds the domestic record when, during the 1995-96 season, he used the most number of players ever fielded by any club in a League season since the Second World War, an amazing 46.

Were the first English League club (in 1960), to reach a European final, the old Fairs Cup. 'The Blues' lost to Barcelona.

Were the first club to sell a player to another British club for £1million when they sold Trevor Francis to Nottingham Forest in February 1979.

Appointed the first female football club managing director in 1992, Karren Brady, then 25 years of age. She was instrumental in the return of old City favourite, and past

Birmingham City...

England international, Trevor Francis, to become manager of the club in 1996.

Received £1.2million from Leicester City for Steve Claridge in 1996.

Sacked their then, new manager Willie Bell a mere 16 days into the 1977 season.

Bought their first stand second-hand in 1897 from nearby neighbours Aston Villa.

St Andrew's ground is said to suffer from a curse placed upon it when the club evicted gypsies from the site during the latter years of the last century.

Manager Ron Saunders blamed the gypsies' curse for the on-going absence of silverware from the board room and ordered the bottom of the players' boots to be painted red in a desperate attempt to improve the club's luck.

Blackburn...

Were founded in 1875 when some old boys of various Public Schools organised a meeting at which the current club colours, blue and white, were decided upon.

Founder member, John Lewis became a founder of the Lancashire FA, the referee of two FA Cup Finals and a vice-president of both the FA and the Football League.

Was originally called Blackburn Grammar School Old Boys. They appeared in the FA Cup Final of 1882 losing to The Old Etonians.

Home ground is Ewood Park. However, during the 1875-76 season all the club's games were played away. They then acquired a pitch at the Oozehead Ground prior to moving on to Pleasington Cricket Ground in 1877. The following year found the aptly named 'Rovers' at Alexander Meadows. A move to Leamington Road in 1881 preceded the club's arrival at their present home, Ewood Park, in 1890,

Was the first club, ever, to win the FA Cup; way back in 1884.

Broke the English transfer receipt record when they sold Alan Shearer to Newcastle in 1996 for £15 million.

England international striker, Alan Shearer scored an amazing 122 goals in 138 games.

Have won the FA Cup on no less than six occasions.

Hold the record for the longest unbeaten run in the FA Cup's history; 24 matches while in the process of winning a hat trick of FA Cup Finals between December 1883 and November 1886.

Long-time servant, Derek Fazackerley has made the most appearances for 'The Rovers', playing in 596 games between 1970 and 1986.

Blackburn...

Most capped international is Bob Crompton who turned out for England on no fewer than 41 occasions between 1902 and 1914.

Took part, in 1891, in probably one of the strangest games, ever. Blackburn were playing their arch enemy, Burnley. After two mass punch-ups all the Rovers' players walked off the pitch in a mass protest; all except Rovers' goalkeeper, Herby Arthur. The referee abandoned the game after Herby refused to take a free kick for an offside infringement when he argued that he had no fellow team mate left on the pitch to whom he could pass the ball.

Chris Sutton became Britain's most expensive signing when he joined Blackburn from Norwich City in 1994 for £5 million. The strike partnership of Chris Sutton and goal ace Alan Shearer brought the Premier League title to Ewood Park by the end of that season.

Defeated Rossendale in the FA Cup, 11-0, way back in 1884; this is still Blackburn Rovers' biggest winning margin.

Blackpool...

Were founded in 1887 when some old boys from St John's School, who were playing the odd game of football, held a meeting at the Stanley Arms Hotel. Blackpool FC, based at Raikes Hall Gardens, won the Lancashire Junior Cup and the Fylde Cup during its first season.

Previous club name was Blackpool St Johns. Blackpool FC joined forces with the South Shore club in 1899.

Rejoice in the nickname, 'The Seasiders'.

Play at the Bloomfield Road ground. Previous grounds include the Athletic Ground and Bloomfield Road.

Are planning a new dream stadium. However, even if they do move they have already spent 100 years at Bloomfield Road having played their first game on the site in 1899.

Greatest day in their entire history was the 2nd May 1953 when 'The Seasiders' won the FA Cup, beating Bolton Wanderers 4-3 , in 'The Matthews Final'. Stan Mortenson scored a hat-trick in this legendary Cup Final and the entire country seemed to rejoice that at-long-last the 38-year-old 'Wizard of Dribble', Stanley Matthews, had won an FA Cup Winners' medal.

Stanley Matthews was the first footballer aged over 50 to play in the First Division, Blackpool's opponents on that occasion were Fulham.

In 1956, Stanley Matthews was the first player to be voted European Footballer of the year.

Went eight years, a total of 13 games, without winning an FA Cup match between the years 1960 and 1968.

Blackpool...

Play in what must be one of the most easily recognisable strips in the English League, tangerine shirts and socks and white shorts.

Jimmy Armfield was an apprentice at Blackpool during the time of 'The Matthews Final' and has always said that this match was all the inspiration he needed to sign on as a professional when the opportunity arose. He went on to play in 568 matches between the 1952-71.

Most capped international is Jimmy Armfield who turned out for England 43 times

Played in the first League game that was ever shown on British television. The date was 10th September 1960, their opponents oddly enough, were Bolton Wanderers.

Biggest victory happened in 1948 when they beat Preston 7-0.

Have been beaten 1-10 twice in their history, by Small Heath in 1901 and Huddersfield in 1930.

Signed Preston's Tony Ellis in 1993 after he had scored six times in three matches against 'The Tangerines'. Blackpool sold him a year later; during that period Ellis had failed to score in three return games against his old club, Preston.

Jock Dodd's scored a hat-trick for Blackpool against Tranmere Rovers in an incredible two and a half minutes in February 1942.

Bolton Wanderers...

Were one of the founder members of the Football League in 1874. A teacher at the Christ Church Sunday School, Blackburn Street formed a church team from his boys' class; the first club president was the vicar, membership was set at six old pennies. Problems arose when the vicar restricted the use of the church premises and started laying down too many rules and regulations. The members broke away and formed Bolton Wanderers, based at the Gladstone Hotel, in 1877.

Were originally called 'The Wanderers' because they did not have their own ground until they moved to Burden Park, a former rubbish tip, in 1895.

The club's previous grounds include Park Recreation Ground, Cockle's Field and Pike's Lane Ground.

Burden Park is the ground represented in LS Lowry's famous painting, 'Going to the Match'.

Burden Park was the site of domestic football's first serious disaster when, in 1946, 33 people died after a barrier gave-way mid-way through a cup tie with Stoke City.

Bolton Wanderers...

Moved to the Reebok Stadium in 1997. The stadium won the Institute of Structural Engineers Special Award for Design in 1998.

Were previously known as Christ Church.

Are nicknamed 'The Trotters'

Were once known as 'The Reds'. In 1883 they wore white shirts with red spots for a while because it was thought that it made the players look bigger.

Won the FA Cup three times, in 1923, 1926 and 1929. A mere 17 players, in total, appeared in all three Finals.

Top striker is footballing legend Nat Lofthouse with 255 goals. Bolton was the only club he ever played for.

Most capped international is Nat Lofthouse who played 33 times for England

Came close to being the first club in League history to do 'a double', accumulate 100 points, and score 100 goals in one season when they became First Division Champions during their 1996/7 campaign . They scored 100 goals but drew their last game against Tranmere finishing on 98 points.

Bournemouth...

Can claim to date as far back as 1875. There was certainly a Bournemouth FC in existence by this date. With the closure of the Boscombe St John's FC in 1899 a meeting was held in a private house in Gladstone Road. Boscombe FC was born and straightway entered the Boscombe and District Junior League.

Became known as Bournemouth and Boscombe Athletic before settling for its present title.

First home was at Castlemain Road, Pokesdown. The club moved to Dean Court in 1910.

Are nicknamed "The Cherries'.

Record club score was 11-0 against Margate in the first round of the FA Cup on the 20th November 1971.

Ted MacDougal holds the record for goals scored in an FA Cup tie by finding the back of the net nine times in the same FA Cup match against Margate in 1971.

Are famous for finding footballing talent who later go on to find fame at other clubs.

Bournemouth...

Former players are also famous for their loyalty to their old club. Ted MacDougal went on to find fame at Norwich and Manchester City but he flew back from Canada to support "The Cherries' during their difficult financial problems in 1997.

Reached the Sixth Round of the FA Cup in 1957 while propping up most of their fellow teams in the Third Division.

Harry Redknapp acquired his management skills at Bournmouth. He moved on to take the helm at West Ham United.

Sold future England star Jamie Redknapp to Liverpool for £350,000; he had played only 13 games for Bournmouth. Canny Scot, Kenny Dalglish had initially taken Jamie on trial at Anfield as a 15-year-old and had carefully watched his subsequent progress.

During one particularly bad injury spell, Harry Redknapp, the manager at the time played himself at No 7. He hadn't played League football for six years prior to that game which they won 3-1.

Bradford City...

Owe their existence to an archery contest organised by Manningham RFC in 1903 to raise money for the cash strapped Bradford club.

Were originally a rugby league club until 1903 when they made the switch to Association Football.

Were granted their application to join the Football League well before Bradford had even assembled a squad of players because the League were enthusiastic about establishing the game of soccer in a strong rugby area.

Greatest achievement was in 1911 when 'The Bantams' beat Newcastle United 1-0 to lift the FA Cup.

Scored 128 goals during the 1928/9 season sharing the record for the most goals scored in a 42 match campaign with Aston Villa.

Will always be remembered for the fire that burnt down the old main stand on 11th May 1985 in which 56 fans were tragically killed. Ironically, the old stand was due to be demolished to make way for a brand new structure the very next day.

Roll of honour includes being champions of Division Two in 1908, Division Three (North) in 1929, and Division Three in 1911.

Were honoured by the presence of the Queen when she officially opened the refurbishment of Valley Parade. It is thought that this is the first time the Queen had officially visited a Football League ground.

Midfield teenage star, Shaun Murrey has won the most international caps as an England Schoolboy.

Brentford...

Most famous apprentice is the pop star Rod Stewart. He was at Brentford during the 1960s.

Are a club with a tidy mind. They ended the 1954/5 season with 46 points from the same number of games, having won 16 games and lost 16 games, and netted 82 goals with 82 goals conceded

Are one of two London clubs (the other is Barnet) with the nickname 'The Bees'.

Were founded in 1889 as a small amateur club, they won the West London Alliance championship in 1893 and lifted the West Middlesex Junior Cup in 1894 and the Senior Cup in 1895. In 1898 'The Bees' joined the Second Division of the Southern League having captured both the London Senior Amateur Cup and the Middlesex Senior Cup.

They played their first full League game in 1920.

The club has had six previous grounds prior to its present home at Griffen Park.

Put out a forward line of international players during the 1937-38 season consisting of Idris Hopkins of Wales, Bill

Brentford...

Scott and George Eastham of England, and David McCullock and Bobby Reid of Scotland.

High point in their history is when they finished 5th in the old First Division at the end of the 1935/6 season.

Are the only League club to win all their home games, a total of 21, in one season, in 1930.

Honours include Division Two champions in 1935, Division Three champions in 1992, Division Three (South) champions in 1933, Division Four champions in 1963.

Brentford reached Wembley in 1985 when they challenged for the Freight Rover Trophy Final.

Club Chairman Ron Noades is also the manager.

Goalkeeper, Jack Durston rushed back from Lords having taken five Surrey wickets for Middlesex in order to keep a clean sheet in Brentford's opening home win (1-0), against Millwall on the 30th August 1920.

Brighton...

Suffered a number of false starts during the early days of the club's history. A professional club, Brighton United, had been formed in November 1897 during a meeting held at the Imperial Hotel, Queen's Road. By 1900 this club had closed down after a mere two seasons playing in the Southern League from the County Ground. Almost immediately some supporters of the now defunct United started up an amateur team, Brighton and Hove Rangers. After a season based at the Withdean ground the club became semi-professional and moved to the County Ground. Brighton and Hove Rangers joined the Southern League but closed down within a year. Within a month, former United manager, John Jackson, called a public meeting at the Seven Stars pub, Ship Street. The result of this evening was the formation of Brighton and Hove United ; they straightway took on the County Ground and joined the Southern League. However, they were forced to change the club name, before a ball could be kicked in anger, to Brighton and Hove Albion because of objections raised by a local club, Hove FC.

Most capped player is Steve Penney with 17 appearances for Northern Ireland between the years 1983-91.

First hat-trick, ever, was scored by Brighton's Irish international, Jack Doran, in the 1921-22 season during a 3-0 away win against Exeter.

Second hat-trick was scored only seven days later by the self-same Brighton player in the return home game against Exeter.

Survived relegation to the Vauxhall Conference in 1997 when they drew 1-1 at Hereford in the final game of the season. The result sent their opponents down instead.

Highest transfer fee received was £900,000 from Liverpool for Mark Lawrenson.

Brighton...

Having survived relegation Brighton ended the 1996-97 season groundless after the Goldstone Ground had been sold-off to developers.

Ernie 'Tug' Wilson has made the most appearances for 'The Seagulls', playing in 509 games between the years 1902-36.

'Tug' Wilson was twice on the verge of turning out for an unbroken 100 games straight- off, but on both occasions was stopped by injury while on 99.

Came as close as the width of a cigarette paper of beating Manchester United in the 1983 FA Cup Final.

Howard Wilkinson, the FA's current Technical Director,is one of their past players. He once scored a goal after only 15 seconds, the fastest ever League goal.

Can also list among its past players a certain Steve Gatting, brother of England cricket captain Mike.

Brian Clough, the one-time manager of the Seagulls, scored five goals in a 9-0 thrashing of Brighton by Middlesbrough in 1958.

Bristol City

Put five goals past Luton during the 1996/7 season. Luton's manager, Lennie Lawrence was so upset that he described his own players as 'gutless'.

Lost in the Second Division play-offs in 1997 to Brentford even though Bristol City's team contained four internationals; Paul Agostino of Australia, Clayton Blackmore of Wales, Greg Goodridge of Barbados, and Shaun Goater of Bermuda.

Was founded in 1894.

Previous name was Bristol South End. The club decided to turn professional after a meeting held at The Albert Hall, Bedminster. The club brought in Sam Hollis from Woolwich Arsenal as their first manager and voted him a grand total of £40 to go out and buy new players.

In 1901 Bristol merged with another local club, Bedminster FC, the same year as they played their first League game.

'The Robins' moved from St John's Lane to Ashton Gate in 1904

Were promoted to the old Division One in 1906. Three City players contributed to this achievement by scoring 20 odd goals each.

Andy Cole is the club's most expensive purchase, Bristol City paid-out £500,000 when the player moved from Arsenal in June 1992. City made a sizeable profit when they sold him to Newcastle for £1,750,000 in March 1993.

Highest League position was second in the First Division in 1906/7 season.

Reached the FA Cup Final in 1909 (they lost 1-0 to Manchester United).

Bristol Rovers...

Fielded the youngest player ever, just 15 years and 180 days, to score in the English League. In 1928 Ronnie Dix put a goal past the Norwich keeper in only his second game for the club.

Were later to be known as Eastville Rovers up until 1898 when the present club name, Bristol Rovers was adopted.

Between 1986 and 1997 Rovers fans were forced to travel to Bath after their team had quit their old home ground at Eastville.

Now play their home games at Bristol FC's rugby union team's Memorial Ground.

First official club name, in 1883, was the 'Purdown Poachers'.

A change of strip, which included black shirts, inspired a club name change to 'The Black Arabs'.

Present nickname is 'The Pirates'.

Old-timer player, Joe Riley was the first Rovers player to score a hat-trick on his debut. He helped 'The Pirates' beat Bournmouth 4-1 way back in 1932.

Received a cool £1 million when they sold England international goalkeeper, Nigel Martyn, to Crystal Palace in November 1989.

Memorial Ground is the smallest pitch in the English League; it measures a mere 101 x 68 yards, which is not so surprising when the site was originally intended for the oval ball game.

Bristol Rovers...

In 1936 Luton's Tommy Payne scored 10 goals in his team's 12-0 win over 'The Rovers'; still the League record for goals scored in a single game by one player.

Blackburn Rovers player, Tommy Briggs put seven past Bristol Rovers in 1955 during their 8-3 win.

Club record for the most unbeaten games in a season (1973/4) is 26.

Honours include Division Three (South) Champions in 1953 and Division Three Champions in 1990.

Burnley...

Striker, George Beel was Burnley's top scorer in six of the nine seasons from 1923 to 1932.

Appeared to be in a free-fall down through the divisions during the 1970s and 80s. 'The Clarets' only saved themselves from the final descent into non-league football by winning their last game of 1987.

Played in the 1914 Cup Final, the first to be attended by a reigning monarch, the then George V. Burnley won the Final beating Liverpool 1-0 at the Crystal Palace ground.

Are nicknamed 'The Clarets' because of the colour of the club shirts.

Were runners-up in the FA Cup Finals of 1947 and 1962.

Play at Turf Moor.

Are a founder member of the Football League.

The club, then known as Burnley Rovers, was formed in 1881 out of the ashes of a rugby club. They carried on playing the oval ball game for another year before, at a meeting held at the Bull Hotel in 1882, the club changed its name to just Burnley and moved from Calder Vale to Turf Moor.

Were Division One Champions twice, in 1921 and 1960, a gap of 39 years.

Used a squad of a mere 17 players when Burnley won promotion to Division One in 1973. Six team members were ever-present.

Have the honour of being the first top flight club in 55 years to suffer defeat on their home ground by non-league opposition when Wimbledon beat 'The Clarets' 1-0 in 1975.

Burnley...

Lost their first three games of the 1920-21 season but then embarked upon an unbeaten run as they went on to win their first League title.

Run of 30 undefeated games that led to Burnley winning the First Division League title in 1921 is still the record for the longest unbeaten run ever during a single League season.

Bury...

Have the shortest name of any team in the entire Football League.

Neville Neville the commercial manager at Bury is the father of Manchester United players Gary and Phil. Their mum, sister, aunt, uncle and cousin also work behind the scenes at Bury.

Completed a club record of 29 unbeaten home League games in September 1997.

Had their FA Cup third round match against Birmingham postponed a record 14 times during the winter freeze-up of 1962/63.

Achieved their highest ever points total, 84, in one season (1984-85), but still ended-up as Division Four runners-up behind Chesterfield.

Equalled this highest ever points total in 1997 when they won the Division Two title.

Owes its existence to a meeting held at the Wagon and Horses Hotel called by members of a Wesleyan and a Unitarian football club. This resulted in the foundation of Bury FC at a subsequent meeting at the Old White Horse Hotel, Fleet Street.

Home ground is Gigg Lane.

Won the FA Cup in 1900 and 1903, but have never been able to reach such heights since.

Achieved the record for the highest score in any FA Cup Final in 1903 when they beat Derby County 6-0.

Cambridge United...

Were voted "Best Ground for Away Supporters" in 1997.

Were also voted the club that sold the "Best Football Food" in the following year, 1998.

Lost a record 31 games on the trot during the 1983-1984 season. They were, not surprisingly, relegated to Division Three.

Can trace its origins back to a team called Abbey United that was founded in 1919. As late as 1949 the club decided to turn professional and change its name to Cambridge United.

Play at the Abbey Stadium.

Have the nickname, the 'U's; a contraction of 'United'.

Lost nine United players, in 1992, when the 'U's manager, John Beck took over the hot seat at Preston. He took all nine United players with him.

Became Division Three champions in 1991.

Were Division Four champions in 1977.

Were about to join the big boys in the top division in 1992, just 22 years after joining the Football League, but lost in the play-off against Leicester. Some five years later Cambridge were fighting to avoid non-league football.

Includes in its list of former managers the flamboyant Ron Atkinson who took the club from the Fourth up to the Second Division during the years 1974-78.

Recorded a 2-1 win over Swansea during the 1996-97 season. Nothing much remarkable about that, except that caretaker manager, Paul Clark resigned after just this one successful game in charge.

Cambridge United...

Players were obliged to take freezing cold showers before every game under Cambridge manager, John 'Long Ball' Beck. His love of 'route one' football explains his instructions that the grass was kept long in all four corners of the pitch. Beck maintained that long balls put over the opposition's full backs were much more likely to stay in play; a form of poor man's back spin.

One-time club captain, Steve Spriggs, holds the club record for the most League appearances, a total of 416 games between 1975-87.

Cardiff City...

Are the only club to have taken the FA Cup out of England. In 1927 City beat Arsenal 1-0 in the FA Final. This Welsh team included in its line-up, four Irishmen, three Scots and one Englishman, but only three Welshmen.

Were founded in 1899 as Riverside, after the cricket club of the same name. They played at Sophia Gardens, now the home of Glamorgan county cricket. Later home venues were Old Park and Fir Gardens.

After the later addition of Albion they changed their club name to Cardiff City in 1908 after Cardiff had become a city in 1905 and permission had been obtained from the local FA.

In 1910 they moved to their present ground, Ninian Park.

Are nicknamed 'The Bluebirds".

Lost out on goal average at the end of the 1923-4 season, missing out on the League title by a mere 0.024 of a goal.

Have benefited by being the victim of an odd co-incidence. City were drawn away to Leeds in the Third Round of the FA Cup three years running, in 1955, 1956 and 1957. Amazingly they not only won each tie they won all three games by the same score, 2-1.

Mid-field inspiration, Fred Keenor, served Cardiff City for 20 years.

Finished 90th in the League at the end of the 1995-96 season.

In this same season, Carel Dale scored an amazing 21 goals out of the club's total of 41.

They were the Division Three (South) champions in 1947 and the Division Three Champions in 1993.

Won the Welsh Cup in 1993 under manager Eddie May.

Carlisle United...

Record sale was ex-England international Peter Beardsley's transfer to Canadian Whitecaps in 1981.

Was the first club outside London to install floodlights.

Were formed in 1903 by the merger of two local clubs, Shaddongate United and Carlisle Red Roses.

Became members of the Lancashire Combination in 1905, despite the fact that Carlisle's Brunten Park ground is some 80 miles north of this particular county.

Are nicknamed 'the Blues'

Have had their fair share of ups-and-downs. They won promotion to the First Division in 1974, topped the table during August of that year, yet still went straight back to the Second Division at the end of the season.

Loyal travelling supporters have further to travel to away games than any other fans in the country. Brunten Park is some 58 miles away from the nearest League ground, that of Newcastle United.

Between 1961 and 1965 Carlisle played in a different division for five seasons in a row.

Extrovert chairman, Michael Knighton once claimed that he had seen a UFO. He has been known, on more than one occasion, to have assisted in the team selection.

Won the Division Three championship in both 1965 and 1995

Made good use of an injury crisis. Gareth McAlindon only played because nobody else was available. He scored the winning goal during extra time in the match against Wigan Athletic on 2 September 1997.

Winger, Chris Balderstone, was one of the last of the old pros who played both football and cricket for a living.

Charlton Athletic...

Youngest club player to make his Football League debut, in 1997, was Paul Konchesky at 16 years and 92 days.

Sold future England midfielder, Rob Lee to Newcastle for just under £775,0000.

Are nicknamed 'The Addicks'.

Valley stadium was the first to host a live televised FA Cup tie when they entertained Blackburn in the fifth round in 1947.

Provided a home venue for the rugby league team, London Broncos, in 1966. When the initial attendance of 10,000 dropped dramatically the Broncos moved on.

Have only won twice away to Birmingham City at St Andrews, first back in 1939, the second in 1996. On both occasions 'The Addicks' won 4-3.

Have two other nicknames, 'The Robins' and 'The Valiants'. The fans' favourite, 'The Addicks' derives from the name of a local chip shop owner whose chippy was often patronised by the team players for post-match meals during the early years of this century.

Valley stadium had the largest capacity in England during the early 1970s, holding some 67,000 fans. Charlton were obliged to leave the ground in 1985. Initially they shared Selhurst Park with Crystal Palace then moved on to West Ham's ground, Upton Park before returning to a much smaller Valley ground in 1992. Altogether, Charlton have played their home games on seven different grounds.

Fans felt obliged to form their very own political party in order to get Greenwich Council's decision to oppose the refurbishment of the stadium reversed. The Valley Party polled 14,838 votes in the ensuing local council election, more than an average Charlton 'home' gate that season.

Charlton Athletic...

Were the first team to play in an FA Cup Final after having lost in an earlier round. In 1946 Charlton had been beaten 2-1 at Fulham but won 3-1 at home. The tie was played over two legs so Charlton went through on aggregate.

Went on to lose in the Final 4-1 to Derby County. Charlton defender, Bert Turner became the first player to net the ball for both sides in an FA Cup Final. He followed-up his own goal 5 minutes from the end of the match by scoring a goal for Charlton just one minute later.

Bert Turner acquired yet one more record in this Cup Final of 1946. At 36 years and 312 days he became the oldest player ever to score in a Final.

Charlton won the FA Cup in the following season, a 1-0 win over Burnley.

Legendary shot stopper, Sam Bartram was one of the best goalkeepers, ever, who has ever been passed over for international duties.

Manchester United legend, Bobby Charlton, scored twice on his 1956 debut against Charlton

Was formed in 1905 by some 14 and 15 year olds living close to the Thames in the region of the present-day Thames Barrier. Soon after the First World War they joined the Kent League then turned professional and joined the Southern League in 1920. In the following year the club was elected to the Football League.

Chelsea...

Have never believed in the old adage of starting at the bottom and working your way up. Chelsea were granted immediate entry into the League's Second Division when they were founded in 1905.

Stamford Bridge often plays host to its own first eleven of famous fans for many of 'The Blues' home games. John Major has been known to drop in, Sir Richard Attenborough is Chelsea's Life vice-president, comedian David Baddiel is a loyal supporter, as is Damon Albarn of the pop group, Blur. The most famous must be the former politician and Heritage Secretary, David Mellor.

Allegations in the press that David Mellor enjoyed sex romps with an actress clad in little else but a Chelsea shirt was a contributory factor in his eventual resignation from the Cabinet.

Are one of only three London clubs, the other two are Arsenal and Tottenham, to have won the League title. However, "The Blues' only success came in 1955. In so doing they accumulated the lowest points total, ever, a mere 52.

Roberto Di Matteo is 'The Blues' record buy, to date. Having arrived at the club in the summer of 1996 for £4.5 million he repaid his new club's faith in him by scoring just 43 seconds after the start of the 1997 FA Cup Final.

Shared the Prince Philip Cup when, in 1975, they drew at home with the Italian Under-23 team .

Were jeered at by Blackpool fans back in 1931 for being 'Southern Softies'. By the end of an away game on a freezing cold and rain- swept Saturday afternoon in October five Chelsea players had left the field unable to carry on because of the Arctic conditions. Blackpool won the tie 4-0.

Chelsea...

Hold the record for the most points accumulated in one season while gaining promotion from the Second to the First Division, 99 points during the 1997/89 season. Is so doing Chelsea also hold the record of suffering a mere five defeats during a 46 match spell.

Fans invented a new terrace chant of "Can we play you every year?" when, during the 1997/98 season 'The Blues' won the League Cup by beating Middlesbrough 2-0. At the end of the previous season Chelsea had won the FA Cup. Their opponents had been the self-same Middlesbrough, and Chelsea had won by the self-same margin, 2-0.

Are the first team to have won the FA Cup at a venue other than Wembley, post-war when, having drawn 2-2 in the first Final, they defeated Leeds 2-1 in the replay held at Old Trafford.

Were also the first team to win the Cup Winners Cup after a replay (defeating Real Madrid 2-1 in Athens). This was prior to the introduction of penalties. Indeed, this was also the last time that a major European trophy was decided by a replay.

Under new player/manager, Gianluca Vialli, became the first English club to bring home the European Cup Winners' Cup, twice, by beating Stuttgart 1-0. The only goal of the match was scored by Zola's first touch of the ball.

Chelsea's Peter Osgood is the only player to have scored in every round of the FA Cup.

Chelsea...

Youngest ever captain is Ray Wilkins, he was only 18 years of age when he was appointed to lead the team in 1975.

Were the first English club to pick up the FA Cup under a foreign (non-British) manager.

Had three managers, one following on from the other during the 1990s, all of whom had netted the winning goal in previous FA Cup Finals; Ian Porterfield (for Sunderland), and David Webb and Glen Hoddle (both for Chelsea).

Defeated Manchester City in 1986, at Wembley, to become the first team to win the old Full Members' Cup.

Leading scorer of all-time is Bobby Tambling with 164 league goals between the years 1958 and 1970.

In the 1960-61 season all-time legend Jimmy Greaves scored the most club goals in a single season, a grand total of 41. This included a post-war record of six hat-tricks.

Chelsea...

Jimmy Greaves began his career at Stamford Bridge. By the age of 21 he was the youngest player, ever, to score the grand-total of 100 League goals. He was to double-up this record at the grand old age of 23 years and 290 days. Amazingly this was the self-same age, exactly, at which the great Dixie Dean reached the same total with Everton.

Were the very first club in the history of the Football League to let in seven goals scored by seven different players in one match, against Leeds during the 1967/68 season. To add insult to injury one strike was an own-goal by Chelsea's Marvin Hinton.

Former manager, Glen Hoddle, is the first English player to have won a French League championship medal.

Fulham turned down a Mr HA Mears' offer to rent them Stamford Bridge, a property he had owned since 1904. However, he was determined to establish a football stadium on the site rather than sell it to the Great Western Railway. He teamed up with Frederick Parker and formed Chelsea Football Club.

The club joined the Second Division of the Football League having been refused membership of the Southern League.

Appointed World Cup hero Geoff Hurst as their manager but he was released because under his guidance Chelsea seemed unable to score goals.

Chester City...

Were founded in 1884, despite the historical records of the game being played in the city streets during the High Medieval period. The first Chester City was formed by the combination of two local teams, King's School old boys FC and Chester Rovers.

During the 1931-32 season, just prior to being elected to the Football League, 'The Blues' scored an unbelievable 170 goals in the Cheshire County League; Arthur Gale, a schoolteacher netted an incredible 73 of this total.

Played at non-league Macclesfield's ground while waiting for the completion of their new Deva Stadium.

The Deva Stadium straddles the Welsh/English border. Chester moved from Sealand Road to this new stadium at Bumpers Lane in 1990. It is the third smallest ground in the League with room for a mere 6,000 fans.

Have a hat-trick of wins in the Welsh FA Cup, 1908, 1933 and 1947. However, despite the dual nationality of their ground, the Welsh FA have not lifted the decree that Chester City can no longer enter this particular competition.

Another honour for 'The Blues' was a semi-final place in the League Cup of 1975 in which they were narrowly beaten 5-4 on aggregate over both legs.

"The Blues' were Debenham Cup winners in 1977.

Discovered and nurtured the great Welsh striker Ian Rush. As a teenager he scored 14 goals in just 34 matches. They then sold him for £300,000 to Liverpool.

Manager Kevin Ratcliffe met Ian Rush a total 20 times when he was Everton's centre half.

Chester City...

Acquired Cyrille Regis, ex-England striker on a free transfer.

Have never been higher than the Second Division (the old Third Division) to which they were elected in 1931.

Record win was 12-0 over York City in 1936;

Worst defeat was 11-2 in a match against Oldham Athletic in January 1952.

League statistics for both the 1995-96 and 1996-7 seasons reads as, won 18, drawn 16, lost 12. The points total for both seasons was 70.

Midfielder, Gary Talbot scored three times in three minutes against Crewe in November 1964, one of the quickest hat tricks in the history of the game.

During a match played on New Years Day 1966 both of Chester's full backs broke their left legs. Their names were Ray Jones and Bryn Jones, but were not related.

Long-time club servant, Ray Gill holds the club record for the most League appearances, a total of 408 games between the years, 1951-62.

Chesterfield...

Hold the Football League record of having scored in 46 consecutive games from 25th December 1929 to 26th December 1930.

Are considered to be something of a footballing academy, specialising in producing great goalkeepers - two such old boys being Sam Hardy and Gordon Banks.

Roll of honour includes winning the old Division Four championship twice, and the Third Division (North) championship twice.

Fielded the youngest player to have ever appeared in a Coca-Cola Cup game played in October 1993. Kevin Davies was a mere 16 years and 104 days old.

Sold Kevin Davies to Southampton for £1 million in May 1997.

Finest hour occurred during their FA Cup run of the 1996/7 season. 'The Spireites' were mid-table in Division Two (formerly the old Division Three). A ref-eree's decision denied Chesterfield the singular honour of being the first club from outside the top two divisions to reach  the FA Cup Final. During the semi-final referee David Elleray disallowed Jonathon Howard's goal. TV replays show that the ball had actually crossed the goal line. Middlesbrough, with only ten men, scored half-way through the second half to scramble a 2-2 draw. Chesterfield lost the replay 3-0 and the chance of becoming footballing legends.

Chesterfield...

Were founded in 1866, the fourth oldest League club in the country. However, they initially played just a few friendlies each season.

Their Rule Book for 1871 still exists; annual membership was two shillings.

The club lifted its first trophy in 1891, the Barnes Cup. Having finally acquired the taste for success Chesterfield won three more trophies in the following year. In 1884 Chesterfield moved from the Spital Ground to the Recreation Ground.

Record defeat was 10-0 inflicted by Gillingham in September 1987.

Chesterfields's record win was way back in 1903 when they beat Glossop North End 10-0.

Highest League position, ever, was 4th place in the old Division Two during the 1946-47 season.

Colchester United...

Fielded the first brothers, David and Neil Gregory, ever to appear in a team's starting line-up for a Wembley play-offs Final.

Scored 15 seconds after kick-off and 15 seconds before the final whistle on New Year's Day 1996 in the 3-2 win over Torquay.

Were founded in 1937 as Colchester Town, based at their current Layer Road ground, but did not play their first Football League game until the 19th August 1950.

Have won no major trophies and have never had a player capped for international duty.

Having been relegated to the Conference in 1990 Colchester, won promotion back into the League in 1992; the same year they completed the non-league double, the Conference title and the FA Trophy.

Traveled to Wembley again in 1997 but lost in the Final of the Auto Windscreens Shield to Carlisle on penalties.

Colchester United...

Proudest moment was in 1971 when the 'U's, from the Fourth Division, scored a notable 3-2 victory at home in the 5th round of the FA Cup over a Leeds team studded with international stars and then currently perched on top of Division One. Incredibly the 'U's had, at one point, led Leeds 3-0. Colchester's moment in the sun was short-lived, they lost to Everton 5-0 in the quarter-finals.

Had reached the Third Round of the FA Cup back in 1948 as a non-league team by beating Huddersfield, then a Division One side. Colchester lost to Blackpool in the next round.

Beat Scunthorpe United 4-3 in February 1995. Nothing much remarkable about this statistic? The Colchester come-back kids had been three goals down without reply after just 18 minutes!

Player, Micky Cook, holds the club record for the most league appearances, 613 during the years 1969-1984.

Coventry City...

Gave as their reason for having beaten Division One Nottingham Forest 3-1 in their 1910 Third Round match in the FA Cup as their previous week's training regime of brisk long walks followed by brine baths at Droitwich.

Were originally named Singers FC. The club was born in 1883 as the works team of the Singers bicycle factory.

While still Singers FC won the Birmingham Junior Cup in 1891 and were elected to the Birmingham and District League in 1894.

The name change to Coventry City occurred in 1988.

Joined the Southern League in 1908. During this period they played in a strip of blue and white quarters.

First top League game, in 1919, was a Division Two home clash in which they were defeated 5-0 by Tottenham Hotspur.

One-time manager, Jimmy Hill, brought Coventry up out of the old Fourth Division to Division One.

Jimmy Hill's imaginative marketing style brought the club a high media profile. He dressed the players in a new sky blue strip, painted a stand sky blue, employed sky blue caterers and insisted upon the establishment of a sky blue radio station and shop, even instituting a sky blue train for away games.

Highfield Road ground received three direct hits durind the Second World War. Amazingly all three bombs landed on the pitch; the stands and offices suffered only minor damage.

Have enjoyed, since 1967, the fourth longest stay in top-flight football. Only Arsenal, Liverpool and Everton have a better record.

Coventry City...

Back in 1958, prior to the use of substitutes, Coventry achieved the highest victory score with less than the full complement of players (they had lost their goalkeeper!) by beating Aldershot 7-1.

Won the FA Cup in 1987 by beating Tottenham 3-2; some 12 months earlier the club had only just saved itself from relegation through a last gasp goal on the last day of the season by Gary Bennett.

Billed their away match against Cardiff in 1965 as 'The first game ever to be staged in two separate stadiums'. Coventry relayed the action, live from Wales, onto a large screen at Highfield Road. Just over 12,000 watched the game live; a crowd of 10,000 home fans saw the match on screen back in Coventry.

Teenage Kevin Keegan was once rejected by Jimmy Hill's Coventry.

Went 11 games without scoring a single goal during the 1919/20 season; the club won its first point on Christmas Day.

Player with the most international honours is Northern Ireland's David Clements with 48 caps.

Coventry's past star player, Reg Matthews was one of very few Third Division players to have received the call to play for England.

Peter Ndlovu scored a hat-trick at Anfield against Liverpool in March 1995. The first by an away team for 33 years.

Crewe Alexandra...

Were formed in 1877, Prior to this they had been a cricket club.

The addition, of 'Alexandra' was in honour of the, then Princess Alexandra.

Crewe's first football success was winning the Crewe and District Cup in the year of the football club's inception.

They reached the semi-finals of the FA Cup in the following year, 1878, only to be beaten 4-0 by Preston North End.

Have the nickname 'The Railwaymen'

Crewe did not play their first league game at Gresty Road until 1892.

Won the Welsh Cup in both 1936 and 1937.

Have been beaten more times in FA Cup games by non-league opposition than any other League team, apart from Exeter City.

Home grown talent includes ex-England mid-fielder, David Platt, Liverpool's Rob Jones and Irishman, Danny Murphy

Manager, Dario Gradi was awarded the MBE in 1998. He is the League's longest-serving manager; he has been in charge at Crewe since 1983.

Played in front of the biggest crowd in the club's history when they visited Sunderland on 18th April 1998. Both sets of fans totalled just over 40,000.

Liverpool and Crewe were the first clubs to form the League's 'Alliance' between football clubs' for the mutual benefit of both clubs'.

Crewe Alexandra...

Revived old glories when, in 1997, they won the Second Division plays-offs. This was the first time they had attained such dizzy heights since being original members of the old 'Second' Division back in 1892

Have matching league records for the 1995/6 and 1996/7 seasons

Beat Hartlepool 8-0 on October 17th 1995 in the Auto Windscreens Shield, all 8 goals were scored by different Crewe players.

Are one of just four League clubs who have never finished top, or runners-up, in any Division.

Are the only English League club to have the letter 'X' in their name.

Crystal Palace...

Were founded, around 1861, by the staff who manned the Great Exhibition.

They reached the semi-final of the first ever FA Cup competition ten years later.

Present set-up dates from 1905, the brainchild of the organisation that controlled the Crystal Palace building. The FA had rejected the idea of the usual Cup Final hosts running their own club so a separate limited company was formed to run the football club. Palace played all their home games on the old Cup Final ground until 1915.

Were Division One Champions in 1994, Division Two Champions in 1979, and Division Three (South) Champions back in 1921.

Future star striker and England international Ian Wright was brought off the subs bench and scored 2 goals in the 3-3 draw with Manchester United in the FA Cup Final of 1990. 'The Eagles' were beaten 1-0 in the replay.

Crystal Palace...

Were beaten, in 1989, 9-0 by the League Champions, Liverpool. Palace's goalkeeper, Perry Digweed suffered the indignity of having eight different Liverpool players slot the ball past him.

Eight months later 'The Eagles' gained a sweet revenge by beating Liverpool 4-3 in an FA Cup semi-final.

Stuart Hall, BBC's eccentric commentator for the now defunct 'It's a knockout', turned out for Crystal Palace reserves back in 1953.

Fans used to sing, "When Jim goes up, to lift the FA Cup, we'll be dead, we'll be dead", during the 1980s. Jim Cannon, the Palace captain, played a record of 571 games for 'The Eagles', but the club never has won the FA Cup.

Record sale was Chris Armstrong to Tottenham for £4.5 million in 1995.

Hold the record for being the only club to have been relegated three times from the Premier division during its relatively short six season's existence.

Are one of the few Third Division clubs to have supplied England with a full international, 'Eagles' centre forward, Johnny 'Budgie' Byrne in 1962.

Darlington...

Have languished in the bottom two divisions since 1927, the only exception being the 1989/90 season when they dropped down into non-league football.

Made the most of this setback by topping the Vauxhall Conference that season. Indeed, having gained promotion back into the League in just one season they went on to win the Division Four title in 1991.

Are one of only seven League clubs to have never produced a player for international duty.

Worst defeat was in 10-0 by Doncaster in 1964. The club's biggest win was against Lincoln City, 9-2, way back in 1928.

Striker, Gary Innes played for ten different teams in just twelve months. Prior to joining Darlington he played in a number of school sides, England Schoolboys, and then had a trial for Middlesbrough. From Darlington he was sent on loan to Waterford in Ireland and then to Gateshead.

Believe in doing things the hard way. In 1958 they defeated Chelsea 4-1 in an FA Cup fourth round replay. "The Quakers' had previously drawn 3-3 at Stamford Bridge, after leading by 3-0.

Was formed in 1861. The club was refounded in its present form in 1883. 'The Quakers' reached the Durham Senior Cup in their first season. They lost to Sunderland after a replay. The replay was the result of an appeal by Darlington that the Sunderland players had 'intimidated' them. They did win this competition the following season and went on to become one of the top amateur teams in the north.

Brian Little was their manager during their short stay in the Vauxhall conference.

Darlington...

Sacked their new manager in 1971, Len Richley, 12 days after the start of the season

Turned professional in 1908 and became founder members of Division Three (North) in 1921. They won this division's title in 1925.

Possess a club historian with a wry sense of humour. Frank Tweddle maintains that the only twin towers the club's fans will ever have cause to pass between to watch their team play are not those of Wembley Stadium but those that adorn the ornamental gates at the entrance to Darlington's 'Feethams' ground.

Derby County...

Striker, Dai Astley scored 49 goals in 98 League and Cup games between 1936 and 1939. His tally included 29 in his first 30 matches for "The Rams'.

Was formed by members of Derbyshire County Cricket Club in 1884. They had no great burning ambition to play the game but soccer was booming in the area and the cricketers hoped to improve their club's finances by including this sport among their activities. The football team initially played in the cricket club's colours, amber, chocolate and pale blue.

Later changed their strip to navy and white before adopting their present-day home colours of white and black.

In 1884, the year the football club was formed, they took part in the FA Cup campaign.

The club were losing FA Cup finalists three times, way back in 1898, 1899 and 1903.

Were, also, founder members of the Football League.

Were obliged to evict a gypsy family from their Baseball Ground when they first took over the site back in 1895. The fans usually blame the curse uttered by the departing Romanies for any run of bad luck.

Although 'The Rams' have reached the FA Cup semi-finals on 13 occasions they have only won the trophy once, in 1946, a 4-1 win over Charlton. Just prior to this first post-Second World War Cup Final the team captain crossed a local gypsy's palm with silver. Seemingly the curse was lifted, if only on a temporary basis.

Vacated the Baseball Ground in 1997. Having moved into their new stadium at Pride Park the fans are still debating whether they have brought the gypsy curse with them.

Derby County...

During the 1945/46 season a record 80,000 plus had turned up to watch Derby play Birmingham City at Main Road. Because of the size of the crowd the government banned mid-week afternoon matches in the immediate post-war period for fear of loss of industrial production.

Gained promotion to the First Division in 1969 and won the League title for the first time in 1972 under charismatic manager, Brian Clough. Having played all their matches 'The Rams' fate was in the hands of other clubs. The players heard of their success while sunning themselves on a beach in Majorca.

Won the League title again three years later, in 1975. The manager was the previous successful club captain Dave Mackay.

Record victory came in their opening tie in the UEFA Cup in 1976; 'The Rams' thrashed Finn Harps of Ireland 12-0.

Worst defeats include a 1-6 thrashing during a home tie in the Second Round of the FA Cup by non-league Boston United in 1955; and losing to Everton 11-2 in the League in 1890.

Faced the drop down into the Fourth Division during the club's centenary year, 1984. Although publisher, Robert Maxwell moved-in to save 'The Rams' the fans became angry at the lack of money made available for new players and started a new terrace chant in honour of their chairman, "He's fat, he's round, he's never at the ground".

Doncaster Rovers...

Were made an unusual offer during the 1970s. Wembley asked if they could buy the entire Doncaster pitch and re-lay the turf in London as the surface was so good, indeed it was considered the best in Britain, they politely declined the offer. The secret of the perfect turf was said to be the base formed by ash from the local coalfields.

Held the world record for the sale of a goalkeeper when they sold legendary Harry Gregg to Manchester United for £23,500.

Had reached the 5th round of the FA Cup, prior to Harry Gregg's departure, a total of four times during the 1950s.

Famous past managers include Lawrie McMenemy, Maurice Setters, Dave Mackay and Billy Bremner.

Have languished down in the lower reaches of the league, the bottom two divisions, since 1958.

Fans sang "Would you like a piece of cake?" to the visiting fans during a home game in 1981. The police became very suspicious but eventually realised that the chant was not a challenge to open warfare on the terraces. The following week the Rovers' fans away at Burnley offered slices of cake to the police and sang, "And so this is Burnley, and what have we

Doncaster Rovers...

done. We've lost here already, would you like a cream bun?"
to the John Lennon tune, 'So This is Christmas'.

Were formed in 1879 and turned professional in 1885.

Were previously based at the Intake Ground from 1880 until
1916. In 1920 'Rovers' moved to the Benetthorpe Ground,
arriving at their present home, Low Pasture, Belle Vue, in
1922.

Were relegated to the Vauxhall Conference in May 1998.

The club's last taste of glory was in 1969 when they lifted the
Fourth Division title, a feat they had last achieved in the year
of England's World Cup triumph, 1966.

**Still hold the all-time English record, 33 wins from 42
matches during their 1946/7 campaign in Division Three
(North).**

Doncaster have won this divisional title on two other
occasions, in 1935 and 1950.

Everton...

Organised an athletics meeting and a fireworks display to celebrate the official opening of Goodison Park, in 1892. The only thing missing to complete a perfect day was a football match!

Initially played in Black shirts with a white sash, thus acquiring the nickname, 'The Black Watch'. The club tried out various different coloured strips prior to settling for Royal Blue in 1901.

Have spent 95 seasons, in the top flight of the League, this is more than any other club.

Are probably the only club to have a member of their board of directors who has appeared in Coronation Street. Theatre producer Bill Kenwright once played barmaid Betty (Turpin) Williams' son.

Have, between the years 1891 and 1987, lifted the League title on no fewer than nine occasions and the FA Cup five times between 1906 and 1995.

Were the first to install undersoil heating. The total cost of £70,000 was wasted as the system was unsuitable.

Keeper Neville Southall, made 91 appearances for Wales.

Set a club record of 28 consecutive games unbeaten, including 18 League, six FA Cup and four European Cup-Winners' Cup matches.

Are nicknamed 'The Toffees'.

Started life in 1878 as the football team of Sunday School based at St Domingo Church who played at Stanley Park. By November 1979 the club had grown to such an extent that they changed the name to Everton. They moved to Priory Road in 1882, on to Anfield Road in 1884 before arriving at their present venue, Goodison Park, in 1892, one year after winning their first League title.

Everton...

Have the honour of being the first team to turn-out with numbers on the backs of their shirts. The match was at Wembley in 1933, the 'Toffees' opponents in this FA Cup Final were Manchester City. Everton players were numbered 1-11, Manchester City's 12-22.

Won the 1915 Championship with a mere 46 points, the lowest total ever.

Have played more FA Cup semi-final ties than any other, a total of 23 times.

Acquired their nickname, 'The Toffees' from 'Ye Ancient Everton Toffee House', situated next door to the pub on whose premises the club was formed.

Record goalscorer is still the great Dixie Dean, with 349 goals in 399 games between 1925 and 1937.

He also scored 60 times, 40 with his head, during the 1927/8 season, a League record. In so doing he scored nine goals in the last nine games.

Dixie Dean died at Goodsion Park after watching a Merseyside derby against Liverpool in 1980.

Goodison Park ground is just 840 yards away across Stanley Park from Anfield, the home of Everton's great rivals, Liverpool.

Former manager Harry Catterick died at Goodison Park.

Once delayed a match because the minister in a local church, a staunch Evertonian, didn't want his Harvest Festival disturbed by people going to the game.

Exeter City...

Are nicknamed 'The Grecians'

Ground name is St James Park, the same as Newcastle, but the latter's stadium can hold an extra 26,000 fans.

Played hosts to US soldiers during the Second World War. The troops lived in the main stand and used the pitch for square bashing.

Record win was way back in 1926 when they beat Coventry City 8-1.

Record defeat was 9-0 back in 1948 against Notts County. Exeter repeated this feat when losing by the same margin to Northampton Town in 1958.

Highest position in the League, ever, was sixth place in the old Third Division in 1980

Record goal scorer was Jim 'Daisy' Bell. During three seasons in the Southern League between 1908 and 1911 he found the net on 52 occasions.

Fans were told over the ground's tannoy system, during a 1-1

Exeter City...

draw against Bury in 1996, that the local council had bought St James's Park and in so doing saved the club from extinction.

Were formed in 1904, an amalgamation of St Sidwell's United and Exeter United. The team joined the East Devon League then the Plymouth & District League. To test local interest in the game of soccer in a predominately rugby playing area the club arranged an exhibition match between West Bromwich Albion and the Woolwich Arsenal.

Exeter City decided to turn professional in 1908 at a meeting held at the nearby Red Lion Hotel.

Played their first full League game (Division Three) in 1920 against Brentford.

Most capped player is Eire international, Dermot Curtis.

Were Division Four Champions in 1990, and lifted the Division Three (South) Cup in 1934.

Sir Stanley Rous, past secretary of the FA and past president of FIFA, turned out for Exeter between the sticks a few times for the reserve team in 1919 while studying at nearby St Luke's Teacher Training College.

Fulham...

Hold the record for the number of grounds the club has occupied, a total of 10 sites prior to moving to Craven Cottage in 1896. These being Star Road, Eel Brook Common, Lillie Road, Putney Lower Common, Ranelagh House, Barn Elms, Purser's Cross, Parsons Green Lane, a short return to Eel Brook Common, the Half Moon at Putney and then Captain James Field at West Brompton.

Are nicknamed 'The Cottagers'.

Previous name was Fulham St Andrews until 1888.

Was founded by two clergymen, in 1879, in an attempt to bring more men into the congregation of the local church.

Fulham won the West London Amateur Cup in 1887 and were the first champions of the West London League in 1892.

Was bought outright by Harrods' owner and multi-millionaire, Mohamed Al Fayed in 1997, making the club the richest in the lower two English divisions.

Are the first Second Division club, ever, to pay £1 million for a player, Paul Peschisolido, who was transferred from West Bromwich to Fulham during the 1997/98 season.

Smashed the £2 million barrier by buying Chris Coleman from Blackburn Rovers just a few months after breaking the £1 million Second Division transfer deal record in 1997.

Became the first club in Britain to pay a player £100 a week when they offered this wage to Johnny Haynes following the abolition of the maximum wage in 1961.

Is unique in that it is the only football club, ever, to have been managed by two men both having the same name; William Dodgins Snr and his son, William Dodgins Jnr.

Fulham...

Midfield star and captain, Johnny Haynes, holds 'The Cottagers' record for having played the most games for the club, 594 between the years 1952-70.

Most honoured international player is Johnny Haynes with 56 England appearances, many as captain of his country.

Only FA Cup Final appearance was in 1975. Fulham lost 2-0 to West Ham even though they had former Hammers and England skipper Bobby Moore as the cornerstone of their defence.

Leading League scorer in a single season, 1931-32, was Frank Newton with 43 goals, Fulham was languishing in the Third Division South at the time.

Gillingham...

Captain, Mark Weatherly, walked six miles through a snowstorm to play in a match against Wigan Athletic on the 13th January 1987. On arrival at the ground he discovered that the match had been postponed!

Was founded back during the heady days of Chatham's Royal Engineers' football team's continued success. The interest generated throughout the Medway Towns caused the creation of a good number of soccer clubs throughout the general area. One of whom, Excelsior, decided to go for the big time and, in 1893 during a meeting at the Napier Arms, Brompton, New Brompton FC was formed. This club was soon to buy and improve the present Priestfield ground.

Back in 1938 they had dropped-out of the league and were not re-elected until 1950.

Were almost declared bankrupt in 1994, only to celebrate their escape from the clutches of the Official Receiver by gaining promotion into the Second Division at the end of the 1995/6 season

Won the Division Four Championship in 1964. In so doing 'The Gills' broke the League record for the most consecutive home wins without defeat, an amazing 52

Gillingham...

games, which was only overtaken some 17 years later, in 1981, by Liverpool with an unbeaten total of 85 home wins.

Record goalscorer is Tony Yeo who found the net 135 times between the years 1963-75.

Goalkeeper, Jim Stannard kept an amazing 29 clean sheets during the 1995/6 season, setting a new club record.

Goalkeeper Fred Fox is 'The Gills' only player to have won an England cap when he made just one appearance for England in 1925.

Gillingham's most capped player is Tony Cascarino. He turned out three times for the Republic of Ireland while a 'Gills' player.

Acquired Tony Cascarino from local Kent club, Crockenhill for a set of football shirts.

Long-time servant, John Simpson holds the club record for the most League appearances; 571 over a period of 15 years at Priestfield between 1957-72.

Hot-shot striker Robert Taylora record £500,000 buy from Brentford scored five goals in a League game against Burnley in 1998/99

Grimsby Town...

Previous ground, Clee Park, was actually situated in the town of Grimsby. The players were obliged to change in bathing huts wheeled-up from the beach. They later moved to Abbey Park.

Present ground, Blundell Park, is not actually situated in the fishing port of Grimsby but in nearby Cleethorpes. It could be argued that 'The Mariners' are the only League club to have played all their home games over the last 90 years 'away from home'.

Were originally called Grimsby Pelham FC. The club was formed at a meeting held at the Wellington Arms on September 1878. The takings at the gate for the first game amounted to the grand total of 6s. 9d. (Around 39p. in today's money).

In 1879 the name was changed to Grimsby Town. Pelham was the family name of the Earl of Yarborough, large landowners throughout the surrounding area.

Striker, Tommy McCairns scored six goals in a 7-1 win against Leicester Fosse on 11 April 1896.

Famous past managers include the legendary Bill Shankly and Laurie McMenemy .

Grimsby Town...

The latter led 'The Mariners' to the Fourth Division title in 1972. In so doing Grimsby ended-up as the highest scorers in the entire English League that season.

Father and son, J and W Butler, played together in the same game against Burnley in 1909.

Lost to Burnley 2-0 in an FA Cup in 1909. Grimsby's goalkeeper, Walter Scott had saved three out of four penalties.

Blundell Park is situated closer to the sea than any other English League stadium.

Won the Division Two Championship in 1901 and 1934, the Division Three (North) Championship in 1926 and 1956, the Division Three Championship in 1980, and the Division Four Championship in 1972.

Striker, Clive Mendonca scored a hat-trick against Ipswich, in April 1996, only his second game after being out with injury for 16 months.

Won the Auto Windscreen Shield Cup in 1998.

Halifax Town...

Was founded, it could be argued, by a certain A E Jones, in 1911. Signing himself 'Old Sport' he wrote to the Halifax Evening Courier suggesting that the town might wish to consider setting-up a football club. A spirited correspondence ensured and at a public meeting held at the Saddle Hotel on the 23rd May 1911 Jones' suggestion was taken-up.

The team's first pitch was initially at Sandhill until the club moved to Exley.

Are the only fourth League team to have regained League status when, in 1998, 'The Shaymen' won the Vauxhall Conference Championship in 1998.

Had been relegated from Division Three back in 1993

Are one of only a handful of League clubs who have never won a Divisional title.

Takes its nickname, 'The Shaymen', from the name of the club ground, the Shay.

Halifax Town...

Fans invented the terrace chant of "hee-haw" to indicate that they thought that a particular opposition team player moved with all the grace of a donkey. This abusive chant caught-on and was taken-up by clubs all over the country. The most famous target being Arsenal's captain and centre back, Tony Adams.

Suffered the worst defeat in League history, 13-0, during a Division Three (North) game against Stockport County back in 1934.

Played before their biggest crowd, ever (36,885), on the 15th February 1953, in a Fifth Round FA Cup tie against Tottenham Hotspur.

Most famous victory happened on the 31st July 1971. A home crowd of over 19,000 witnessed the defeat of Manchester United 2-1 in a pre-season Watney Cup match. This United team included such all-time greats as Bobby Charlton, Denis Law and George Best.

Hartlepool United...

Have been forced to apply for re-election to the Football League a record 14 times. They have always been successful.

Fielded an Egyptian inside right, a certain Tewik Abdallah, on 11 occasions during the 1923/4 season. His previous career had included spells with International SC (Cairo), Derby County and Cowdenbeath. Upon retirement he became a Soccer coach in the USA.

Player who has been accorded the most international honours is Ambrose Fogarty who won just one international cap for the Republic of Ireland.

Drew 0-0 at Torquay in 1996, despite having had two players sent-off in the first 32 minutes.

Former manager during the 1960s, Keith Houchen's main claim to past fame was that he netted a vital goal for Coventry against Tottenham in the 1987 FA Cup Final.

Were called Hartlepool United up until 1968, then, in line with a current PR fad, contracted the club name to just 'Hartlepool'. The club reverted back to the original Hartlepool United in 1977.

Can trace its origins way back to 1905 when West Hartlepool FC (established back in 1881) won the Amateur Cup. This cup success initiated the formation of a professional team in 1908. West Hartlepool joined the North-Eastern League and won the Durham Cup in 1909 and again in 1910.

Can claim to be the very first club to be bombed. During the First World War, on the 17th November 1916, German Zeppelins jettisoned their bombs over the ground. 'The Pools' applied for £2,500 compensation for damage caused to the stadium at Victoria Park upon the termination of hostilities. The German government ignored the club's repeated requests.

Hartlepool United...

Hold the record for having been knocked out of the FA Cup four years running between the years 1927-30 by non-league sides.

Hold another League record. They are the only club never to have reached the last 16 in the FA Cup.

Knocked Premier Division Crystal Palace out of the FA Cup during the 1992/93 season then went on to achieve the British club record of 13 league and cup games without finding the net.

Huddersfield Town...

Appointed Peter Jackson as manager during the 1997/8 season. At that time 'The Terriers' had accumulated a mere four points from 15 games. By the end of the season Huddersfield had avoided the drop and Peter Jackson had won a Vauxhall Conference Championship medal as a Halifax Town player.

Leeds Road space-age ground, the Sir Alfred McAlpine Stadium is the most modern and well appointed in the entire country.

Owe their existence to a meeting called by the Huddersfield & District FA held at the Imperial Hotel in 1906 to discuss forming a football club in a rugby stronghold. A couple of years later a man with both the finances and the vision, Mr Hilton Crowther called a meeting at the Albert Hotel. In 1908 the present club was formed with capital of £2,000 and joined the North-Eastern League.

Were the first team to win the League on goal average when they took the title in 1924.

Player who holds the record for the most games is Billy Smith with 520 appearances for the club between 1914

Huddersfield Town...

and 1934.

Beat future European Champions, PSV Eindhoven, 4-1 and the French club, Rennes, 5-1 in the Festival of Britain tournament back in the early 1950s.

Most famous fan was the Labour Prime Minister, Harold Wilson. A life-long fan of 'The Terriers' he always kept a photograph of the great team of the 1920s in his wallet.

Were the first club to win the Football League Championship three times in a row. The club achieved this record hat-trick in 1924, 1925 and 1926 under Herbert Chapman.

Also won the FA Cup in 1922, the Division Two Championship in 1970 and the Division Four Championship in 1980.

Were, during the 1972-75 season, the first past League Champions to free-fall down into the Fourth Division.

Hull City...

Were sponsored by Hull University during the 1997/98 season; the first League club to have been sponsored by an academic establishment

Almost went bust in 1997. In this year, during a 2-0 home defeat by Scarborough, 'The Tigers' attracted their lowest crowd ever, a mere 3,774.

Are well travelled. They started out, in 1904, at Boulevard Ground (the home of Hull's Rugby Football Club), then a year later, 1905, were moved on to Anlaby Road (Hull Cricket Club's ground). Between 1944 and 1945 'The Tigers' found themselves back at the Boulevard Ground. It was in the following year, 1946, that the club arrived at its present site, Boothferry Park.

Have never played in the top flight. Indeed, Hull is the biggest city in England, with a population of 270,000, whose football team has always languished in the lower divisions of the League.

Past star players who have turned out in the black and amber strip include Raich Carter and a former England manager Don Revie.

Hull City...

Was founded in 1904 by a collection of very courageous individuals. Hull was a stronghold of the oval ball game and Hull City's founders actually had sufficient cheek to enter into a three-year rental agreement with the city's rugby league club to share their ground. Too many Rugby players changed to the round ball code and the Rugby League issued an edict that forbade the future use of their club pitches by soccer clubs.

Entered the FA Cup in their first professional season.

They were elected to the Second Division in 1905.

Most capped player is Terry Neill with a total of 59 caps for Northern Ireland, 15 while a Hull City player. While occupying City's hot seat he almost succeeded in taking 'The Tigers' into Division One, before leaving to manage Arsenal and Spurs.

Can boast that during the 1970/1 season Hull had two future international managers in their line-up, Terry Neill and Tommy Docherty of Scotland. Terry Neil has the distinction of being the only International team manager to have scored the winning goal against England at Wembley. Neill was not only Northern Ireland's manager he picked himself, and appointed himself captain.

Were the first club to lose a first class match on penalties. City and Manchester United had drawn 1-1 at the close of open play in the semi-final of the Watney Cup in 1970. City lost the subsequent shoot-out 4-3.

Ipswich Town...

Joined the Football League as late as 1938. However, the club was formed in 1878 when a meeting was held at the Town Hall at which Mr T C Cobbold MP became the club's first president.

The original name was Ipswich Association FC to distinguish it from the much older rugby playing Ipswich Football Club. The two clubs amalgamated in 1888; the oblong ball game was dropped in 1893.

Player who made the most appearances in an Ipswich shirt was full-back and captain Mick Mills, a total of 591 between 1966 and 1982. He was also captain of England.

Youngest ever team, average age 22 years and nine months, took the field against Tottenham on the 21st August 1976. Ipswich won 3-1.

Play their home games at Portman Road.

Record win was 10-1 against the Maltese club Floriana during their European Cup campaign of 1962.

Ipswich Town...

Record defeat happened around 12 months later, a loss of 1-10 against Fulham.

Manager, Bobby Robson led the club to its greatest success, the FA Cup in 1978 and the UEFA Cup in 1981, when Ipswich beat the Dutch club, AZ Alkmaar.

Were taken, by manager Alf Ramsey, up from the Third Division (South) through to the old Division One Championship between the years 1957 and 1962. Ramsey left to take up the England manager's job.

Roger Osborne was so exhausted by scoring the winning goal against Arsenal (and by being submerged under his celebrating team-mates) that he had to be substituted during the club's 1978 Cup Final victory.

Player with the most international caps is Alan Hunter with 53 caps for Northern Ireland; he won 47 of them while at Ipswich.

Domestic League honours include the Division One Championship in 1962, the Division Two Championship in 1961, 1968 and 1992. and the Division Three (South) Championship in 1954 and 1957.

Were the first club to have an all-seater stadium.

Leeds United...

Striker, Ian Rush started off with a four-month dry spell in the first team before he found the net.

Had South African international, Lucas Radebe between the sticks for a couple of games as a stand-in keeper in 1996.

Were merely maintaining an old South African link. The Spion Kop at Elland Road is so-named after a hill on which 322 British soldiers were massacred during the Boar War.

Scored the fewest League goals ever in one season, 28 in 1996/7, and still managed to avoid relegation.

Were the last club to win the old First Division prior to the establishment of the present Premier Division.

John Charles scored 11 hat-tricks while a Leeds player.

Was founded in 1919, the same year that Leeds City FC was closed down by the FA because of financial irregularities as regards payments to their players. Almost at once a Leeds solicitor, Mr Alf Masser, called a meeting, and Leeds United was born. The club joined the Midland

Leeds United...

League in 1919 and in the same year had discussions with
the directors of Huddersfield Town as regards move to
Leeds and an eventual amalgamation. Neither option was
taken-up.

Fans had a new song to sing from the terraces during
manager George Graham's tour of duty, "We'll score again,
don't know where, don't know when".

Won the European Fairs Cup twice, in 1968 and 1971.

Fans rioted after their team's 2-1 defeat by Bayern Munich
after the European Cup Final of 1975. This resulted in the club
being banned from all European competition for three years.

**Manager , Don Revie so admired Real Madrid that he
changed the club strip to all-white.**

John Charles is the club's record goal-scorer in one season,
he netted 42 goals.

**Centre-back, Jack Charlton holds the club record for the
most League appearances, 629 outings between the years
1953 and 1973.**

Entered into a ground share with Hunslet Rugby League club
between 1982 and 1994. In 1982 Eland Road ground was the
first football stadium to stage the Rugby League Challenge
Cup Final, apart from Wembley.

Leicester City...

Can trace its origins back to 1884 when some old boys of Wyggeston School met up at a house on the Roman Fosse Way and formed the Leicester Fosse FC. A collection was made and 9d was collected towards the cost of a football, plus the same amount in membership fees.

The club's first professional, Harry Webb was signed from Stafford Rangers in 1888 for 2s. 6d. (12p) per week, plus his travelling expenses.

While playing as Leicester Fosse the club suffered its worst defeat, 12-0 to East Midland neighbours Nottingham Forest, in 1909.

First ground was at Victoria Park; the club moved to Belgrave Road in 1887 for just one year then back to Victoria Park in 1988.

'The Foxes', AKA "The Filberts', arrived at Filbert Street in 1891.

Leicester Fosse became Leicester City in 1919.

Have taken part in more play-off finals, four, than any other club since the system was introduced in 1987.

Leicester City...

Goalkeeper, Mark Wallington did not miss a single game between the years from 1975 to 1981, and 1982 to 1983.

Won 13 consecutive home games in Division towards the end of 1906.

Installed a bubble-type weather protection system in the 1980s. When inflated the plastic sheeting was of sufficient height for the City players to train comfortably underneath it.

Record buy was Mark Draper from Notts County, for £1.25 million in 1994, they later sold him for £3.25 million to Aston Villa in 1995.
Players, Stan Milburn and Jack Froggatt, were both credited with but did not claim an own goal during a game against Chelsea in 1954.

Were knocked out during the early rounds of both the UEFA Cup and the Cup Winners' Cup by the same team, Atletico Madrid.

Roll of honour includes the League Cup twice, in 1964 and 1997.

They have also won the Division Two Championship an amazing six times between 1925 and 1980.

Have never won the FA Cup even though they have reached the Final on four occasions.

Striker, Alan Smith had three teeth replaced in hospital after a foul during a match in 1984 against Stoke City. They had been found in the grass after a careful search of the pitch.

England striker Gary Lineker, won no honours until he left Leicester .

Leyton Orient...

Player with the most international honours is John Chiedozie of Nigeria.

The 'O's can boast of having beaten Wales, 2-1, in a friendly international held in May 1996.

Are somewhat confused about their origins. Although 19th century clubs such as Leyton and Clapton are sometimes put forward as the inspiration behind the foundation of the'O's it seems more likely that the club was formed by members of Homerton Theological College. They had set-up Glyn Cricket Club back in the Spring of 1881 then, needing a winter pastime, formed a football team.

The club turned professional in 1903.

Roll of honour includes just two items; Division Three (South) Champions in 1956 and Division Three Champions in 1970.

Owes the addition of 'Orient', in 1898, to the fact that the club attracted as playing members a large number of the Orient Shipping Line's employees.

Previous club names include Glyn Cricket and Football Club, Eagle Football Club, Orient Football Club, Claptam Orient and then, in 1946, Leyton Orient. Between 1966 and 1987 the club, in tune with a current PR fad, wished to be known as just the Orient.

Former player and vicar, Alex Comfort conducted the first wedding ceremony ever to be held in a football club stadium , at Brisbane Road, in 1995.

Previous home grounds include Glyn Road, Whittles Athletic Ground, Millfields Road, Lea Bridge. In 1930 the 'O's, moved into Brisbane Road.

Leyton Orient...

Serve up the worst food sold in any League stadium, according to The Coleman's Football Food Guide for 1998!

Sacked England goalkeeping legend, Peter Shilton "because he couldn't kick the ball far enough". Shilton was to play between the sticks for the Orient on only 10 occasions.

In December 1996 Shilton became the first player to play 1,000 League games when he played for Orient in their 2-0 victory over Brighton.

Are still the only Football League club to have played home games (two) at Wembley Stadium. During the 1930/31 season the condition of the club's Lea Bridge ground failed to come up to League requirements. Clapham United's two home games against Brentford and Southend were played beneath the famous twin towers.

Survived its third financial melt-down when, in 1995, boxing and snooker promoter Barry Hearne took over as chairman.

Lincoln City...

Appointed, in 1993, the first black manager in the history of the English game when they invited Keith Alexander to take the hot seat.

Can trace its origins back to 1861. The present club was formed in 1880 and won the Lincolnshire Senior Cup just four years later.

The club were founder members of the Midland League in 1889 and were championship winners by the end of that first season.

In 1892 they turned pro-
fessional and played their
first League game in
Division Two.

**Previous ground was
John O'Gaunt's. The club
moved to Sincil Bank in
1894.**

Nickname is 'The Imps', or
'The Red Imps'. They have
been well provided with
nicknames over the years;
another was the 'Citizens', or just the 'Cits'. The earliest was
'Window Blinds', a reference to the club's red and white strip's
similarity to the striped awnings that then adorned many high
street shop fronts.

Were, in 1987, the first club to be relegated from the League when automatic promotion from the Conference League was first introduced.

Went 621 minutes during the 1995-96 season without conceding a single goal at home. This equalled a 64 year club record.

Lincoln City...

Tony Emery turned out in the club's colours for a record 402 times between 1946 and 1959.

Appointed the youngest ever manager in the history of the League. Graham Taylor was just 28 years of age when he arrived in 1972.

Won their last six matches in 1958 to avoid relegation from Division Two.

Scored 7 goals in twenty-one minutes against Halifax Town in 1932.

Boasted a 6ft 3ins centre-half called Ray Long and a 5ft 2ins outside-left called Ray Short in the 1958/59 season.

Liverpool...

Were born out of a local difference of opinion between Everton and the landlord of their Anfield Ground. Most of the Everton players left Anfield and set up shop in nearby Goodison Park. The landlord, John Holding tried to retrieve his financial loss by attempting to reform the club. He was unsuccessful in keeping the name 'Everton' and Liverpool Association Football Club was born on the 5th March 1892.

Have the most successful record of any English club. The 'Reds' have won 18 League titles (a record in itself), five FA Cups, and four European.

Reached an amazing total of 100 victories in Europe when they defeated Strasbourg during the 1997/98 season.

Did the 'double' of Cup and League in 1986, only the third side to achieve this since 1900.

Ian Rush is the club's leading international with 65 caps for Wales while an Anfield player.

Had two graduates on the playing staff during the 1970s, Brian Hall and Steve Heighway.

Manager, Graham Souness, made a loss of £9 million from his dabbling in the transfer market.

Their second leg European Cup quarter-final against Cologne in March 1965 was abandoned because of snow on the pitch.

The fog was so thick during a European game against Ajax in the 1960s that Bill Shankly walked onto the pitch and talked to two of his players without the referee noticing.

Liverpool...

Were involved, back in 1899 with opponents Sheffield United, in an epic struggle to complete an FA Cup semi-final. The first game at Nottingham was a 2-2 draw, the reply at Bolton a 4-4 draw and the third attempt, held at Manchester's Fallowfield ground was abandoned after a first half lasting 105 minutes. The ground could not hold the 30,000 fans and they continually ended up spilling onto the pitch. The tie was finally decided in Liverpool's favour at the next and last replay.

Legendary manager, Bill Shankley changed the Liverpool strip from red shirts and white shorts to all red in time for the start of the 1964-65 season. He thought it made the players look bigger.

Striker and England World Cup hero, Roger Hunt holds the club record for the most League goals, 245, and the most goals scored during a single season, 41.

Full back Tom Cooper died in June 1940 when the England international's motorbike was involved in a collision with a bus.

Kevin Keegan is the first English player to have been sent off at Wembley; the event being the 1974 Charity Shield.

Ian Rush informed the Press that, "It was like playing in a foreign country", when he returned from his spell with the Italian club, Juventus.

Worst defeat was a 9-1 drubbing by Birmingham during a Second Division clash back in 1954.

Bill Shankly took over a struggling Second Division side in 1959 and by 1965 brought the First Division Championship to Anfield and led Liverpool to its first FA Cup triumph.

Under 'Shanks', won two more League Championships, another FA Cup, and the club's first European honour, the UEFA Cup.

Liverpool...

Gave English football its most unforgettable quote when Shankly informed the press that "Some people believe football is a matter of life and death. I am very disappointed with that attitude. I can assure you it is much, much more important than that".

Manager, Bob Paisley's first season as manager of Liverpool was not a taste of things to come. It was the only season under his leadership that Liverpool added no silverware to the trophy cupboard. His total haul whilst in the hot-seat included a UEFA Cup and an incredible three European Cups. (But not the FA Cup.)

Won its first European Cup by beating Borussia Moenchengladbach 3-1 in Rome. Upon the team's arrival in the Eternal City, Second World War veteran, Paisley commented "The last time I was here I was in a tank".

Kenny Dalglish is the first player/manager to win the 'double' in his first season in charge. A feat he achieved with Liverpool in 1986.

'King Kenny' guided Liverpool to three League Championships in just five seasons.

Graham Souness, who succeeded Kenny Dalglish as manager won the FA Cup in 1992.

Lost the last game they ever played on Christmas Day. A 3-1 defeat by Grimsby back in 1958.

Cyril Sidlow, in an attempt to improve his distribution, was the first goalkeeper to throw, rather than kick, the ball to his team mates.

Michael Owen, at only 17 years and five months, is the youngest Liverpool player to have scored for the club. He first found the back of the net for 'The Reds' in April 1997 when he came on as a substitute against Wimbledon.

Liverpool...

Michael Owen scored on his League, League Cup, FA Cup and International debuts.

Goalkeeper Bruce Grobbelaar was a full international with the Zimbabwe national team.

Rev. James Jackson combined playing for Liverpool during the 1920s with his training to become a clergyman. The 'Parson', as he was affectionately know by the fans, was ordained in 1933.

Jan Mobley was not available for selection to Liverpool's first team for part of 1988 because he was serving a prison sentence for a driving offence.

Striker, Gordon Hodgson also played cricket for Lancashire around 1930.

Beat Arsenal 3-2 in 1964 in what was Match of the Day's first game

Goal scoring legend Ian Rush holds the record for the most goals in the FA Cup with a total of 43. (39 for Liverpool, 3 for Chester and 1 for Newcastle).

Liverpool...

Fielded an incredible 10 Scottish players for their first ever competitive game. Only the goalkeeper was English.

Conceded just 16 goals in their title-winning campaigne of 1978-79. This established a record for a 42 match programme.

Amassed 68 points in the same season, again another record before the introduction of 3 points for a win

Won 13 trophies under manager Bob Paisley - but never the FA Cup.

Became the first ever club to win the European Cup on penalties when they beat Roma in 1984

Kenny Dalglish was 39 years and 54 days when he played in a game against Derby County on 1 May 1990.

Beat Stromsgodset of Norway 11-0 in the European Cup-Winners' Cup with nine players finding the back of the net.

Fielded an unchanged team for the first 12 league games of 1967/68. They used only 18 players that season and made only four substitutions.

Player Ian Callaghan played a record 88 FA Cup games, 79 of them for the Reds.

Won the League Cup four years running - 1981/1984.

Never finished lower than 2nd in the league during Kenny Dalglish's time in the manager's chair.

Goal-machine Roger Hunt scored 245 League goals between 1959 and 1969, including 41 in season 1961/62.

Luton Town...

First game at Kenilworth Road in 1905 was nicknamed 'The Green Game'. Their opponents on the day, Plymouth, wore a green strip, the referee was a certain Mr Green and the game was kicked-off by a local brewer whose surname was Green.

Was formed by the eventual amalgamation of two local clubs, the Wanderers and a works team called Excelsior following a meeting at Luton Town Hall in April 1885.

The Wanderers had won the first ever FA Cup. Three months earlier this famous club had changed its name to Luton Town Wanderers.

Entered for the FA Cup in its first full season and turned professional in 1890, the first club to do so south of Birmingham.

Most famous supporter was comedian Eric Morecombe. He was a director of 'The Hatters' from 1976 until his death in 1983.

Luton Town...

Played at various grounds, Excelsior, Dallow Lane and Dunstable Road until their final move to Kenilworth Road in 1905.

Forward, Joe Payne scored 10 goals in 'The Hatters' record 12-0 thrashing of Bristol Rovers in 1936. The crowd was just over 13,000. After Joe Payne's exploit over 23,000 packed into Kenilworth Road for 'The Hatters' next home game. He scored the goal in the 1-1 draw with Coventry.

Bob Hawkes became the club's first player to be called up, in 1970, for full international honours. He was already a well-established England amateur international.

Most capped player is Mal Donaghy with 58 appearances for Northern Ireland.

Were the first League club to ban away supporters, in 1986, after visiting Millwall fans rioted inside the stadium. Luton's unilateral action resulted in the FA banning them from the League Cup competition of that year.

Won the League Cup in 1988 and reached FA Cup Final in 1959.

Macclesfield Town...

Goalkeeper, Ryan Price was voted Man-of-the-Match after 'The Silkmen' had beaten Leyton Orient 1-0 in 1998. He had just made it to the ground in time for the kick-off having dashed back from hospital after the birth of his first child.

Were a rugby club from the 1850s until 1874.

In 1891 the club moved to Moss Rose, they were

champions of the Manchester and District League in 1906 and 1908. By 1911 they had lifted the Cheshire Senior Cup five times.

Became a founder member of Cheshire County League in 1919.

In 1886 they recorded their best win by thrashing Chester St Marys 15-0 in the second round of the Cheshire Senior Cup.

Are only the second team ever to have won promotion from the Vauxhall Conference to the Third and then the Second Division in successive seasons.

Almost joined the League when they won the Vauxhall Conference for the first time, in 1995. Despite Chester City

Macclesfield Town...

having played all their home games at Macclesfield's Moss Rose ground from 1990 until 1992 the League considered the pitch and facilities to be below the required standard and refused them their hard won opportunity for League football.

Are nicknamed 'The Silkmen'.

Manager, Jimmy McIlroy was capped 88 times for Northern Ireland.

Worst defeat was back in 1929, a 15-0 thrashing by Tranmere Reserves.

Paid a club record transfer fee of £30,000 to Stevenage Borough for Efetobore Sodje, in 1997.

Received a record £40,000 from Sheffield United for Mike Lake, in 1988.

Manchester City...

Winger, Nicky Sumerbee holds the record for possessing the hardest shot in League football, an amazing 87 mph. This is listed in the Guinness Book of Records and was confirmed live on the TV programme, Record Breakers.

Have the largest pitch in the entire English League, it measures 117 yards by 78 yards.

The club have had five previous grounds, Clowes Street, Kirkmanshulme Cricket Ground, Queens Road, and as City, Pink Bank Lane and Hyde Road. The club moved to Main Road in 1923.

Can trace its origins back as far as 1880 when St Mark's church at West Gorton added a football club to its list of sporting activities. Amalgamation with Gorton Athletic occurred in 1884 and Gorton FC was founded. Because of a change of ground the club became Ardwick FC in 1887.

In 1892 Ardwick thrashed Bootle 7-0.

Manchester City was formed as a Limited Company in 1894, the same year that Ardwick was declared bankrupt.

Were the first club, in 1926, to play both in the FA Cup Final and be relegated in the same season.

Main Road ground played host to 2.2 million fans during the 1946/47 season. In addition to the normal League and Cup schedule the stadium was chosen as the venue for the FA Cup semi-final replay between Liverpool and Burnley and the Rugby League Challenge Cup Final.

Manager, Peter Reid equalled the League record for the shortest period in the hot seat. He was sacked after only 12 days in charge.

Main Road Stadium was packed in 1996 when City fans, the pop group Oasis played live.

Manchester City...

Comedian Bernard Manning is a big fan of City.

Are the first and the only current holders of the League Championship, in 1937, to be relegated from Division One.

Striker Tommy Johnson is the club's record top scorer, 158 between the years 1919 and 1930; he also holds the record for the most goals in a single season, 38 in 1928/29.

Legend, Billy Meredith appeared in "The Citizens' colours in an FA Cup semi-final of 1924 when aged 49.

Played 34 away games in the League without a single win during the 1986/87 season.

Highest honour was achieved in 1970 when City lifted the European Cup Winners' Cup.

'The Citizens' domestic honours include lifting the FA Cup on four occasions between 1904 and 1969, and winning the League Cup twice, in 1970 and 1976.

Glyn Pardo was just 15 years and 315 days old when he played his first game for City in 1961.

Signing of Georgian international George 'Kinky' Kinkladze in 1998 by City manager Alan Ball inspired the tabloid headline, "Ball gets Kinky". The fans adapted the words of a current hit single, Wonderwall, and the terraces resounded to the refrain, "And all the runs which Kinky makes are winding" whenever their hero turned on the magic.

Manchester United...

Could argue that the club was founded way back in 1878 when the dinning room committee of the carriage and waggon works of the Lancashire and Yorkshire Railway Company set up Newton Cricket and Football Club.

The football team lifted the Manchester Cup in 1886 and were elected to the League in 1892 as Newton Heath FC. This club was declared bankrupt in 1902, was reformed, and Manchester United were born.

First League goal, while still called Newton Heath FC, was scored by Robert Donaldson against Blackburn Rovers in September 1892. The same player scored the club's first ever hat-trick later that same season.

Most unusual recent craze have been T-shirts bearing the legend 'Uwe Rosler's dad bombed Old Trafford'. During the years following the end of the Second World War 'The Red Devils' had been forced to play at neighbours Manchester City's Maine Road ground until 1949 as Old Trafford had suffered from the close attention s of the Luftwaffe.

Played in front of the biggest crowd ever (83,260) to attend an England ground when they entertained Arsenal at Main Road in 1947 during their period of post-War enforced exile.

Previous home grounds include North Road, Monsell Road, and Bank Street. United moved to Old Trafford in 1910.

Were the first English club to win the European Cup when they defeated Benfica 4-1 in 1968.

Welsh wizard, Ryan Giggs started his career at rival's Manchester City's Main Road.

Hold the Premiership record for the Premiership's biggest win, a 9-0 thrashing of Ipswich in 1995.

Manchester United...

United racked up another Premiership record during this demolition job. Andy Cole's five-goal tally is the Premiership record for the most goals scored in a game by one player.

Are arguably the most successful English club ever, with a record nine FA Cups plus 11 League titles.

Biggest win ever during a European Cup campaign was a 10-1 drubbing of RSC Anderlecht in 1956.

Three worst defeats, all by seven goals without reply, were by Blackburn Rovers, Aston Villa and Wolves. However, all three games were played prior to 1932.

Bobby Charlton holds the club record of having scored 247 goals in 754 games, 199 of his goals were in his 606 League matches.

Are Britain's richest club. The most up-to-date figures available indicate that United have a current turnover of around £88 million and a gross profit of £27.5 million.

Sir Matt Busby's 24 years as manager (1945/69) of the football club he turned into one of the most famous in the world is a post-War record. During his tenure of office he brought seven domestic honours back to Old Trafford, two FA Cups and five League Championships.

Defenders Gary and Philip Neville are the first pair of brothers to have played in a 'double-winning' post-War team.

Supporters could well argue that United could have won the European Cup a decade earlier if it had not been for a 'plane crash, usually referred to as the Munich Disaster, in 1958, when eight players, including Duncan Edwards, died. The Busby Babes made a stopover after returning from an away match against Red Star Belgrade. Sir Matt Busby and Bobby Charlton were two of the 20 survivors.

Manchester United...

Enigmatic genius and European Footballer of the Year for 1968, George Best was once reported to have said, "I was so embarrassed that I played the last 20 minutes at left back". He was referring to a Fifth Round tie in the FA Cup against Northampton in 1970 during which he found the back of the net six times, still a club record, in United's 8-2 win.

George Best never appeared in Manchester United's (or any other club's) colours in an FA Cup Final or the final stages (with Northern Ireland) of either the World or European Cup.

Were the first English club to score in the San Siro (Giuseppe Meazza) Stadium during a European Cup tie, in March 1999.

Denis Law holds the record for the most hat-tricks in European competition, an incredible five.

Most capped player was Bobby Charlton who made 106 England appearances. He also scored a record of 49 goals for his country, most of them pile drivers from outside the penalty area.

Record holder for having scored the most goals for "The Red's' in one season is Denis Viollet with 32.

Not only enjoys world-wide adulation with supporters clubs in many countries but, closer to home, have welcomed around a million supporters to Old Trafford in recent seasons.

Attracts a host of celebrity fans, including Simply Red's front man Mick Hucknall, TV presenter Zoe Ball, the actor and satirist Angus Deyton, and Mike Atherton one-time England cricket captain.

Manchester United...

Diversification into the noble art of kick boxing was short lived. Indeed, it was more a unilateral declaration by maverick French genius Eric Cantona when, sick of the mindless taunts from the terraces, jumped into the crowd and scissor-kicked Crystal Palace supporter Mathew Simmons during an away game against Crystal Palace in January 1995. He was fined a total of £30,000, banned from the game for eight months and sentenced to 120 hours of community service for this 'retaliation'. Upon his return United went on to 'do the double', again.

Current boy wonder, David Beckham, yet one more product of United's successful home-grown youth policy, was actually born within the sound of London's Bow Bells. He was voted the PFA's Young Player of the Year in 1997.

David Beckham scored from the half-way line in a match against Wimbledon on the first day of the 1996-97 season.

Were on the wrong end of the record long distance goal ever scored in the Charity Shield of 1967 when United had to suffer the indignity of watching Spurs' keeper Pat Jennings find the back of their net having dropped kicked the ball from well within his own area.

One-time captain and central defender, Steve Bruce was not a player to duck-out of physical contact. His reward was a career best of over 100 stitches.

Were winners of the highest scoring Charity Shield encounter ever when, back in 1911 United drubbed Swindon Town 8-4.

Famous ground hosted the game with the official lowest ever attendance, a grand total of 13 fans. In 1921 Leicester City and Stockport County were forced to transfer a meaningless end-of-season game to Old Trafford.

Manchester United...

Supporters often trace the start of the club's incredible amazing modern-day success from their Cup Final victory over Blackpool in 1948. 'The Red Devils' twice came back from behind to beat the great Stanley Matthew's team 4-2.

Defied the English football establishment when Matt Busby entered his famous 'Busby Babes' for the European Champions Cup in 1956. Their first foray into Europe resulted in a 10-0 thrashing of Anderlecht.

George Best, 'El Beatle' entitled his autobiography, 'The Good, the Bad, and the Bubbly'.

Alex Ferguson sold his son, Darren, who was a player on United's books, to Wolves.

Kevin Moran carries the shame of having been the first player, ever to be sent off during an FA Cup Final at Wembley, in 1985.

Part-exchange of Keith Gillespie was included in the deal that brought Andy Cole to Old Trafford from Newcastle.

Legendary manager, Sir Matt Busby was born in Scotland.

Denis Irwin was the only player to have played in every League game for 'The Reds' during their progress towards lifting the 1994 Premiership title.

Ryan Gigg's father was a professional Ruby League player.

Double-winning captain Steve Bruce never played for England.

Mansfield Town...

Most famous unused substitute was Olympic and World Champion Decathlete Daley Thompson.

Owes its existence to the foundation of the Mansfield Wesleyans FC back in 1897. The club became Mansfield Wesley in 1906 when it turned professional and changed its name to Mansfield Town in 1910.

Are nicknamed 'The Stags';

Played their first League game in 1931.

Fielded both their youngest and their oldest player ever during the same year, 1997, but not in the same game. Jonathan Milner played for the first team at the age of 16, Tony Ford was still playing at the ripe old age of 38.

Record in the transfer market was back in 1989 when they spent out £80,000 to bring Steve Wilkinson from Leicester. "The Stags' more than recouped their outlay, within the month when they sold Simon Coleman to Middlesbrough for £600,000

Highest League win was 9-2 against Rotherham back in 1932. Just over a year later 'The Stags' were thrashed 8-1 by Walsall, the club's worst defeat, ever.

Enjoyed a well-earned promotion in 1977 to the (old) Second Division. This was a first for Mansfield. Unfortunately, the club followed this achievement with yet another first, they were relegated the following year.

Long-time servant, Rod Arnold has turned out in the club's colours on more occasions than any other Town player, 440 League appearances between 1970 and 1983.

Player with the most international honours is John McClelland who won six of his 53 caps for Northern Ireland while still on Mansfield's books.

Mansfield Town...

Ted Harston, who turned out for 'The Stags' during the 1930s holds the club record for having scored the most goals in one season, 55. The club's top scorer of all time is Harry Johnson with his tally of 104.

They won the Freight Rover Trophy in 1987.

Middlesbrough...

Paid Juventus a club record of £7.5 million when they signed Fabrizio Ravanelli from Juventus in 1997. He rewarded his new club's faith in him by scoring a hat-trick against Liverpool in his first game for 'Boro, a 3-3 draw.

Supporters often hold to the local legend that Middlesbrough FC was formed during the course of a tripe supper held at the local Corporation Hotel.

More prosaic club historians will insist that Middlesbrough's birth pangs can only be traced back to 1875 when members of Middlesbrough's Cricket Club held a meeting in the gymnasium of the Albert Park Hotel in an effort to find a sport to occupy them during the   winter months.

Do not believe the old adage regarding 'too many cooks'. During the 1997/98 season 'Boro broke two of their post-War club records. They fielded 36 players, 20 of whom were to find the net.

Raked in a cool £12 million when they sold the Brazilian Juninho to Atletico Madrid in 1997.

Can perhaps thank an outbreak of smallpox for having won the Amateur Cup twice during the early years of the club's history. The first success, in 1895, was a normal cup run, but the second, in 1898, was a somewhat bizarre affair. The semi-final against Thornaby was switched from Darlington to the village of Brotton, miles from anywhere in the Cleveland hills.

Hold the record for having reached three major Wembley finals in two years, only to lose all of them.

Can sometimes demonstrate an amazing consistency, 'The Ironsides' played 33 games and went four and a half years without registering a single away League victory.

Middlesbrough...

Still holds the record for the most League hat-tricks ever scored by one player. Back in 1926/27 George Camsell scored eight hat-tricks, which constituted 24 of his 59 goals.

The 59 League goals scored by George Camsell in the 1926/27 season was also a record until a certain Dixie Dean scored 60 in the following season.

Most honoured international was Wilf Mannion who played 26 times for England.

Were the first club to smash the English transfer record way back in 1905 when they signed England international Alf Commons from Sunderland, for the cool four figure sum of £1,000.

Famous old boy, Brian Clough is one of three 'Boro players who have scored five goals in a single match.

Followed-up their relegation from the Premiership in 1997 by signing a certain midfielder call Paul Gasgcoigne and gaining promotion at their first attempt at the end of the next season.

Record win occurred as far back as 1890 when they thrashed Scarborough 11-0.

Millwall...

Are still the only English club team ever to have won or drawn every home game for a full season in all four League divisions.

Had a record run of 59 games unbeaten at home for three years in the 1960s.

Might have been known as London Scottish rather than Millwall Rovers when the club was first formed in 1885. The leading lights of this venture, employees of Morton and Company, a jam and marmalade factory in West Ferry Road, were mostly Scots.

Team tactics in the very early days were discussed in the Islanders pub in Tooke Street.

The home ground was at Glengall Road,

Won their first trophy in 1887, the East End Cup.

Second home, by 1866, was the rather large back garden of a local pub called the Lord Nelson.

Changed the club name to Millwall Athletic in 1889 and moved to East Ferry Road in the following year.

Turned professional in 1893 and, by 1901 was based in North Greenwich.

Acquired 'The Den' at Cold Blow Lane in 1910. 'The Lions' moved to their present home, also called 'The Den', at Zampa Road in Bermondsey in 1993. The club can now boast of having one of the most modern stadiums in the country.

Old ground, the old 'Den', can claim the distinction of having been closed down on a record number of occasions (5) by the FA because of crowd trouble.

Millwall...

Best results ever were two 9-1 wins against Torquay and Coventry, both matches having been played in the 1927/8 season.

Worst defeat was 9-1 in a 1946 FA Cup tie against Aston Villa.

Leading scorer, with 93 League goals, was Teddy Sherringham.

Defender Barry Kitchener holds the club record for the most appearances for 'The Lions', 523 league games between the years 1967 and 1982.

Most capped player, with 23 Republic of Ireland caps, Eamonn Dunphy became the most loathed journalist in Ireland having voiced his criticism of Jack Charlton's tactics at the 1990 World Cup Finals.

Newcastle United...

List of famous fans includes the Prime Minister Tony Blair, the Roman Catholic Primate of Britain, Cardinal Basil Hulme and Channel Four's horse racing expert, John McCririck.

Player with the most international honours is Alf McMichael with 40 caps for Northern Ireland.

Owned the most expensive player in the world in 1996 when Newcastle bought Alan Shearer from Blackburn for £15 million .

Played 13 games in seven weeks in 1950 on their way to reaching the semi-final of the FA Cup and 11 games in four weeks after reaching the semi-final of the FA Cup in 1955. On both occasions Newcastle reached the Final and lifted the trophy.

Can trace the club's formation back to a club called Stanley, founded in 1881 and based at South Byker. In October 1882 the club changed its name to Newcastle East End so as not to be confused with two other clubs with similar names, Stanley Nops FC and Stanley Albion FC. After a merger by these two clubs and another local team, Rosewood FC, this greatly enlarged club adopted the club name Newcastle West End in August 1882.

Initially their pitch was at Town Moor but they moved to Brandling Park in 1885 and St James' Park in the following year, 1886, the home of local team, Newcastle Rangers. Newcastle East End FC were based at Chillingham Road, Heaton between 1886 and 1892, they turned professional in 1889. Newcastle West End FC suffered an extended run of bad results and by the early 1890s voted itself out of existence. A few members of the committee invited Newcastle East End FC to move to St James' Park. This offer was accepted at a meeting at the Bath Lane Hall in 1892 during which the club changed its name to Newcastle United. The club played its first League game in 1893.

Newcastle United...

Qualified for the Fairs Cup despite finishing 10th in the First Division. Amazingly they defeated Ujpest Dozsa 6-2 on aggregate in the final, the club's only success in European competition .

Worst defeat was way back in 1895, 9-0 by Burton Wanderers.

Record win was in 1946 when they drubbed Newport County 13-0. Len Shackleton netted six of the 13 and a club record.

Scored six without reply by Fulham back in 1908. This score is still the record for an FA Cup semi-final.

Failed to win the Premiership title for the 1995/96 season despite holding a 12 point lead in January 1996. No other club with such a safe margin has ever failed to go on to win the title.

Oldest player to represent the club was William Hampson. He was almost 45 when he turned out against Birmingham City in 1927.

Youngest player to represent 'The Magpies' is Steve Watson at only 16 years of age on his debut game in 1990.

Manager Frank Watt led Newcastle to six FA Cup Finals between the years 1905 and 1924, a record that still stands today.

All-time legend, "Wor' Jackie Milburn is commemorated by a large bronze statue situated in the city centre. He is Newcastle's record goalscorer with a grand total of 178.

Northampton Town...

Lost 8-2 to Manchester United in an 1970 FA Cup tie; with George Best scoring six of United's goals.

Player with the record number of appearances, 521, for 'The Cobblers' is Tommy Fowler.

Was formed, in 1897, by a group of schoolteachers who were members of the Northampton and District

Elementary Schools' Association. The club experienced and survived a financial crisis at the end of its first year of existence. Although Northampton was £675 in debt the club still applied for, and was accepted as, a member of the Midland League.

Joined the Southern League in the same year as the club turned professional, 1901, and played its first League game in 1920.

Striker, Ralph Hotel netted five goals for Northampton Town in their 8-1 defeat of Crystal Palace in October 1928.

First ever, Wembley appearance was in 1997 when Northampton Town reached the Third Division Play-offs. They

Northampton Town...

beat Swansea in the Final and were promoted to the Second Division.

Were unable to entertain other teams at home during the month of August while based at the old County Ground because they shared the stadium with Northants Cricket Club who had first claim on the use of the pitch.

Beat Sutton Town 10-0 in an FA Cup tie in the 1900s. Herbert Chapman scored twice and had three other goals disallowed.

Became Division Three Champions in 1963 and Division Four Champions in 1987.

'The Cobblers' became the first team to reach the top division via all the other three.

Appear to have suffered from vertigo after this exploit and, by 1969, the club found itself back in the bottom Division again.

Norwich City...

Was nicknamed 'The Canaries' because of its green and yellow kit and because the team were based between the years 1908 and 1935 at a ground in Rosary Road called 'The Nest'.

Most famous fan, and a director of the club since 1996, TV cook Delia Smith, brought in a top fashion designer, Bruce Oldfield, to design a new club kit for the 1997/98 season

Were formed in 1902 by two local schoolteachers during a meeting at the Criterion Cafe. Two years later the FA Commission decided that the club, based at Newmarket Road, was being run on professional lines and was thrown out of the FA Amateur Cup.

Appointed new officers and a professional club was properly established at a meeting in the Agricultural Hall during March 1905.

Played its first Football League game in 1920.

Moved to its present-day Carrow Road ground until 1935. Prior to this Coleman's mustard company had kept horses on the site.

Carrow Road stadium was constructed during the summer of 1935. The project took a mere 82 days. It was suggested that this was perhaps the largest building project the city had seen since the medieval period when Norwich castle was built.

Player with the most international honours is Mark Bowen. He won 35 of his total of 41 caps for Wales while a Norwich player.

Sale of striker Chris Sutton to Blackburn Rovers brought 'The Canaries' its record transfer fee in July 1994, £5 million.

Norwich City...

Did its bit during the Second World War; two anti-aircraft gun emplacements platforms were constructed in the club car park.

Best win happened in 1930 when Norwich beat the Midlanders FC 10-2.

Worst defeat was by the same scoreline back in 1908 against Swindon.

Put out an unchanged side for a club record of 21 matches during the 1950/51 season.

Striker, John Gavin is the club's leading scorer with 122 League goals between the years 1949/58.

Ralph Hunt netted 31 goals in a single season during the mid-50s.

Set a club record, during the 1970s, of playing 41 away League games without registering a single victory

Qualified for Europe in 1985 by winning the League Cup but were excluded from the UEFA Cup following the Heysel disaster.

Qualified for a second time, again by winning the League Cup, and in 1992 had a good run in UEFA beating such top opposition as Bayern Munich before being knocked out by Inter Milan.

Won the Division Two Championship in 1972 and 1986, and the Division Three Championship (South) in 1934.

Are the most Easterly League team in England.

Nottingham Forest...

Is one of the oldest football clubs in the world and was formed in 1865 when the players of a hockey-like game called 'shinny', based at a local pub the Clinton Arms, decided to switch to football and became the Forest Football Club. In 1865 the club bought the players a set of red caps to complete their on-field strip.

Was the first team to play to the sound of a referee's whistle during a home game in 1878 against Sheffield Norfolk.

Old time player, Sam Widdowson, came up with the idea of shinguards in 1874.

Went one whole calendar year undefeated in the league after having won the League Championship in the 1977/78 season.

All-time hero, Stuart Pearce, nicknamed by the fans, 'Pyscho' was the club's leading international player with 76 England caps.

Ground is only 330 yards from that of local rivals Notts County. The two clubs are the nearest neighbours in English football.

Have had six different grounds, including Forest Racecourse, The Meadows, a two-year spell at Trent Bridge Cricket Ground between the years 1880-82, Parkside then Gregory, both in Lenton, and the Town Ground, before arriving at the City Ground in 1898.

Most successful manager was Brian Clough. Having taken Forest into the First Division in 1977 Cloughie led the club to the league title the following season. Forest are the only newly promoted English club to have achieved this.

Were only the third English club to lift the European Cup when they beat Malmo in 1979. Under Cloughie they retained the trophy the following season with a 1-0 win over Hamburg.

Nottingham Forest...

Won the League Cup an amazing four times, in 1978, 1979, 1989 and 1990.

Won the FA Cup twice, the first in 1898, the second in 1959, a gap of some 61 years. The scorer of Forest's first goal in that game was Roy Dwight, uncle of Reg Dwight, better known as pop star and Watford chairman Elton John. Unfortunately Roy also broke his leg in the game.

Were the first side to win the League and League Cup Final in the same year, 1978.

Finished the 1977 Christmas holiday programme five points clear of their nearest rival. Brian Clough commented, "The last time Nottingham were five ahead of anybody was in a cricket match".

Notts County...

Are the world's oldest football club still in business. Notts were formed in 1862 and became a founder member of the League in 1888.

Are the first post-War club to have been uncatchable as early as March when, during the 1997/8 season, 'The Magpies' had clinched the Division Three title and promotion.

Can lay claim to be the club who has suffered relegation in the Football League on more occasions than any other, an amazing 14 times.

First ground was The Park, next to the Castle, prior to moving to the Meadows Cricket Ground in 1864. From 1877 the club played out of Beeston Cricket Ground, moved on to the Castle Ground in 1880 and three years later arrived at Trent Bridge. The club set up home at the County Ground, Meadow Lane in 1910.

Played its 4,000th League game in 1998 and celebrated with a 2-1 win over Rochdale.

Celebrated its centenary in 1962. Later research work by historian, Keith Warsop indicates that initially the club appears to have played little more than scratch matches with teams made up from its own members; presumably because Notts was one of the few football clubs in existence by this early date.

Notts County...

The name Notts Football Club was adopted at a meeting held at the George IV Hotel on December 1864. Notts turned professional in 1885 and played its League game three years later.

Took a penalty kick three times and still did not score. In 1974 three different players took the same penalty during a game against Portsmouth. The first Notts player scored but the referee ruled that the goalkeeper had moved. The second shot found the net but the referee disallowed the goal because he said it had been taken before he had signalled. The third spot kick attempt was saved by the 'keeper.

Goalkeeper, Albert Ironmonger appeared for 'The Magpies' in 564 matches between the years, 1904 and 1926, a club record. He was almost 42 years of age when he last played between the sticks, another club record.

Paddy Mills scored five goals for County in 9-0 win against Barnsley in 1927.

Henry Cursham, who often took the field with two of his brothers also listed on the teamsheet, scored a record 48 goals for Notts County in FA Cup competitions between the years 1880 and 1887.

Roll of honour includes the Division Two Championship in 1897, 1914, 1923, the Division Three (South) Championship in 1931 and 1950, the Division Three Championship in 1998, and the Division Four Championship in 1971.

Lifted the FA Cup way back in 1894.

Won the Anglo-Italian Cup in 1995.

Were watched by a mere 300 fans when they played Crewe in the League way back in 1894.

Oldham Athletic...

Thrashed Newton-le-Willows 11-0 back in 1905 with one Oldham player netting the first five goals and another scoring the last six.

Are nicknamed 'The Latics'.

Was formed in 1895 when the landlord of the Featherstall and Junction Hotel, John Garland decided that he should form a football club, which he named Pine Villa FC and entered the Oldham Junior League.

In 1899, when a local professional club called Oldham County went out of business, a liquidator convinced the officials of Pine Villa to take on Oldham County's Sheepfoot Lane ground, turn professional and change their name to Olham Athletic FC.

Moved to Boundary Park in 1905. The club still keeps, behind glass in the VIP suite, the silver spade that was used to turn the first turf cut.

Reached the League Cup Final in 1990, FA Cup semi-finals in 1990 and 1994, and promotion to the top Division in 1991.

Frankie Bun scored a League Cup record six goals in Oldham's 7-0 Third Round win over Scarborough.

Roger Palmer is the club's all-time record scorer with 141 goals scored between the years 1980 and 1994.

The player who holds the record for having scored the most goals in one season, 1937/7, is Tom Davies.

Beat Manchester United 3-2 back in 1924. Defender Sammy Wynne netted four of the five goals, including two own goals.

Oldham Athletic...

Hammered Southport 11-0 back in 1962, a record for the Fourth Division that still stands.

Worst defeat was in 1935, a 4-13 defeat by Tranmere Rovers. The 17 goal aggregate total in a single game is still the League record.

Are one of only four League clubs to have ever replaced their grass pitch with an artificial one.

One-time manager, David Ashworth (easily recognisable by his bowler hat) always watched the game from the flat roof of the stand. He would run up and down keeping up with the game until on one fateful day he fell over the edge of the roof. Luckily the flat roof of the stand was a much-favoured perch for many of "The Latics' supporters and they managed to grab him and pull him back to safety.

Oxford United...

Were obliged to share their Manor Ground around 1925 with a cricket club, a bowls club, a tennis club, an occasional flock of sheep and the odd horse.

Won the Division Two Championship in 1985, the Division Three Championship in 1968 and 1984, and lifted the 1986 League Cup, beating QPR 3-0.

Are building a new all-seater stadium on the Minchery Farm site. The project is behind schedule, the main problem being a lack of sufficient funds rather than the adjacent sewage farm.

Created League history when they became, in 1964, the first Fourth Division club to reach the quarter-finals of the FA Cup.

Created another record in the early 1970s when it took the 'U's six matches, and 11 hours, to complete their FA fourth round tie against Alverchurch.

Charismatic football manager and TV pundit Ron Atkinson and his brother, Graham, were both one-time team mates for the 'U's.

Netted their first goal in 10 hours and 44 minutes of open play when they drew 1-1 with Notts County in April 1996.

Were still known as Headington United when Manor Ground hosted its first floodlit match on the 18th December 1950.

Are a much travelled team. Between 1893 and 1925 the club has had six previous grounds, returning to one, the Sandy Lane Ground, twice.

Could claim to be able to trace their origins back to a certain Oxford United FC who were active in the Oxfordshire Thursday League from as early as 1893 up until the First World War. Whether this mid-week league for shopkeepers and shop assistants on their half-day off is the true forerunner of today's Oxford United is somewhat debatable.

Oxford United...

Sometimes prefers to consider its true forerunner to be a club called Headington FC, founded in 1893. A year later Headington United was born. At first it played on a pitch on Quarry Fields, then moved to Wootten's Fields in 1894. The efforts of a certain Dr Hitchings, around this period, were somewhat responsible for the club's continued existence. The club turned professional in 1949 but did not play its first League game until 1961.

Former club chairman Robert Maxwell, the Czech-born media tycoon, proposed a merger between Oxford United and Reading to form a new club called Thames Valley Royals. The plans were dropped after protest from fans and League disapproval.

Worst defeat was a 6-0 drubbing by Liverpool in a First Division game in March 1986.

Most famous celebrity fan is ITV's Jim Rosenthal.

Peterborough Utd...

Were nicknamed, 'the Posh', back in 1934 when a completely new team strip was paraded by the players for a match against Gainsborough Trinity.

Fans sometimes maintain that the club nickname derives from a comment made by Pat Tirrel, a former manager, when he said: "I'm looking for posh players for a posh new team".

Reached the third round of the FA Cup twice and the fourth round twice in seven seasons.

Eventually joined the League, in 1960, at their 21st attempt.

Were elected to the League along with three other clubs, Oldham, Southport and Hartlepool.

Won the Fourth Division in their first season in the Football League ('The Posh' lifted the same title again, in 1974), scoring a club record for one season of 134 goals. Terry Bly netted 52 of these goals, yet another club record.

Had 19 points deducted during the 1967/8 season because of alleged illegal pay-outs to certain players.

Peterborough Utd...

Played-out the rest of the season knowing that the club's fate had already been decided, an automatic relegation to the bottom Division from the Third.

Goalkeeper, Mick Drewert kept seven consecutive clean sheets during the 1970s.

Can trace its early history back to the old Peterborough and Fletton club that had been founded in 1923. The FA closed down this club in 1933. Local die hards formed a new professional club in 1934. Peterborough United was a member of the Midland League by 1935.

Were forced to replay an FA Cup tie against Kingstonian in 1922 because a member of the crowd had thrown a coin and struck their goalkeeper. The first match had finished 9-1; the second match, played in a deserted stadium, ended in a 1-0 win for Peterborough.

Hot-shot striker Giuliano Grazioli scored five goals for Peterborough in a League match against Barnet in the 1998/99 season.

Hammered Oldham Athletic 8-1 in a Fourth division match in 1969 recording their biggest ever win.

...Lost 8 -1 against Northampton in a 1946 Cup tie.

Chris Turner, the club's most successful manager ever, having won back-to-back promotions with the club in 1991 and 1992 became chief executive after leading a financial buy-out at the club.

Plymouth Argyle...

Originated as Argyle FC back in 1886. The team was composed of old boys of both public and private schools who had no desire to give up the round ball game just because they had left school. The name, Argyle Athletic was decided upon during a meeting held in a Coffee House called the Borough Arms in Bedford Street later that same year.

Decided upon their present name, Plymouth Argyle in 1903, the same year the club turned professional.

Played their first League game in 1920.

Forward, Frank Richardson scored a hat-trick on his League debut against Bristol Rovers on 27 August 1921.

Turned professional in 1903.

Are nicknamed 'The Pilgrims'.

Have the most southerly-situated stadium in the entire English League.

Are the second largest English city (the largest is Hull) never to

Plymouth Argyle...

have possessed a football club who have occupied the top League Divisions.

Were only the sixth Third Division club to reach an FA Cup semi-final, in 1984.

Hold a double club record. In both 1932 and 1994 'The Pilgrims' netted 8-1 wins, against Millwall and Hartlepool, respectively.

Worst defeat in the club's history was a 9-0 defeat by Stoke City in 1960.

Sam Shilton was the youngest player to turn out for Plymouth when he made his debut against Gillingham in 1994. His father, goalkeeping legend, Peter, is the clubs oldest player when, as manager, he picked himself to play against Burnley in 1993, he was a mere 44 years old.

Malcolm Allison, the fedora-wearing, cigar-smoking, champagne-supping charismatic football manager started his League career at Home Park.

Finished second in the Third Division (South) a record six consecutive times in the 1920s, but with regionalisation, only the Champions went up.

Port Vale...

Was managed by footballing legend Sir Stanley Matthews from 1965 until 1968.

Was formed in 1876 as Port Vale, named after the name of the house at which the inaugural meeting was held, based at Limekin Lane, Longport. In 1881 the club moved to Westport. The club adopted the addition, 'Burslam' in 1884 when they moved to Morland Road, Burslam.

Turned professional in 1885 and moved to the Athletic Ground, Cobridge the following year. 'The Valiants' had dropped the prefix, 'Burslem' by 1909 and four years later were playing out of the Recreation Ground, Hanley, only taking over the Vale Park site as late as 1950.

Played their first League game as early as 1892, being a founder member of Division Two. They were in and out of the League until 1919.

Ejected manager Dennis Bulter from the 'Vale' a mere 12 days into the 1979 season.

Record League victory was a 9-1 thrashing of Chesterfield in 1932.

Port Vale...

Completed a League double over Stoke City during the 1995/6 season, the first time 'The Valiants" had scored such a success over their rivals and close neighbours for 70 years.

Manager, John Rudge was in charge from 1984 to 1999.

Record transfer sale was Ian Taylor when he was sold to Sheffield Wednesday in 1994 for £1 million.

Most capped player is Sammy Morgan who won 7 of his total of 18 for Northern Ireland while a Port Vale player.

Worst results were both 10-0 drubbings, the first by Sheffield United in 1892 and the second by Notts County in 1895.

Most famous fan is pop star Robbie Williams.

Enjoyed a run of 30 matches without conceding a goal during the 1953/54 season; this is still a Football League record.

Were expelled from the league in 1968 for making illegal payments to players... they were immediately re-elected but Stanley Matthews, their manager at the time, resigned.

Wilf Kirkham scored 38 League goals for the club in the 1926/27 season - a record which still stands today. He netted a total of 154 League goals for the club.

Roy Spronson made an unbelieveable 761 appearences for the club between 1950 and 1972.

Portsmouth...

Defender, Andy Awford scored against Sheffield United on the 9th March 1999. It was his first home goal for 'Pompey' in nine years.

Celebrated the club's 100th birthday in style when, on the 4th April 1998 Portsmouth scraped in with an injury time equaliser against Birmingham.

Alan Knight holds the League record for the most appearances by a goalkeeper for one club when, on the 13th January 1996, he notched-up 601 games between the sticks.

Caused a rule change by the League authorities. Matthew Reilly, who had played Gaelic football back in Eire and was well-used to bouncing a ball, was so good at such possession that the FA banned goalkeepers from using their hands outside the penalty area.

Was formed in 1898 when solicitor and alderman, JE Pink called a meeting in his High Street offices with five business and professional colleagues. They bought a market garden site next to Goldsmith Avenue for £4,950 and the Fratton Park Stadium at Frogmore Road was very quickly developed.

Portsmouth...

First manager, Frank Brettell signed on a team of professionals and the club played its first game in the Southern League on September 1899.

Played its first full League game in 1920; a 3-0 home win over Swansea.

Won the League twice in a row, in 1949 and 1950, a post-war record.

Played the first League game, ever, under floodlights in 1956, their opponents being Newcastle United.

Won the 1939 Cup Final, beating Wolves 4-1 and, because of the outbreak of hostilities held on to the title for seven years. Manager Jack Tinn had worn his lucky white spats throughout the Cup run.

Most famous past-president must be the great war-time leader Field Marshal Montgomery.

Took just seven years from their election as founder members of Division Three to reach the top flight.

Guy Whittingham scored 42 League goals in the 1992/93 season for Pompey.

Record appearance holder for the club is Jimmy Dickinson with 764 outings. The second highest number of appearances for any one club. He is also the club's most capped player, winning 48 caps for England.

Preston North End...

Were the last club to lose its unbeaten away record in the 1995/96 season, a run of 21 unbeaten games.

Can trace its origins from the foundation of the North End Cricket and Rugby Club in 1863. The members were playing most sports, including football, by 1879. In 1881 the club decided to specialise in the round ball game, despite having just been thrashed 16-0 by Blackburn Rovers during an invitation friendly at Deepdale. A few weeks later Preston were an affiliated member of the Lancashire FA.

Turned professional in 1885 and played their first League game in 1888 which they won 5-2 against Burnley.

Were not only one of the founder members of the League in 1888 but they took the Championship that very first season without losing a single game.

Record League win was 10-0 against Stoke in 1889.

Pitch is one of the smallest in the League.

Handed out an incredible 26-0 thrashing to Hyde FC during an FA Cup First Round tie in 1887. This all-time record win by 'The Lilywhites' includes the legend that the match had lasted over two hours because the referee had lost his watch.

Scored a round 100 goals while in Division Two during the 1927/28 season. 'The North End' accumulated the same tidy amount while in Division One during the 1957/58 season.

Tom Finney played for England 76 times whilst on the books of Preston.

Preston North End...

Former manager, John 'Long Ball' Beck, was unable to let the grass grow longer in the corners of the pitch because Deepdale had installed a plastic pitch. Refusing to be beaten he ordered the ground staff to place more sand in the corners under the plastic pitch so that the ball would hold up for his forwards to run onto whenever the ball was pumped over the opposition's defence.

Was the last club to replace its plastic pitch when it returned the Deepdale Stadium to good old-fashioned grass in 1994.

Have occupied their Deepdale Ground since 1881, third in the all-time list.

Manergerial legends Bill Shankly, Tommy Docherty and Howard Kendall have all played for Preston North End.

Won the League and Cup double in the League's first year, retained the League for the following year and before finishing runners-up for the next three seasons.

QPR...

Were, in 1981, the first English League club to lay a plastic pitch.

First player to achieve international recognition was Evelyn Lintott who won three England caps. The 'R's sold him to Bradford City in 1908 for a, then, cool £1,000.

Most capped player, 52 for Northern Ireland, is Alan McDonald,

Hold the club record for having had more grounds than any other in the League. These include Welford's Fields, the London Scottish Ground at Brondesbury, Home Farm at Kensal Rise Green, the Gun Club Wormwood Scrubs, Kilburn Cricket Ground, Kensal Rise Athletic Club, Latimer Road in Notting Hill, the Agricultural Society at Park Royal, the actual Park Royal Ground, Loftus Road in 1917, then White City, back to Loftus Road in 1933, back to the White City in 1962, and a final return to Loftus Road a year later , in 1963.

Were formed in either 1885 when Christchurch Rangers and St Jude's Institute FC pooled their resources under the guiding influence of George Wodehouse. The family had maintained close links with 'R's up until quite recently.

QPR...

Name was changed, within the first year of the club's foundation, from St Jude's Institute to its present form because the club players, in the main, came from the Queens Park area.

Turned professional in 1898 but did not play its first full League game, as a founder member of Division Three, until 1920.

Record transfer fee received was for Les Ferdinand when 'Rangers' sold him to Newcastle United in 1995 for £6 million.

Record pay-out for a player was in 1995 when 'Rangers' paid £1.5 million for Mark Hateley.

Have had four different strip designs.

Hero, Rodney Marsh, netted a club record of 44 goals when the 'R's won the unique 'double' of the Third Division Championship and lifted the League Cup in 1967.

Highest ever League position was second in 1976 under manager Dave Sexton.

Record League victory was 9-2 against Tranmere Rovers in a Division Three match in December 1960.

Lost 8-1 to Manchester United in a Division One match in March 1969.

Reading...

Record defeat was a whacking-great 18 goals against, without reply, against Preston North End in an FA Cup tie back in 1893.

Received a record transfer of £1.5 million for goalkeeper Shaka Hislop when he left for Newcastle United in 1995.

Record win was back in 1946 when Crystal Palace was defeated 10-2.

Most famous fan must be the psychic, Uri Geller who maintains that his attendance at Reading's matches can affect the final result, as well as the condition of the canteen cutlery.

Former grounds include Reading Recreation Ground, the Reading Cricket Ground at Coley Park, Caversham Cricket Ground, and then, in 1896, 'The Royals' moved to Elm Park in Norfolk Road.

Worst defeat was an 18-1 thrashing by Preston way back in 1890s.

Were formed as far back as 1871 at a public meeting held in the Bridge Street Rooms.

They first entered the FA Cup early in 1877 after having joined forces with The Reading Hornets. The enlarged club were the first winners of the Berks and Bucks Cup in 1879. By 1889 they had linked-up with Earley FC.

Turned professional in 1895 and by 1920 were founder members of Division Three.

Most capped player, with 17 out of his total of 46 for Northern Ireland while with 'The Royals', is Jimmy Quinn.

Striker, Jimmy Quinn has hidden talents; in 1995 Reading recorded its first win over West Bromwich Albion in 67 years when he took over in goal for the second half.

Reading...

Rejected plans for a merger with Oxford United put forward by Robert Maxwell in 1983.

Beat First Division Luton 4-1, in 1988, in the final of the Simod Cup.

Played 55 home matches between the years 1933 and 1936 without losing a single match to set another club record.

Most famous fan is probably cricket commentator John Arlott.

Play at the Madejski stadium. Named after the millionaire club chairman John Madejski.

Goal-scoring ace Jimmy Quinn joined forces with Mick Gooding and led the team to the 1995 promotion play-offs.

Rochdale...

Achieved the club's first away win at a London club, ever, in 1995 when 'The Dale' beat Barnet 4-0.

Most famous fan is comedian Tommy Cannon, who was also a director of the club for a time.

Are one of a handful of League clubs who have never supplied any country with a full international.

Was formed as Rochdale Town in 1900 but, because this was a rugby stronghold, had gone out-of-business by 1907. The present club was founded from the ashes within a few weeks and straightway joined the Manchester League.

The club turned professional in 1907, was a full member of the Lancashire Combination by 1908, but did not play its first League game until 1921.

Reached the final of the League Cup in 1962 where they lost by 4-0 to Norwich.

Did not win a FA Cup tie between November 1927 and November 1945, a total of 13 matches and 18 years.

Suffered 13 successive home defeats and recorded, in total, a mere four wins in 1931.

Hold the Division Three record for having won just two matches throughout the 1973/74 season.

Worst defeat was a 1-9 drubbing by Tanner back in 1931.

Best FA Cup victory was an 8-2 win against Crook Town in 1927.

Rotherham United...

Played their first League game in 1893 but did not turn professional until 1905.

Most capped player is Bermuda's Shaun Goater with 18 appearances for his country.

Played at the Red House Ground until 1907 when 'The Merry Millers' moved into their Millmoor Ground.

Can trace their foundation back to a certain Rotherham FC, formed in 1870, which became Rotherham Town in the late 1880s. In 1877 another local club, Thornhill United, was formed. By 1905 United had become Rotherham County. Rotherham Town had joined forces with Rotherham County to become Rotherham United by 1925.

Went 15 League and Cup games unbeaten during the 1950-51 season, during which the club lifted the Division Three (North) title.

Defeated Shrewsbury at Wembley 2-0 in 1996 when they lifted the Auto Windscreens trophy.

Beat Crewe Alexandra 8-1 in 1873, the Fourth Division record for an away win.

Best win was over Oldham in 1947, an 8-0 victory.

Worst defeat occurred in 1928 when Bradford City thrashed 'The Merry Millers' 11-1.

Became Division Three (North) champions in 1951, Division Three champions 1981 and Division Four champions in 1989,

Appeared in the first ever final of the League Cup in 1961.

Scarborough...

Are one of the League's 'new boys', having won promotion from the GM Vauxhall Conference in 1987.

Turned professional in 1926.

Have the honour of being the first club to have enjoyed automatic promotion from the Vauxhall Conference to the League.

Goalkeeper, John Burridge is the oldest player to have turned out for 'The Boro', a few weeks short of his 42nd birthday when he played against Doncaster Rovers in 1993.

Are one of a handful of League clubs who have not supplied any country with a full international.

Pitch is the third largest in the League.

Record victory was a 6-goal thrashing, without reply, of Rhyl in a Cup tie back in 1930

Can list their first League club victim in the FA Cup as Lincoln City, who they beat in a second round tie 6-4 back in 1930 while 'The Boro' were still languishing down in the Midland League.

Worst defeat was back in 1919 when 'The Boro' were crushed 16-1 by Southbank FC of the Northern League.

Was founded by the town's cricket club and initially the club played under the name of Scarborough Cricketers' FC playing their home games on the North Marine Road Cricket Ground. By 1887 the club had moved to the Recreation Ground, moving to the Athletic Ground in 1898.

Are one of just four League clubs who have never finished top, or runners-up, in any Division.

Scunthorpe United...

Eight goals against Torquay in 1995 is a club record.

Most famous footballer is actually a cricketer, the legendary
Ian Botham who turned-out as the team's centre forward on
11 occasions during the early 1980s.

**Was founded in 1899 when Brumby Hall FC, who played
on the Old Showground, joined-up with other local clubs
to become Scunthorpe United. Under the chairmanship of
WT Lockwood this club linked-up with North Lindsey
United to become Scunthorpe and Lindsey United in 1910.**

Turned professional two years later but did not play its first full
League game until 1950.

**Did not leave the Old Showground for Glanford Park until
1988. 'The Iron' did not drop the suffix, 'Lindsey' until
1958.**

Players who were to find future international fame with
England, but only after they have left 'The Iron', include
goalkeeper Ray Clemence and Kevin Keegan.

**Are one of a handful of League clubs who have never
supplied a football international to any country.**

Record FA Cup win was a 9-0 victory over Boston FC in 1953.

**Record defeat was by Carlisle, eight goals without reply in
1952.**

Full back Jack Brownsworth not only holds the record for
having played more League games, 595, for the club than any
other but is also the oldest player to have ever turned out in
the club colours at the age of 41 years.

Sheffield United...

Most famous fan is actor Sean Bean. He achieved a lifetime dream when he played the part of a footballer and got to tread the sacred Bramall Lane turf in the 1996 film, When Saturday Comes.

Was founded and turned professional in the same year, 1889. Charles Stokes of the Yorkshire County Cricket Club set-up the club a mere six days after having watched an FA Cup semi-final between Preston North End and West Bromwich Albion. This had convinced him that the formation of a football team would be a financial success at Bramall Lane. Initially,

the cricket club's secretary, a Mr JB Wostinholm doubled-up in the same position for the new football club.

Played their first League game, in Division Two, in 1892.

Bramall Lane has played host to both FA Cup Finals and Test Match Cricket.

Were the first League club to record a victory in double figures during an away match when they put ten past Burslem Port Vale in 1892.

Are nicknamed 'The Blades'.

Sheffield United...

Were the last club to win the FA Cup before the start of World War One.

Took part in the so-called 'Khaki Final', losing 3-0 to Chelsea in front of a crowd consisting of mainly soldiers.

All-time legend, Billy 'Fatty' Foulke is said to have punched his fist through a dressing room door because a referee had given a 'bad' decision against him. Even more apocryphal is the tale of when Billy arrived at the team hotel before his team mates and polished off six other player's dinners as well as his own.

Record defeat was by 13 goals during a game against Bolton in 1890.

Most capped player, Billy Gillespie, was awarded 25 international caps by Northern Ireland.

Are one of three clubs to hold the record for playing the most drawn games in the Premier League, 18 during the 1993/94 season.

Sheff Wednesday...

Collected an incredible five trophies during the 1902-03 season; The First Division Championship, the Midland League, the Sheffield Challenge Cup, the Wharncliffe Charity Cup and the Plymouth Bowl.

Were originally nicknamed 'The Blades', the present nickname of their arch rivals, Sheffield United.

Played a game that lasted five months when, back in 1898, 'The Owls' game against Aston Villa was called-off after 79 minutes because of bad light. It was not until an astonishing five months later that the last 11 minutes were eventually played. Wednesday added another goal during this final period of play to win 4-1.

Were known as just 'The Wednesday' until 1929, and are the only League club to be named after a day of the week.

Turned professional in 1887 and played their first League game just four years later, in 1892.

Fans include two Labour politicians, Roy Hattersley and Joe Ashton.

Were based at Highfield from 1867, moved to Myrtle Road in 1869 and on to Sheaf House in 1877. From here they moved to Olive Grove and Owlerton in 1899. The latter has been called Hillsborough since 1912.

Can trace its origins back to the Sheffield Wednesday Cricket Club (itself formed as early as 1825). The members, mainly shop workers, played on the Wednesday half-holiday in the High Street shops as they had to work all-day Saturdays. The first meeting to form the football club was held at the Adelphi Hotel; the original committee included Charles Stokes who was to go on to be a founder member of Sheffield United. The club's colours have always been blue and white.

Sheff Wednesday...

Player with the most international honours is Nigel Worthington who won 50 of his 64 caps for Northern Ireland while at the club.

Record transfer fee received was for Des Walker's move to the Italian club, Sampdoria in 1993. In the same year 'The Owls' sold Andy Sinton to QPR for the same amount.

Shrewsbury Town...

Have won the Welsh Cup on six occasions, the first being back in 1891, the latest in 1985. This is a record for an English club.

Was founded in 1886, their early matches being played on the Old Shrewsbury Racecourse.

Shrewsbury School had supplied a good number of both Welsh and English international players during the early years of the modern game; there appears to have been a 'Town' FC as early as 1876 which lifted the Birmingham Senior Cup in 1879.

Are based at Gay Meadow.

Turned professional in 1905 but did not play its first full League game until 1950.

Equalled a club record when, on the 25th November 1995 'The Shrews' recorded seven consecutive wins in all competitions which was extended, in the League only, to seven consecutive wins in that competition as well.

Record win is a 7-0 defeat of Swindon in 1955.

Created a club record when they went 14 League games without defeat in 1994.

Worst defeat was an 8-1 drubbing by Norwich in 1952, a feat 'The Shrews' repeated against Coventry in 1963.

Record goal scorer is Arthur Rowley with 152 goals between the years 1958 and 1965. In doing so he reached the all-time League record of 434 goals, having played for four other clubs.

Arthur Rowley also holds 'The Shrews' club record for having netted the most goals in one season, 1958/59.

Southampton...

Supplied a custom built section of the stand at the Dell during the early years so that the supporters could store their bicycles under cover from the elements.

Welsh striker, Ron Davies netted 37 goals for 'The Saints' during the 1966/67 season, exactly half the club's total.

Became the first Southern League club, in 1900, to reach the FA Cup Final since The Old Etonians back in 1883.

Cup tie against Leeds in 1960 started as usual at 7.30pm, had the normal 90 minutes of action, plus 62 minutes in total darkness due to a floodlights failure, during which time two players were carried off by torchlight. Nine goals were scored with the winning 'Saints' finally walking off the Dell pitch at ten minutes past ten o'clock.

Were based at the Antelope Ground from 1885, the County Cricket Ground from 1897, moving to the Dell in the following year, in 1898.

Was formed by players from a local club, the Deanery FC. This appears to have been set-up by local school teachers back in 1880. Many of these were members of a Young Men's Association attached to St Mary's church. At a meeting held in November 1885 the club was established as Southampton St Mary's FC. The church's curate was elected as the first president of the new football club.

Turned professional in 1894, playing their first League game in 1920 as founder members of Division Three.

The Dell has got the smallest capacity of any Premiership ground.

England striker, Mike Channon is the club's record goalscorer having found the net on 185 occasions.

Record victory was 9-3 against Wolves in 1965.

Southampton...

Record defeat occurred in 1936 when Spurs put eight past 'The Saints'. They lost by the same total to Everton some 35 years later, in 1971

Most capped player was Peter Shilton who turned-out for England 49 times (out of a total of 125) while a 'Saints' player.

Player with the most League appearances of 713, is Terry Paine.

Record transfer fee received was £3.3 million for England striker Alan Shearer from Blackburn Rovers in 1992.

Bobby Stokes won a brand new car after having hit the winning goal when 'The Saints', then in Division Two, won the FA Cup in 1976, by beating Manchester United 1-0. Unfortunately, he had never passed his driving test.

Southend...

Rootes Hall Ground has a long history of human occupation; Anglo-Saxon graves were uncovered and Viking and Roman coins unearthed when the pitch was excavated back in 1914.

Record transfer sale of Stan Colymore to Nottingham Forest in 1993 for £2 million included a clause negotiated by manager Barry Fry to the effect that 'The Shrimpers' would receive an extra £25,000 if 'Stan the Man' scored 20 or more goals for the club that season.

Turned professional in 1906 but did play their first League game until 1920 when they became founder members of Division Three.

Went for nine games without defeat in 1996, a club record.

Most famous star supporter is ex-Yazoo front lady Alison Moyet.

Worst defeat was by Brighton, a 1-9 drubbing in 1965.

Record FA Cup win was a 10-1 thrashing of Golders Green back in 1936.

Played at Rootes Hall in 1906, Prittlewell in 1906, moved to the Kursaal in 1920, on to the Southend Stadium in 1934, arriving back at Rootes Hall in 1955.

Were founded in 1906 as a modern go-ahead professional club. Bob Jack was appointed as secretary-manager and straightway United became members of the Second Division of the Southern League.

Won the Fourth Division Championship in 1981, 'The Shrimpers' only title success.

Did not have a single player sent off between 1920 and 1952, a total of 1,027 matches.

Stockport County...

Played an astonishing 67 games during the 1996/97 season.

Have only supplied one international player, goalkeeper Henry Hardy played one game for England in the 1920's.

Were founded during a meeting held in 1883 at Wellington Road, South by members of the congregation of the Wycliffe Congregational Chapel at which the Heaton

Norris Rovers FC was set-up.

The team were based at the Heaton Norris Recreation Ground, then the Heaton Norris Wanderers Cricket Ground by 1884, moved to Chorlton's Farm, Chorlton's Lane the following year, Heaton Norris Cricket Ground in 1886 and Wilkes' Field, Belmont Street in 1887.

Broke the club rule of having a different ground every year and stayed put for two years prior to moving to the Nursery Inn, Green Lane in 1889. However, they did indulge in a name change to just Heaton Norris FC in 1888.

Stockport County...

Joined the Football Combination and turned professional in 1891, a year after having become Stockport County.

Best win was back in 1934, a 13-0 thrashing of Halifax.

Worst defeat was an 8-1 drubbing by Chesterfield in 1902.

Fielded the first father and son combination in a League game in 1951, Alec and David Herd.

'The Hatters' played their first League game in Division Two in 1900 and moved into Edgeley Park in 1902.

Reached the semi-finals of the Coca-Cola Cup in 1997 having seen-off the likes of Blackburn Rovers, West Ham United and Southampton on the way.

Defender, Tony Dinning made an important contribution to 'The Hatters' 2-0 win against Carlisle in 1995 when he was forced to deputise between the sticks for 55 minutes for County's injured goalkeeper.

Stoke City...

Are something of a goalkeeping academy. During the 1970s both Peter Shilton and Gordon Banks played for 'The Potters'.

Striker, Mike Sheron found the opposition's net in seven successive League games during the 1995- 96 season.

Fielded the oldest player ever to have played in the top division; Stanley Matthews was 50 years of age when he turned out for 'The Potters' in 1965 against Fulham.

Most famous fan is probably the chairman of the TV show, *They Think It's All Over*, Nick Hancock.

Are the second oldest League side in England. They have been based at their Victoria Ground for 119 years, an English League club record.

Were originally based at Sweeting's Field by 1875. In 1878 Stoke moved into the Athletic Club Ground which had just been re-named the Victoria Ground.

Have always claimed 1863 as the year of their formation. Local historian, Wade Martin has been unable to find any

Stoke City...

evidence for the club's existence prior to 1868 when a couple of Old Carthusians apprentices at the local works of the North Staffordshire Railway called a meeting to form Stoke Ramblers. A local Stoke FC club went bankrupt when this new club was formed.

Turned professional in 1885 and played their first League game in 1888 as founder members of Football League.

Were not re-elected to the League in 1890, bounced back the following year only to be relegated in 1907. Having been forced to resign from the League because of money problems in 1908 Stoke City re-joined the League for keeps in 1919.

Played in the shortest match on record when it was abandoned after four minutes because of a snowstorm.

Record defeat was ten goals without reply by Preston North End in 1889.

John Ritchie was shown the red card during a European tie during the 1970s without having touched the ball, having just been sent on as a substitute.

Player with the most international honours is Gordon Banks who won 36 out of his total of 73 England caps while a Stoke player.

Sunderland...

Went a total of 18 games without defeat during the 1995/96 season, a club record.

Were the first League club to win the Championship three times. They achieved their hat-trick of wins in 1892, 1893 and 1895.

Was founded by Scottish schoolmaster James Allan who taught at the Hendon Boarding School. He was the leading light in the establishment of the Sunderland and District Teachers' AFC when he called a meeting at the Adults' School, Norfolk Street in 1879. Money problems forced the club to widen its membership and try to attract more than just schoolmasters, and in so doing had changed its name to Sunderland AFC.

Did not appoint an English manager for 60 years prior to the arrival of Alan Brown in 1957.

Goalkeeper, Jim Montgomery pulled-off what is arguably considered to be the greatest save in Cup Final history during the 'The Rokermen's' win at Wembley over Leeds in 1973. They accomplished this FA Cup Final upset without fielding a single international player. This was also the first time a Second Division club had lifted the FA Cup during the post-war period.

First played at the Blue House Field, Hendon from 1879. In 1882 the club moved to Groves Field, Ashbrooke, Horatio Street in 1883, Abbs Field, Fulwell in 1884, Newcastle Road in 1886, arriving at Roker Park in 1898.

Turned professional in 1886 and played its first League game in 1890.

Became the first club to have had points deducted because they had used an illegal player, back in 1890.

Sunderland...

Hold the 19th century record for the most points accumulated in one season, 48.

Most famous fan is an athlete who dominated middle-distance during the 1980s, Steve Cram.

Worst defeats were an eight goal thrashing without reply by West Ham United in 1968, and Watford in 1982.

Best victory was an 11-1 destruction of Fairfield FC in a Cup tie of 1895.

Have never lost to Preston North End in the FA Cup, despite meeting them an incredible seven times in the competition?

Oldest player fielded by 'The Rokermen' is 'Pop' Robson, just over 38 years of age when he turned out against Leicester in 1984.

Striker David Halliday scored 30 or more League goals for four years running in the 1920s. He remains the only player to have achieved such a feat.

Swansea City...

Were known as Swansea Town until February 1970.

Were founded in 1912, the same year 'The Swans' turned professional.

First game in League Division Two was played on the 29th August 1925, 'The Swans' first game in Division One was played on the 29th August 1981. This co-incidence did not stretch back to the club's first game in Division Three (of which the club was a founder member) which was played on the 28th (not 29th) August 1920.

Was formed at a public meeting held in June 1912 and straightway took over the Vetch Field.

Player with the most international honours is Ivor Allchurch who won 42 of his caps for Wales out of his total of 68 while a 'Swans' player.

Worst defeat was an eight-goal drubbing by Liverpool, without reply during a 1990 Cup tie.

Made seven appearances in the European Cup Winners Cup competition, the last being in 1991, by virtue of having winning the Welsh FA Cup on nine different occasions.

John Toshack guided the team from Division Four to Division One in four seasons in the early 1980s.

Recorded a 12-goal victory, without reply, against Sliema Wanderers of Malta during their European Cup Winners' Cup campaign of 1982.

FA Cup exploits include knocking out Arsenal in 1926 and Liverpool in 1964.

Swindon Town...

Turned professional in 1894 and played their first League game in 1920 as an original member of Division Three.

Thrashed Luton 9-1 in their first League game in 1920.

Were founded in 1881 by the Rev. William Pitt, captain of the Spartans FC, an offshoot of a local cricket club with the same name. The team was based at The Croft until 1896. The club name had changed to Swindon Town back in 1883 when it had amalgamated with St Mark's Young Men's Friendly Society FC.

Worst defeat was a 10-1 thrashing by Manchester City in a 1930 cup tie.

Player with the most international honours is Rod Thomas who won 30 of his 50 Welsh caps while a 'Robins' player.

Lifted the League Cup in 1969, mainly due to winger Don Rogers, and the Anglo-Italian Cup in 1970.

Forward, Archie Brown was the club's top scorer for successive Southern League seasons between the years 1911 and 1915.

Original nickname was "the Moonrakers', a back-handed compliment denoting a mixture of feigned stupidity and a countryman's guile.

John Trollope represented 'The Robins' on 770 occasions between the years 1960 and 1980, a League record.

Hold the Premiership record for 100 goals conceded in a season and the least wins with five in their only season amongst the country's elite in 1993/94.

Torquay United...

Was founded by a group of old boys of Torquay College and Torbay College. Initially they discussed the idea while sitting in Princess Gardens listening to the band. A meeting was called at the Tor Abbey Hotel in 1898 and they decided to take over the Teignmouth Road ground. The club entered the Eastern League, later known as the East Devon League.

Occupied the Torquay Recreation Ground pitch from 1900, moving to Cricket Field Road in 1904. In 1906 'The Gulls' moved to Torquay Cricket Ground, arriving at their present Plainmoor Ground in 1910 as Torquay Town. The club adopted its present name in 1921.

Are one of a handful of clubs who have never supplied an international player to any country.

Worst defeat was by Fulham in 1931, a 2-10 drubbing, the same scoreline achieved by Luton Town in 1933.

Turned professional in 1921 and 'The Gulls' played their first League game some six years later.

Striker, Jimmy Trotter's 26 League goals during the 1930-31 season was a 25 year club record.

Torquay United...

Have never got beyond the fourth round of the FA Cup or the third round of the League Cup.

Only retained their League status in 1996 because Stevenage, who had won the Conference, did not possess a stadium considered to match up to League standards.

Defender, Pat Kruse holds English football's all-time record for the quickest goal ever scored, just six seconds. Unfortunately it was an own-goal netted in a 1970s match against Cambridge United.

Record transfer sale is £180,000 for Lee Sharpe to Manchester United in 1988.

Tottenham Hotspur...

Was the first club this century to win the League and Cup 'double' way back in 1961.

Hold the record for their winning start to the 1960/61 season with 11 straight wins.

Admired Preston North End, the most successful team of the late 1890s, that in 1899 Spurs changed their kit to the same as that of their heroes, their present-day strip of white shirts and blue shorts.

Goalkeeper, Ian Walker the son of former Colchester' keeper Mike Walker, is a part-time model.

England international, Darren Anderton is nicknamed 'Sicknote' because of his habit of picking up injuries.

Have a liking for a '1' at the end of the year date, having won the FA Cup in 1901, 1921, 1961, 1981 and 1991. Tottenham are the only non-league club this century to lift the FA Cup, being members of the Southern League when they won the trophy in 1901.

Was founded in 1882 as the Hotspur Football Club by a local cricket club. Initially the players were mostly old boys of St John's Presbyterian and Tottenham Grammar Schools. The first goalposts were painted blue and white and supplied by two brothers named Casey. They also donated a football.

First ground was on the Tottenham Marshes, prior to a move to Northumberland Park in 1885. Spurs arrived at White Hart Lane in 1898. The club members met up at the local YMCA but after trying out a few other club rooms decided on their present headquarters, Red House, otherwise known as 748 High Road.

Most capped international is Pat Jennings, he played 74 times for Northern Ireland between the years 1965/1977.

Tottenham Hotspur...

Spurs legend, Jimmy Greaves holds two goalscoring records for the club, 220 league goals between 1961/70 and 37 League goals during the 1962/63 season.

Steve Perryman holds the all-time record for appearances in the famous white shirt, between 1969/86 he played in 655 League games.

Attracted the biggest TV audience for an FA Cup Final, 14.9 million people, when they played Nottingham Forest in 1991.

Were the first British club to bring home a major European trophy when, in 1963, 'Spurs beat Atletico Madrid 5-1 in Rotterdam.

Beat Wolves 3-2 on aggregate in the 1972 UEFA Cup, this is the first and only time two English clubs have met each other in a European final.

Won the Worthington Cup in George Graham's first season in charge. They beat Leicester City 1-0 in March 1999.

Tranmere Rovers...

Preston Park car park did its bit during the Second World War. It was employed as a site from which black smoke was sent-up into the sky in order to confuse the German bombers.

Was founded by cricketers attached to the Belmont and Lyndhurst Wanderers Cricket Club in 1884. Initially known as Belmont FC the club became Tranmere Rovers in the following year. They joined the West Lancashire League in 1889 to celebrate that year's success in the Wirral Challenge Cup.

Almost went out of business in 1899 when most of the players left to join a local rival club.

By 1908 they had won the Football Combination.

Turned professional in 1912, and had won the Lancashire Combination by 1914.

Played at Steeles Field from 1884, moved to Ravenshaw Field, Old Prenton Park in 1887, arriving at Prenton Park in 1912.

Tranmere Rovers...

Left the Central League to join the Football League in 1921.

Worst defeat was 9-1 by Spurs in 1953.

Record victories were a 13-4 win over Oldham in 1935 (the highest aggregate number of goals ever scored in one game), and a 13-0 drubbing of Oswestry in the FA Cup back in 1914.

Harold Atkinson netted six against Ashington in an FA Cup tie in 1952 during an 8-1 win.

Lifted the Welsh FA Cup in 1935 and the Leyland Daf Cup in 1990.
Most capped player is John Aldridge who turned out for the Republic of Ireland 29 times (out of a total of 68 caps) while a 'Rovers' player.

Player-manager, John Aldridge is the record holder for the most goals ever scored in the English Football League, 470. He netted 170 of this total while a 'Rovers' player.

Youngest player was Dixie Dean who played for them whilst aged just 16. He then went on to find fame and glory at nearby club Everton.

Harold Bell holds the English League record for the most consecutive appearances for one club, 401 games.

Walsall...

Michael Ricketts scored with his first touch of the ball in his first League game after coming on as a substitute against Brighton in May 1996, his first and last appearance that season in 'The Saddlers' colours.

Most capped player is Mick Kearns who won 15 out of his 18 caps for the Republic of Ireland while a Walsall player.

Record holder for the most League appearances for Walsall FC is Colin Harrison who played in an amazing 467 matches.

Employed a grand total of nine managers between the years 1926 and 1937.

Was formed out of an amalgamation of the Walsall Swifts (founded in 1877) and Walsall Town (founded 1879) in 1888. The club, which played from Fellows Park until 1895, was known as the Walsall Town Swifts until 1895.

Forerunners, the 'Swifts' had won the Birmingham Senior Cup in 1881, the 'Town' had reached the fourth round of the FA Cup in 1883.

Turned professional in 1888 and played its first League game in 1892, having been elected to Division Two that year.

Worst defeat was in 1892 when 'The Saddlers' were thrashed by 10 goals, without reply, by Small Heath. They lost by the same margin to Darwen just four years later.

Got their revenge for the 1896 defeat by drubbing Darwen 10-0 three years later, in 1899.

Lifted the trophy for the Division Four Championship in 1960.

Watford...

Most famous fan is pop legend Elton John. Under his chairmanship and manager Graham Taylor's guidance 'The Hornets' achieved top-flight football and reached the 1984 FA Cup Final.

Star striker, Luther Blissett arrived at AC Milan's San Siro Stadium in 1984 and is reputed to have enquired; "Where's the dog track?"

Were founded as Watford Rovers in 1891. However, another version of the cub's early history is that, in 1898, Watford was formed by an amalgamation of two local clubs, West Herts FC and Watford St Mary's FC.

Turned professional in 1897 but did not play their first League game until 1920 as founder members of Division Three.

Record defeat was 10-0 to Wolves in an FA Cup tie back in 1912.

Played at the Cassio Road ground until 1922 when the club moved into the Vicarage Road Stadium.

Record League victory was 8-0 against Sunderland in 1982, and their record FA Cup win a 10-1 thrashing of Lowestoft Town in 1926.

Qualified for the UEFA Cup in 1980s.

Most capped players are Wales' Kenny Jackett and England's John Barnes who, in 1984, scored one of the greatest England goals ever, when he danced past the entire Brazilian defence in the Maracana Stadium, Rio.

Won the Division Three Championship in 1969 and the Division Four Championship in 1978.

West Brom...

Record transfer fee was £1.5 million from Manchester United for future England captain and midfield dynamo, Bryan Robson, in October 1981.

Are blessed with various nicknames including the 'Throstles', the 'Baggies', and the 'Albion'.

Secretary, Dr John Evans is one of the few Football League club officials to possess a PhD.

Was founded in 1878 when workers at Salter's Spring Works went to the nearby association football stronghold of Wednesbury to buy a football. Club fees for the newly formed West Bromwich Strollers were set as 2d. per week.

Adopted their present name in 1881, turned professional in 1885 and were founder members of the Football League in 1888.

Achieved their 1,000th home win and their 500th away win in successive matches during October 1995.

Had restless feet during their early years. Albion started out at Coopers Hill in 1878, moved to Dartmouth Park the

West Brom...

following year, Bunns Field at Walsall Street a year later, Four Acres at Dartmouth Cricket Club in 1882, Stoney Lane in 1885, moving to The Hawthorns in 1900.

Were the last team to win the League Cup, in 1966, when it was played over two legs.

Are the first club, in 1931, to have lifted the FA Cup and won promotion to the top divisions in the same season.

Best win was a 12-0 thrashing of Darwen FC back in 1892.

Fielded 11 English players when the club won the FA Cup back in 1888, a League first.
Fan with the highest media profile is Fantasy League presenter, Frank Skinner.

Jeff Astle scored the only goal of the 1968 FA Cup Final against Everton, he also scored in every qualifying round as well.

West Ham United...

Most famous fans include television heartthrob Nick Berry, Warren Mitchell, the leading character in the TV sitcom, *Till Death Us Do Part.*

Was founded in 1895 by workers from a shipbuilding yard on the Thames. The Thames Ironworks FC entered the FA Cup that same year and joined the London League in their second full season.

Found themselves in financial difficulties and the club closed down in June 1900. By July West Ham United was born out of the ashes and turned professional that same year. The club had played its first League game in Division Two by 1919.

Players were involved with the construction of the first ironclad warship, HMS Warrior, However, all links with the shipbuilding yard had been severed by 1904.

Had played at the Memorial Recreation Ground, Canning Town until 1904 when 'The Hammers' moved into the Bolyn Ground.

Record FA Cup victory was a 10 goal thrashing without reply of Bury in 1983.

Player with the most international honours is the late-great Bobby Moore with 108 England caps, most of which were won as captain of the international team.

Lifted the European Cup Winners Cup in 1965, beating Munich 1860 2-0 at Wembley.

Won the FA Cup on three occasions, 1964, 1975, and 1980.

Defender, Alvin Martin netted an odd hat-trick during 'The Hammers' 8-1 drubbing of Newcastle in 1987, with each goal being scored against a different goalkeeper. The first was the normal 'keeper, Martin Thomas, the second was Chris Hepworth, and the third England striker Peter Beardsley.

West Ham United...

Lost 2-0 to Bolton during the famous White Horse FA Cup Final of 1923 when thousands of fans spilled out onto the pitch. This was the first Wembley title so 'The Hammers' hold the dubious honour of being the first team to be defeated at Wembley in an FA Cup Final.

Most successful failure was a certain David Cook. He did not make the grade as a footballer with West Ham but went on to find fame and fortune in the pop music business as David Essex.

Supplied three members of the winning England side that lifted the World Cup in 1966, a League club record. In addition to supplying the winning World Cup captain, Bobby Moore, all four goals in the final against West Germany were scored by West Ham players, Geoff Hurst (3) and Martin Peters (1).

Are the last team to have lifted the FA Cup who were not members of the top flight when, as members of the Second Division, they beat Arsenal 1-0 in 1980. This Wembley victory included a collector's item, a headed goal by midfield general, Trevor Brooking.

Wigan Athletic...

Were the first English League club to included three Spanish players in its line-up, Isidro Diaz, Roberto Martinez and Jesus Seba, two of the trio ended the season as the club's top scorers.

Are one of a handful of English League clubs who have never been called upon to supply an international for any country.

Have appointed a total of 30 managers since the 1940s, a post-war record.

Most famous fan is former president of the Soviet Union, Mikhail Gorbachov.

Entertained the Russian side, Metallist Khartrov during the 1969/70 season. A certain young man in the entourage was 'assistant secretary Gorbachov'.

Were formed upon the demise of Wigan Borough FC and this club's resignation from the Football League in 1931. Following a public meeting at the Queen's Hall in May 1932, Wigan Athletic was born. 'The Latics' bought Springfield Ground for £2,250 but were unable to gain admission to the Football League for another 46 years.

Eventually became members of Division Four in 1978.

Lifted the Freight Rover Trophy in 1985, and won their first ever League title some 12 years later, becoming Division Three champions in 1997.

Biggest win was a 1982 drubbing of Scunthorpe, 7-2.

Worst defeat, 1-6, was by Bristol Rovers in 1990.

Wimbledon...

Were champions of the Isthmian League on a staggering eight occasions. 'The Dons' also lifted the FA Amateur Cup in 1963; Eddie Reynolds netted four goals for 'The Dons', all with his head.

Dean Holdsworth is not just a sharp shooter, having ended more than one season as the club's top scorer, but is a part-time model who is in great demand by the fashion industry, especially the Top Man organisation.

Started out at the aptly named, Plough Lane Ground prior to moving to Selhurst Park, South Norwood.

Were formed in 1889 as the Wimbledon Old Centrals FC by old boys of the Central School, and became Wimbledon FC in 1905. The club turned professional in 1964, playing their first League game in 1978.

Earliest success was winning the Clapham League. The club joined the Southern Suburban League in 1902.

Lifted the FA Cup in 1988, a mere 11 years after having joined the Football League and only 25 years since they lifted the FA Amateur Cup, by overturning all the odds in their 1-0 defeat of Liverpool.

Joined the Football League as late as 1978, won the Division Four title in 1983, gained promotion to the Second Division the following year and entered the top flight, the old Division One, in 1986. 'The Dons' were still there when the Premier Division was formed in 1993. They are one of a very few teams never to have been relegated from the top division.

Record defeat was an eight-goal thrashing, without reply, by Everton in 1978.

Record signing is Efan Ekoku from Norwich for £920,000 in 1994.

Wimbledon...

Goalkeeping hero, Dave Beasant holds two FA Cup records; he is the first goalkeeper to have saved a penalty kick in the final and is the first goalkeeper to have captained Wembley's winning team.

Hard man, and now movie star, Vinnie Jones has been given his marching orders by Premiership referees a record 12 times.

Manager, Joe Kinnear has occupied 'The Dons' hot seat for almost 10 years, the third longest surviving manager in the Premiership.

Attracted the lowest attendance, just over 3,000, at a Premiership match when they entertained Everton in January 1993.

Supporter with the highest media profile is the country's most famous, and long-lasting radio and TV sit-com queen June Whitfield.

Striker, Alan Cork, who holds most of Wimbledon's goal scoring records, inspired the fans chant from the terraces, "He's got no hair, but we don't care". He has also scored goals in all four divisions with the same club, a truly unique record.

Alan Cork also holds an unofficial club, and perhaps League, record. He played, under orders from his manager, in the FA Cup Final suffering with a hangover. Bobby Gould had ordered his players to spend the Friday evening at the pub. Cork maintains he got home at 2am and needed sunglasses while travelling on the club coach to Wembley.

Wolves...

Was formed in 1879 when players from two local clubs, St Luke's FC founded in 1877 and Goldthorn FC founded in 1876, broke away and started up 'The Wolves'.

Were a founder member of the Football League in 1888, the same year that the club turned professional.

Had at least one 'Wolves' player picked to represent England in all the 148 peacetime internationals played between 1938 and 1963.

Started out at the Goldthorn Hill ground in 1877, moved to John Harper's Field in 1879, Dudley Road in 1881, finally arriving at Molineux in 1899.

Record FA Cup victory was a 14 goal thrashing of Cresswell's Brewery work's team during a second round tie way back in 1886.

Legend, Billy Wright won 105 caps for England, mostly as captain.

Striker, Steve Bull is nicknamed the 'Tipton Terror' having scored 240 League goals for the 'Wolves'. Steve was born in the town of Tipton.

Were lauded as the best club side in the world by the home grown media because of the team's success in friendlies against various foreign opposition. 'Wolves' exploits were a contributory factor in the future foundation of the European Cup.

Most famous fan is rock legend and one-time front man for Led Zeppellin Robert Plant.

Were the first club to have become champions of all four divisions when, in 1989, they topped the Third Division.

Wolves...

Youngest ever player to play for the 'Wolves', Jimmy Mullen (just over 16, against Leeds in 1939) was to become the first substitute to play for England.

Worst defeat was a ten-goal thrashing, without reply, by Newton Heath back in 1892.

Manager, Stan Cullis put the club's success during the 1950s down to his philosophy of "kick and rush football".

Have never won any European honours; the club's glory days had gone by the time this country's footballing authorities had been forced to drop their 'Little England' outlook.

Reached the final of the UEFA Cup back in 1972, the only all-English European final so far, which ended with Tottenham Hotspur lifting the trophy. On their way to this final 'Wolves' had beaten Den Haag of Holland 7-1 on aggregate. The Dutch side kindly supplied three own goals to 'Wolves' grand total.

Wrexham...

Welsh international, Micky Thomas was once questioned by the police on suspicion of having passed forged £10 notes to members of the youth team.

Is the oldest Welsh club still in existence having been formed in 1873 by local businessmen in order to raise a squad to play a seventeen- a- side game against a team representing the Provincial Insurance Company. By 1875 Wrexham were fielding only 11 players, presumably because of a dearth of suitable seventeen-a-side opposition.

Were one of the founder members of the Welsh FA, in 1876, playing out of Acton Park. 'The Robins' moved to the Racecourse Ground at a later date, turned professional in 1912 and became founder members of Division Three that same year.

Have reached a record total of 45 Welsh Cup Finals, lifting the trophy on a record 23 occasions.

Most capped player is the Welsh wizard Dia Davies who won 28 of his caps, out of a total of 51, while at Wrexham.

Record defeat was a nine-goal blitz, without reply, by Brentford in 1963.

Record win was a 10-1 victory over Hartlepool in 1962.

Fielded the second youngest League player, ever, when 15 year old Ken Roberts was sent on in Wrexham's colours back in 1951.

Striker, Tom Bamford netted a total of 175 goals between the years 1928 and 1934. He also holds another club record, 44 goals during the 1933-34 season.

Arfon Griffiths, during two periods with 'The Robins' between the years 1959 and 1979, played 592 in the League, another club record.

Wycombe...

Can rarely lack for advice, as the club's director with the highest media profile must be football commentator, Alan Parry.

Can trace their foundation back to 1884 when some young furniture workers from the North Town area played friendlies as North Town Wanderers FC. The club entered an official junior football League and by 1887 Jim Ray, the club secretary, and Datchett Webb, the club captain, had held a meeting at the Steam Engine pub and Wycombe Wanderers FC was born.

Turned professional in 1974 and played their first League game some 19 years later.

First known ground was The Rye. The club moved to Spring Meadow in 1893, Loakes Park in 1895, Daws Hill Park in 1899, back to Loaks Park in 1901, finally arriving at Adams Park in 1990.

Replaced Halifax Town when they won promotion from the Vauxhall Conference in 1993.

Wycombe...

'Chairboys' nickname originates from the town's long-standing tradition of furniture manufacture.

Martin O'Neill guided them to promotion to the Second Division in their first season after having gained entry to the League.

Was named in honour of the famous side of the 1880s, The Wanderers FC, who met the first High Wycombe club in the FA Cup way back in 1877.

Worst defeat was an 8-1 drubbing by Reading, in the Cup back in 1899.

Are one of only four clubs not to have finished as winners, or runners-up, in any Football League Division. The others are Barnet, Scarborough and Crewe.

Best win was a 15-1 thrashing of Witney Town in a preliminary round of the FA Cup.

As a non-League side, became the first British side, in 1956, to entertain a visiting Ugandan side. 'The Chairboys' thrashed their barefoot opposition 10-1.

Were winners of the FA Amateur Cup in 1931 when they beat Hayes 1-0 at Highbury.

York City...

Could claim to have been founded as early as 1903 by a soccer enthusiast from Darlington. This club folded during the First World War. It did not start-up again until 1922, immediately turned professional and played its first League game in 1929.

Were based at Fulfordgate until 1932 when 'The Minstermen' moved to Bootham Crescent.

Knocked Manchester United out of the Coca-Cola Cup with a 0-3 win in 1995. This was the only home defeat United were to suffer all season.

Record defeat was a 12-goal drubbing, without reply, by Chester back in 1936.

Most capped player is Northern Ireland international, Peter Scott.

Beat a Blackpool side, which included the great Stanley Matthews, 2-0 back in 1955 as part of their best FA Cup campaign ever. Newcastle finally knocked 'The Minstermen' out of the competition in the semi-finals.

Were Division Four Champions in 1984.

Record victory was a 9-1 win over Southport in 1957.

Finished the 1996/97 season with the same record as the previous season; finishing one place above the relegation spot, having won 13 games, drawn 13 and lost 20. On both occasions the club had accumulated 52 points.

Player with the most League appearances, 481, is Barry Jackson between the years 1958 and 1970.

SCOTTISH

LEAGUE

CLUBS

Aberdeen...

Were founded in 1903 and have always been based at Pittodrie; the site name is said to be Gaelic for 'dunghill'. 'The Dons' ground was the first in Britain to become an all-seater Stadium.

Was the first club in Britain to introduce 'dug-outs'. Manager Donald Coleman wanted to be able to watch and improve his players' footwork.

Lifted the Scottish Cup on seven occasions between the years 1947 and 1990.

Were Division One Champions in 1955 and, under the guidance of Alex Ferguson, the Premier Division Champions in 1980, 1984 and 1985.

Were only the third Scottish club to lift a European trophy when, in 1983, they beat Real Madrid 2-1 to win the European Cup Winners' Cup.

Went on under manager Alex Ferguson, in less than a fortnight, to defeat Rangers in the Scottish Cup, a unique 'double'.

Nickname is 'The Dons' because the founding fathers of the club included members of the academic staff of Aberdeen University.

The club's first nickname was 'The Wasps" because of its white, black and gold striped shirts.

Record holder for having scored the most goals for 'The Dons' is Joe Harper, he netted 199 during his two periods with the club.

Best win was a whacking great 13-0 victory over Peterhead.

Worst defeat was an 8-0 thrashing by Celtic.

Aberdeen...

Lifted the Scottish League Cup five times between the years 1955 and 1996.

The stadium is the most northerly League ground in Britain. When, in 1980, the footballing authorities brought-in a nation-wide ban on supporters bringing alcohol, bottles and other drinks' containers into football stadiums Aberdeen's fans were livid because they were no longer allowed to bring their hot drinks in thermos flasks into the ground to protect them from the bitter winds blowing in off the nearby North Sea.

Defender, Alex McLeish holds the club record for the most appearances in Scotland's colours, having won 77 caps.

International centre-back, Willie Miller has made more League appearances, 556, for the club than any other player.

Record signing is the £1 million 'The Dons' paid for Oldham's Paul Bernard in 1995.

Celtic...

Reached the final of the Scottish Cup within a few months of 'The Bhoys' formation back in 1888. The pitch was covered in snow but, because of the large crowd, the Scottish Football Association insisted that the game should be played, but only as a friendly. Third Lanark won, 3-0, then they claimed the Cup! A replay was eventually ordered; Celtic lost 2-1.

Brilliant young goalkeeper, John Thomson died in 1931 five hours after having fractured his skull during an accidental clash during an Old Firm game.

Famous pop star fan, Rod Stewart cut the tape to officially open the new North Stand in 1995.

Can list 26 one-time club players who have scored more than 100 goals in the top flight.

Were the first British club, in 1967, to lift the European Cup, a 2-1 win over Inter Milan in Portugal. The 'Lisbon Lions', under the leadership of the late-great Jock Stein, broke down the Italian giants defensive 'big chain', or 'catenaccio' and remain the only Scottish club to have ever lifted this European trophy.

Have won the Scottish FA Cup on a record 30 occasions; they have reached a record 47 finals.

Was founded by two local Glasgow business men and a certain Brother Walfrid, the latter is always credited with having had the idea in the first place.

Won the final of the Coronation Cup against fellow Scots, Hibernian, in 1953. Celtic had beaten both Arsenal and Manchester United to reach the final.

Did not charge Roman Catholic priests to watch the club's home games for the first 110 years of its existence. Women were also admitted free during the early years.

Celtic...

Parkhead ground acquired its nickname when a fan commented on the club's early move from the old ground near the Eastern Necropolis, or cemetery, stating that 'It's like moving from the graveyard to Paradise".

Left-half Jerry Solis, who made just nine appearances for the club during the early 1930s, was the club's only Jewish player. Goalkeeper Joe Cohen was not Jewish.

Jimmy McGrory was Europe's top scorer, with 49 goals, during the 1926/27 season. He is the club's top scorer, having netted a staggering 397 goals between the years 1922 and 1938.

Celtic Park is the largest in the Scottish Premier League.

Went 62 games without defeat from 1915 to 1917, a Scottish League record.

Have won 29 First Division Championships, three Premier Division Championships and have lifted the Scottish League Cup on nine occasions.

Have won the Scottish League Championship on nine consecutive occasions.

Have completed the League and Scottish Cup 'double' on 11 occasions.

Notched-up a record 7-1 win over arch-rivals, Rangers in the 1957 Scottish League Cup Final. When the edited highlights were transmitted on television later that evening only the first-half could be viewed - the camera operator had forgotten to take the lens cap off after the half-time break.

Dundee United...

Were founded as Dundee Hibernian in 1909, changing their name to Dundee United in 1923.

Tannadice Park is the only ground ever used by the club.

Are nicknamed 'The Terrors' after the ferocious lion on the club badge.

Tannadice Park ground and that of Dundee's, Dens Park, may be a mere 100 yards apart but the two local rivals do not hold the world record for physical closeness; two Hungarian clubs' stadiums are actually situated back-to-back.

Lost the UEFA Cup Final, and the Scottish Cup Final, in just two days in 1987.

Reached the semi-finals of the European Cup in 1984, falling at the penultimate hurdle.

Paid the club's record transfer fee, £4 million, for big Duncan Ferguson in 1993 when he joined United from mighty Rangers.

Dundee United...

Have always been at the forefront of football's commercial development; United were the first Scottish club to install glass fronted VIP lounges for the club's sponsors.

Paid out a club record of £6 million to Patizan Belgrade for Gordon Petric in 1993.

Most passionate fan is a GMTV girl Lorraine Kelly.

Have been relegated from the top flight only once, in 1994. 'The Terrors' bounced straight back into the Premiership at the first try, but only after the indignity of a play-off.

Record Scottish Cup win was a 14-0 thrashing of Nithsdale Wanderers back in 1931.
Record League defeat was 1-12 by Motherwell in 1954.

Were the first Scottish club to run its own football pools operation, as early as 1956.

Maurice Malpas is 'The Terrors' player with the most appearances for his country having won 55 Scottish caps.

Player who has made the most League appearances, 612 in United's colours between the years 1974 and 1994, is David Narey. He has also made more club appearances in European matches than any other Scottish player, a total of 76 games.

Player who has scored the most League goals in one season, 1955/56, is John Coyle who found the net for United a total of 41 times.

Striker, Peter Kay has scored the most goals for the club in total, 158.

Dundee...

Have the closest neighbours in all British football; Dundee United's ground is a mere 100 yards away from Dens Park.

Have won the Scottish Cup once, back in 1910, after a second replay with Clyde.

Lifted the League Cup on three occasions, in 1952, 1953 and 1974.

Have won the League just the once, in 1962, since the club's formation back in 1893. 'The Dee's' all-conquering team included the great Alan Gilzean and Ian Ure.

Worst result, ever, was an 11-0 thrashing by Celtic way back in 1895.

Successful manager, Bob Shankly, brother of Liverpool legend Bill, led the club to this triumph.

Striker, Alan Gilzean holds the club record as the top goalscorer, he found the net 113 times.

Record win was a 10 goal drubbing of Aloa, without reply. In so doing Dundee were the first to score double figures in an away tie.

Repeated this record win, by exactly the same scoreline later that that same year, 1947. On this occasion their victims were Dunfermline.

Most capped player is Scotland's Alex Hamilton, his tally is 24.

Record transfer fee received was for Tommy Coyne in 1989. Celtic paid Dundee £500,000 for his services.

Record transfer fee paid out was £200,000 for Scotland goalkeeper, Jim Leighton in 1992.

Heart of Midlothian...

Most famous schoolboy to have had trials with 'The Hearts' - he was rejected because he was too small - was a certain Ronnie Corbett who was to go on to fame and fortune as one half of The Two Ronnies. However, his cousin did go on to become a first team player.

Player with the most international honours, with 29 Scottish caps, is Bobby Walker.

Paid a club record of £750,000 to Rangers for Duncan Ferguson in 1990.

Almost bought-out their local rivals, Hibernian in 1990. The fans of both clubs would not be convinced that such an amalgamation might contribute to the breaking of the two Glasgow clubs' dominance of Scottish football.

Are featured in Sir Walter Scott's novel, The Heart of Midlothian. This refers to an Edinburgh prison of the same name that had actually been razed to the ground some 50 years prior to the club being founded in 1874.

Previous grounds include The Meadows, from 1874, moving to Powderhall in 1878, Old Tynecastle three years later, before arriving at Tynecastle Park by 1886; a new modern stadium is currently being built.

Netted an amazing 21 goals against Anchor FC during a tie in the way back in 1880.

Record defeat in a Scottish Cup tie is 8-1 back in 1888 by the Vale of Leven.

Record goalscorer is Jimmy Wardhough having found the net 206 times between the years 1946 and 1959.

'Terrible Trio' of Alfie Conn, Willie Bauld and Jimmy Wadhaugh were the engine room when the club won the Division One Championship in 1958.

Heart of Midlothian...

Created a number of records on their way to lifting this trophy. 'Hearts' scored record 132 goals, leaked a meagre 29, and in so doing acquired a goal difference of 103 - a Scottish League record.

Were relegated for the first and only time in 1977.

Have lifted the Division One Championship, and the League Cup, on four occasions, and the Scottish Cup on five occasions.

Almost took the League in 1965 but Kilmarnock took the honours by a superior goal average of 0.042.

Enjoyed an unbeaten run of 27 games on their way to the club's first 'double' in 1986. However, 'Hearts' again came so close but failed, yet again. They lost their last game of the season and Celtic took the League title in the cruellest way possible, by goal difference.

Went on, three weeks later, to lose to Aberdeen 3-0 in the Scottish Cup Final.

Rangers...

Hold the world record for having won all 18 of their League fixtures during the 1898/99 season.

Were founded back in 1873; 'The Gers' previous grounds were Burnbank and Kinning Park prior to their eventual move to the Ibrox Stadium.

Have never brought the European Cup back to Scotland but did lift the European Cup Winners' Cup in 1972.

Could claim to be the most successful Scottish club team, ever. By 1997 'The Gers' had equalled Celtic's nine consecutive League Championship wins.

Were forced to share the League Championship once, the very first one ever held in 1891, with Dunbarton. However, this title is included in 'The Gers' record total of 47 League Championship titles.

Hold the Scottish League's record for the number of points accumulated, 76, and the most victories, winning 35 games on their way to lifting the First Division title during the 1921/22 season.

Hold yet another record that of 33 wins out of a total of 44 matches in the two seasons between 1991 and 1993, and that of having accumulated the most points, 73 from 44 matches, in the Premier Division during the 1992/93 season.

Slotted home a Premier Division record of 101 goals during the 1991/92 season.

Striker, Ally McCoist is the club's record goalscorer with 249 League goals; he has netted 339 in all competitions.

The ironically named Sam English holds the club record for the most goals, 44, scored in a season, 1931/32.

Rangers...

Player who holds the record for the most appearances for the club is John Greig having played in 496 League matches between the years 1962 and 1978.

Best defensive record, during the 1989/90 season, is just a mere 19 goals conceded.

Player who has won the most Scottish caps is Ally McCoist with his tally of 54.

Largest victory in the Scottish FA Cup was a 14-2 thrashing of Blairgowrie back in 1943.

Record defeat was a 2-10 drubbing by Airdrieonians way back in 1886.

Record transfer fee received was £5,58 million for Trevor Steven when he was sold to Marseille in 1991.

Goalkeeper, Chris Woods went 1,196 minutes without conceding a single goal between 1986 and 1987, a British Record.

Record transfer fee paid was £4.3 million to Lazio in 1995 for Paul Gascoigne.

THE

INTERNATIONAL

TEAMS

Argentina...

First international was a 3-2 away win over Uruguay way back in 1901, the first international match ever to be played outside Britain.

First World Cup match was a one goal win over France in Uruguay 1930.

Were runners-up in the first World Cup ever played, in 1930.

Were runners-up in the 1990 World Cup as well.

Player with the most caps is Oscar Ruggeri with 98.

Gabriel Batistuta has scored a record 43 goals for his country.

Highest score, without reply is a 12 goal thrashing of Ecuador in 1942.

Most crushing defeat was a 1-6 thrashing by Czechoslovakia in 1958.

Argentina...

Is the oldest footballing country, other than those of the British Isles.

Have played in four World Cup Finals, 1930, 1978, 1986 and 1990.

Claudio Lopez's goal in the quarter-finals of France '98 was their 100th in the entire Competition.

Did not enter the World Cup in 1938, 1950 and 1954.

Did not qualify for the World Cup Finals on only one occasion, 1970.

Antonio Rattin, the Argentine captain was sent off during the quarter-final match against England in the 1966 World Cup.

Players invaded the England dressing room after this match. Having been escorted out they returned to kick the closed door.

Diego Maradona was ejected from the USA '94 World Cup Finals for failing a drugs test.

Belgium...

First international was a three-all draw with France in Brussels back in 1904.

First World Cup game was a 3-0 defeat by the USA in the first World Cup ever, Uruguay 1930.

Player who has won the most caps for his country, 96, is Jan Ceulemans.

Bernard Voorhoof and Paul Van Mimst both hold the record for having scored the most goals for their country, a total of 30 each.

Highest score was a 9-0 victory over Zambia in 1994.

Lost 11-2 against England Amateurs in 1909.

Were playing organised football as early as 1895.

Won the football Gold Medal at the 1920 Olympic Games, held in Antwerp, the first footballing nation to break the monopoly of the English speaking nations.

Were the first non-British team not to be defeated by England. Belgium and England drew 2-2 in a friendly match played in Antwerp.

Has been chosen, with next door neighbours Holland, to host the next European Championship in the year 2000. This is the first time that finals will have joint hosts.

Reached the World Cup semi-finals in 1986, only to be beaten 2-0 by Argentina and ended the competition in fourth place.

Brazil...

Are the only nation to have played in every World Cup Final, all 16.

Most crushing win was a nine goal spree, without reply, over Columbia in 1957.

First international was a three goal defeat by arch-rivals Argentina in Buenos Aires way back in 1914.

The 6-1 defeat by Argentina in 1940 was the country's worst ever result.

Lost 2-1 to Yugoslavia in Uruguay back in 1930 in their first ever World Cup match.

Have scored a record 171 goals World Cup Finals.

Djalma Santos is the most-capped player, appearing for his country 100 times.

Got to hang onto the Jules Rimet trophy when they won their third World Cup at Mexico '70 ...

... However, their hold on the trophy was short lived; it was stolen from the offices of the Brazilian FA and has never been recovered.

Legendary striker Pele scored 77 goals during his international career; he is Brazil's top goal-scorer of all-time.

Have been South American Champions on a mere five occasions, since 1916; and, even more surprising, just twice during the last 50 years.

Brazil...

Are the most exciting and successful footballing nation in the world. They are the only international team to have lifted the World Cup on four occasions. Brazil's first success was back in 1958 when they defeated Sweden 5-2. Their second successful final was in 1962 when they defeated Czechoslovakia 3-1, their third a 4-1 win over Italy in 1970 and the fourth again against Italy, 3-2 on penalties, in 1994.

Were defeated in a World Cup Final for the first time in 1998 when France beat them 3-0.

Finished in second place to Uruguay back in 1950 when the competition was decided on points after a four team final round.

Mario Zagallo was the first person to win the World Cup as both a player and as a coach. He played in the 1958 and 1962 teams and managed the 1970 team.

Pele scored two goals in his country's defeat of Sweden in the 1958 World Cup Final and, in so doing, became the youngest player ever, at 17, to win a World Cup winners medal.

England...

Are, together with Scotland, the oldest international team.

Played the first ever-official international match against Scotland in Glasgow in 1872, which ended in a 0-0 draw.

Supplied all the players for the Great Britain team that won the first Olympic Games football Gold Medal.

Lost to the United States in the 1950 World Cup - a result that shocked the soccer world.

Took fair play to extremes back in 1875 when they played with just 10 outfield players. They had hung on until Bill Carr, the goalkeeper finally did arrive and take his place between the sticks. The match finished 2-2.

The 48-year-old record of never having lost a World Cup qualifying match at home ended when, in 1997, Italy won 1-0 at Wembley.

Fastest goal was scored by Tommy Lawton, just 17 seconds into a game against Portugal in 1947.

Fastest goal during a World Cup competition was scored in 1982 by Bryan Robson against France a mere 27 seconds after the kick-off.

Geoff Hurst netted the first hat-trick during a World Cup Final when England lifted the trophy in 1966. Altogether he grabbed 24 goals in 49 appearances for his country.

One-time great Jackie Milburn described England manager, Alf Ramsey as being like a good chicken farmer as regards players who did not come up to his expectations, "If the hen doesn't lay he wrings its neck."

England...

Alf Ramsey hated social events. When the England squad were invited onto the latest James Bond film set Ramsey made a speech of thanks to "Seen [sic] Connery for his hospitality".

Failed to qualify for the finals of the World Cup three times, in 1974, 1978, and 1994.

First game in the finals of the 1950 World Cup was a 2-0 win over Chile in Brazil.

Bobby Charlton is England's leading goalscorer with 49 goals in 106 appearances.

Highest victory was a 17-0 thrashing of Ireland back in 1882.

Lost at home to Hungary 6-3 in 1953, followed-up the next year by a 7-1 defeat by Austria in Vienna.

Goalkeeper Peter Shilton played a record 125 times for England between 1970 and 1990, keeping an amazing 65 clean sheets in the process. What is even more remarkable about these figures is that Ray Clemence also played 61 times between the sticks during the same period. Indeed, when Ron Greenwood was manager of England he alternated the pair of them.

Were involved in what is probably the most disputed goal in the entire history of the game, when Bakhramov, the Russian linesman decided that Geoff Hurst's shot had crossed the line after having bounced down from the crossbar in the 1966 World Cup Final.

England...

Have never won the European Championship.

Striker, Andy Cole won his first four international caps under four different managers, Terry Venables, Glenn Hoddle, Howard Wilkinson and Kevin Keegan.

Wonder wingers Tom Finney and Stanley Matthews provided centre forward Stan Mortensen with an incredible service, resulting in four goals, during an international against Portugal back in 1948. However, on the two occasions that Tom Finney provided Mortensen with the perfect cross for him to score with a header the striker always fell to the ground holding his head, something he did not do when Matthews provided similar crosses for the other two goals. When Finney asked Mortensen for an explanation at the end of the match he explained that because he and Matthews were team-mates at Blackpool Matthews knew to ensure than when the ball arrived in the penalty area the lace should always be pointing towards the goal.

Still favoured the 'dribbling game' back in 1878 which may explain why they were beaten 7-2 by Scotland with their more modern passing game.

Banned Scottish players who played for clubs south-of-the-border from representing their own country in full internationals until 1896.

Greatest centre-forward of the 1890s, GO Smith was a prep school teacher, a chronic asthmatic, very small and very slow; and was the first England player to win 20 caps. As captain he also refused to head the ball believing that the game should be played on the ground. He scored 11 international goals as well as a century at Lords for Oxford during the Varsity match of 1896.

England...

Fans in HM prison, Parkhurst on the Isle of White, were spared the agony of the cruel penalty shoot-out by being locked back up in their cells by the staff after being allowed to watch the first half of the semi-final against Germany during the European Finals in 1996 on TV.

Were awarded the Fair Play Award at Euro '96 although they did not reach the final.

John Barnes scored what is usually considered to be the greatest goal ever for England after having danced past the Brazilian defence in their Maracana Stadium in Rio in a friendly played in 1984 at the tender age of 20.

Peter Beardsley, with 59 caps to his name, was seemingly Gary Lineker's favourite strike partner.

Gary Lineker, who scored just one goal less than Bobby Charlton during his England career, won the Golden Boot at the Mexico World Cup in 1986 as the tournament's top scorer with a final tally of 10 goals. In all he scored five hat-tricks for England, netted all four England goals twice in wins against Spain and Malaysia, and was never booked throughout his entire career.

Nat Lofthouse was dubbed "The Lion of Vienna" by the British press after his brave display against Austria in 1952.

Tiny striker, Wilf Mannion scored a hat trick against Northern Ireland during his first England match in 1947. "Bloody ridiculous, can't we play them again?" was his comment as he came off the field after England's surprise 1-0 defeat by the USA in the 1950 World Cup.

England...

'Wizard of the Dribble' and one of the greatest footballers of all time, Stanley Matthews not only scored 11 goals (and created many more) for his country during 54 appearances in the famous white shirt in 1956, he was voted the first ever European Footballer of the Year.

Midfield genius, Johnny Haynes won 56 caps and grabbed 18 goals. He scored during his first game for England, a 2-0 victory over Northern Ireland in 1954.

Enjoyed six consecutive wins, and scored 40 goals, under the captaincy of Johnny Haynes from 1960 until 1962, when he was badly injured in a traffic accident.

Bobby Moore made more appearances as captain than any other player, his tally of 108 caps is second only to Peter Shilton.

Gary Neville had played just 19 games for Manchester United when he was picked for his first international against Japan in 1995, an England record.

Philip Neville, his brother, became, at 19 years and four months, the youngest player to have pulled on the famous white shirt since his former Manchester United colleague Lee Sharpe.

Gary and Philip Neville are the first brothers to play together in the same England team since Bobby and Jack Charlton.

Bill Nicholson scored for his country with his first touch in international football in 1951, just 19 seconds into the game. He holds the record for the fastest goal scored by an England debutante, and the second fastest goal ever scored by an England player. It was his one and only cap.

England...

Wonder boy, Michael Owen is the youngest player to wear the famous white shirt, just 18 years and 59 days in 1998 when took the field against Chile. He was just 18 years and 166 days when he slotted home against Morocco in his third game for his country, breaking Tommy Lawton's own 60 year old record to become England's youngest scorer.

The other scorer during the World Cup victory of 1966 was 'the Ghost', Martin Peters. He had a knack of appearing in the penalty area out of no-where at just the right time; "Ten years ahead of his time", is how Alf Ramsey described him.

David Platt scored 27 goals in a total of 62 games, the record for an England midfielder.

'Wingless Wonders', a 4-4-2 formation, was the system developed by Alf Ramsey during the 1966 World Cup Finals because he maintained that he was unable to find quality wingmen.

Alf Ramsey's most famous line is "You have beaten them once now go out and do it again" to his players during the interval just before extra time during the 1966 World Cup Final against West Germany. His description of the Argentinean side as "Animals" after an earlier qualifying match was to come back to haunt him four years later.

Jamie Redknapp's long range shot during his first ever England game, a friendly against Columbia in 1995, produced goalkeeper Rene Higuita's famous 'scorpion kick'. It seems probable that the whistle had already been blown but whether the crazy Columbian had heard it is a matter of debate.

England...

Most hated manager, probably, the late Don Revie did not join the international team on tour so that he could secretly negotiate a coaching job with the United Arab Emirates prior to resigning as the England manager, a latter-day 'Revie Plan'.

Manager with the best record of wins under his belt since Walter Winterbottom is Bobby Robson. His overall record of achievement could be argued to be second only to that of Alf Ramsey's. He led England to the World Cup quarter-finals in Mexico '86 and the semi-finals during Italia '90.

Bobby Robson netted two goals during a four goal victory over France in his first appearance in an England shirt in 1957. He was part of the England squad, playing three games in Sweden, during the World Cup Finals of 1958.

'Captain Marvel', Bryan Robson found the net on 26 occasions for his country during his tally of 90 matches in an England strip. For some time he appeared to be the only England player who knew where the opposition's goal was and the only England squad member capable of scoring goals.

Most successful new boy must be Paul Scholes, who is equally at home in either attack or mid-field. He grabbed a goal himself and set-up Ian Wright in the 2-0 defeat of Italy during the Le Tournoi in 1997 on his debut for his country. He found the net again against Moldova in 1997, and almost silenced 'Gaza Mania' with a spectacular strike on-the-turn against Tunisia in France '98.

Paul Scholes' hat-trick at Wembley against Poland in March 1999 re-kindled hopes that England had some chance of qualifying for the European Finals in the year 2000.

England...

Goalkeeper David Seaman has been a team sheet fixture as first choice between the sticks for his country since the mid-1990s. He has won 44 caps and maintains that he has worked-out a scientific method of saving penalties.

Striker Alan Shearer won the Golden Boot Award in Euro '96 with his final tally of five goals. Prior to this achievement he had not scored for his country in 12 matches, an astonishing lean spell of almost two years. The fact that he was not dropped by the manager is a record for an England player.

Manager, Glenn Hoddle appointed Alan Shearer captain of the international team in 1996. Shearer finished France '98 as England's joint top scorer with Michael Owen.

Striker, Teddy Sheringham was manager Terry Venables' preferred choice to partner Alan Shearer up-front.

Midfielder, Alan Ball is one of just five England players who have ever been sent off while playing for their country. The other four are Alan Mullery, Trevor Cherry (after having his front teeth knocked-out by an Argentinean during a friendly), Ray Wilkins and a certain David Beckham!

'Banks of England', Gordon Banks is arguably the greatest goalkeeper the country has ever produced. During 73 appearances he kept an amazing total of 35 clean sheets.

His international career was ended prematurely when he lost the sight of one eye in a serious car crash.

Gordon Banks pulled off the greatest, and still the most unbelievable save of all time, when he tipped Pele's downward header over the bar during the 1970 World Cup Finals in Brazil.

England...

Gordon Banks holds the record of having kept seven consecutive clean sheets for his country; a run that was only ended by Eusebio's penalty during the 1966 World Cup game against Portugal.

Centre-back and occasional captain, Tony Adams is the first Englishman born after the 1966 World Cup success to be picked to represent his country.

David Batty strode up to take his first ever penalty in anger during the shoot-out against Argentina during France '98. His spot-kick was saved, and thanks to a rush of blood to David Beckham's head, so was his reputation.

David Beckham was the only player to have been picked by Glenn Hoddle for all seven qualifying games for France '98. He is as famous for his engagement to the Spice Girl, Victoria Adams as he is for being only the fifth England player, ever, to be sent off when he lashed out during the Argentinian match in the first round of France '98.

Record goal scorer prior to the First World War, with an amazing total of 28 goals in just 23 games, was Steve Bloomer. He found the net at least once during each of his first 10   internationals.

Midfielder with the silky-smooth skills, Trevor Brooking won 47 caps for England. During his spell as England's creative maestro between 1974 and 1982 the team lost just seven games in which he was picked.

The best player never to have been awarded an England cap must surely be Manchester United captain Steve Bruce. Despite leading his club to three Premiership titles.

England...

Central defender, Sol (short for Sulzeer) Campbell makes a habit of scoring. He almost succeeded in re-writing history during France '98 when his header against Argentina was ruled-out because of a foul by Shearer. The Queen was most upset at the referee's decision and let it be known through her press office.

Bobby Moore's tragic early death in 1993 was greeted by the Sun newspaper with the caption "God can tell Heaven's XI to start getting changed, the captain has arrived".

Bobby Moore had pulled on the captain's armband a record 91 times between the years 1962 and 1973, just once more than Billy Wright.

Caps were first handed out in 1886. England players still receive a hand-made cap manufactured by flag makers, Toye, Kenning and Spencer.

1966 World Cup winning centre-half, 'The Giraffe', otherwise known as Jack Charlton won 35 caps and scored 6 goals for England.

Awarded Brian Clough two England caps before he was forced into early retirement because of injury. His son, Nigel, also played for England. Together they became the first father and son to have both played for their country yet still not scored a goal between them.

Most hated second strip was the grey kit (officially known as indigo blue) worn in place of the normal red during the ill-fated Euro '96 semi-final against Germany.

Centre forward Dixie Dean played for England 16 times during which he scored 18 goals, including 12 in his first five appearances.

England...

Oldest player to make his first appearance in his country's strip is Leslie Compton. His first cap was won against Wales in 1950 when he was 38 years of age. He was to represent England just once more.

Centre forward Ted Drake scored six goals during five appearances for his country. He spent his summers playing first class cricket for Hampshire.

Duncan Edwards was just over 18 when he faced Scotland at Wembley in 1955, just two years after his debut for his club.

Bobby Charlton once stated that "If I had to play for my life and could take one player with me it would be Duncan Edwards". He was considered to be the most complete footballer of his time and it is probable that Edwards would have led the England team during the 1966 World Cup campaign if the Munich air crash of 1958 hadn't occurred.

'Preston Plumber', Tom Finney, was equally at home on either wing which was just as well as whenever he played in tandem with Stanley Matthews he was always forced to play left wing. He still managed to score 30 goals in a total of 76 outings for his country, placing him fourth in the list of England's top goal scorers.

Robbie Fowler collected his first goal for his country during a friendly against Mexico at Wembley in 1997.

Won 'the Battle of Highbury' at Arsenal, in a so-called friendly with Italy in 1934, by three goals to two. After the Italian Monti received his marching orders things got even nastier and England's captain Eddie Hapgood finished the match with a broken nose.

England...

Goal-scoring legend Jimmy Greaves found the net on his international debut in 1959, a 4-1 drubbing of Peru. His 44 goals in 57 internationals included six hat-tricks.

Jimmy Greaves was unable to win back his place after injury in the team for the World Cup Final of 1966 and was so upset that he refused to join in the team's celebrations in a London Hotel later that evening.

Manager Ron Greenwood took charge of the national team for 55 matches; his record reads as won 33, drew 12 and lost 10.

Hot shot striker Trevor Francis scored a surprising 12 goals in a grand total of 52 international appearances for his country.

Captain, 'Crazy Horse', Emlyn Hughes won 62 caps and scored a solitary goal for his country.

Paul Ince was the first black player to have captained his country when he led the team out against the USA in 1993. Better known for his do-or-die defiance he has found the opposition's net a couple of times during his 43 appearances in his country's colours.

Tommy Lawton scored 22 goals in only 23 games for his country; the War interrupted his international career. He netted twice in five successive matches for his country and became the first player since 1929 to grab four for England in one match. He got 16 of his international goals in 15 games and scored after only 17 seconds during a game against Portugal in 1947.

Graham Le Saux is the first Channel Islander to play for England, Matt Le Tissier is the second, coming on as a substitute in the same game, against Denmark in 1994.

England...

Kevin Keegan once described Robert Lee as "the best midfielder in the country". Lee is known by his fellow players as 'Lurker' because of his ability to hang around the opposition's penalty area unnoticed. Because of strong competition for places in England's midfield he has won only 18 caps.

Graham Le Saux clutched his face instead of tackling Romania's Dan Petrescu during a France '98 Group G match. Because of this Petrescu scored, England went on to face Argentina, not the fans so-called soft option Croatia, and were eliminated.

Nat Lofthouse made his first appearance in an England shirt in 1951 scoring both of his country's goals in a 2-2 draw with Yugoslavia at Highbury. He won 33 caps and scored 30 goals for his country, including two goals per game in 12 matches.

Steve McManaman has never scored for his country in 22 outings. His debut match was against Nigeria in 1994. He only made one appearance in France '98.

England...

'Wor' Jackie Milburn scored 10 goals for his country in just 13 appearances; none were headers, he was never able to head a football.

'Clown Prince of Soccer', Len Shackleton was known for love of jokes and this may have been one of the reasons he only wore the England shirt a mere five times, finding the net just once.

Chris Sutton did not assist his chances of adding to his single international cap by upsetting England manager Glenn Hoddle by refusing to turn out for the B team against Chile B in February 1998.

Frank Swift was the first goalkeeper to captain his country. He won 19 caps, became a journalist and was killed in the 1958 Munich air disaster.

Manager Graham Taylor had no friends at the Sun newspaper. The headline "Swedes 2, Turnips 1" after England's defeat in the European Championship Finals was accompanied by a photograph showing Taylor's face merged with a turnip for his head.

Lost only seven matches during Taylor's three year reign. Unfortunately, they were all the wrong matches to lose. The worst result was possibly a defeat by the USA in a friendly of 1993. The Sun's headline was "Yanks 2, Planks 0".

Terry Venables was the first player to represent his country at all five levels, schoolboy, youth, amateur and Under 23 level, plus two full caps for his country.

Terry Venables became the first British manager to lift The World Manager of the Year Award. As England's manager

England...

the country lost fewer games (apart from Joe Mercer's caretaker spell of seven games), just one in 23 games, and that was to the World Champions, Brazil.

Venables took his country to the Euro '96 semi-finals, equalling Alf Ramsey's achievement in the same competition back in 1968.

Winger, Chris Waddle found the net six times during 62 appearances for his country but will always carry the burden of his penalty shoot-out miss in the 1990 World Cup semi-final against Germany.

First player to have been sent off during the World Cup Finals is Ray Wilkins who threw the ball at the referee during a boring no-score tie with Morocco in 1986. He won just two more caps to bring his total to 84.

Long-time servant Walter Winterbottom served his country between the years 1946 and 1962, first as chief coach and then manager.. He was in control of the national team for 139 matches.

Winterbottom guided the country to more wins, 78, than any other England manager, but more defeats as well, 28. He took England to a record four World Cup Finals, 1950, 1954, 1958 and 1962.

Manager Graham Taylor dropped Chris Waddle for a European Championship qualifying tie against Turkey during the 1990s and brought in Dennis Wise in his place. Wise scored the only goal of the game. This is the only time that Dennis Wise has found the net for his country in 10 outings.

England...

Did not join FIFA until after the Second World War. The country had boycotted the pre-War World Cups held between 1930 and 1938.

Billy Wright actually started his playing career as a wing-half before being converted to his club's, Wolves, and England's centre-half.

Captain, Billy Wright was the first player to reach the magic total of 100 caps for his country when he led the team out against Scotland in 1959. He captained his country on 90 occasions, 70 of which were consecutive matches.

Have played more international matches and scored more goals than any other footballing nation.

Billy Wright led his country to three of its worst defeats, by the USA in 1950, and Hungary in 1953 and 1954.

Striker Ian Wright's international career was revived by manager Glenn Hoddle during a World Cup qualifier against Italy in Rome in 1997. He was very unlucky not to appear on the score-sheet and his record of nine goals and 31caps is the result of serious injuries, one of which kept him out of the France '98 World Cup Finals.

Cheerful caretaker manager, Joe Mercer was the perfect antidote to the country's shock at not having qualified for the 1974 World Cup Finals. His record was played seven, won three, drew three and lost one.

Kevin Keegan, the current England manager, made his international debut against Wales in 1972. His next two games were also against Wales.

France...

Were the nation that first thought up the idea of a football World Cup back in 1930, but it was not until 1998 that the country first lifted the trophy.

Had never before even reached the World Cup Final prior to the 1998 tournament.

Failed to qualify for the World Cup Finals six times, in 1950, 1962, 1970, 1974, 1990 and 1994.

Won the third place play-off in the 1986 World Cup.

Reached the semi-final of the World Cup three times, in 1958, 1982 and 1986.

Match against West Germany in the World Cup of 1982, which they lost on penalties witnessed probably the worst foul in international football ever to go unpunished, when Germany's goalkeeper broke Batiston's jaw and knocked out two of his teeth in a truly cynical and illegal challenge. The referee awarded France a goal kick.

First international was a 3-3 draw with Belgium in Brussels back in 1903.

France...

First game in the World Cup Finals was a 4-1 defeat of Mexico in Uruguay way back in 1930.

Player who has won the most caps, 82, is Manuel Amaros.

Legendary captain, Michel Platini has scored a record 41 goals for his country.

Best victory was an eight goal drubbing, without reply, of Iceland back in 1957.

Worst defeat was an astonishing thrashing by Denmark way back in 1908; the final score was an incredible 17-1.

Just Fontaine scored a World Cup Finals record of 13 goals during the 1958 campaign.

Won the Euro '84 defeating Spain 2-0 in the final. Home advantage was a plus but the team were led by their truly great mid-field maestro, Michel Platini.

Are the first team to have put out 12 players during a match. During a game against Northern Ireland, in 1952, Bonifaci of France who had been taken off injured in the first half returned to the pitch not having been told that he had already been substituted. After half-time France just sent out the normal of 11 players, and won 3-1.

Banned Eric Cantona from the national team for a year after he insulted manager Henri Michel.

Germany...

Are the 'come-back-kids' of world soccer. West Germany won the World Cup Final of 1954 after going two goals behind to the great Hungarian team, including Puskas, to run-out 3-2 winners.

Are usually at their most dangerous when they go behind. They reached the quarter -finals of France '98 after coming back against both Yugoslavia and Mexico.

Are the only nation to have won the European Championship on three occasions. As West Germany in 1972 and 1980, and as Germany (after re-unification) in 1996.

Franz Beckenbauer turned out for West Germany on 103 occasions, grabbing 13 goals. 'Der Kaiser' as he was nicknamed practically invented the creative 'sweeper' system and led West Germany to World Cup victory in 1974.

Beckenbauer became the first person to have not only won the World Cup as captain of the national team but to lead his country. to further World Cup victory as manager, the 'double' he achieved in 1990.

Third group match in USA '94 was a tight affair. After being three goals in the lead at half-time the South Koreans hit back with two goals of their own. The crowd jeered at the German team and one of their players, Stefan Effenburg made a gesture to the terraces; he was sent back home to Germany.

Striker Jürgen Klinsmann has scored 47 goals for his country having won 108 caps.

Klinsmann is the only player to have found the net during three different European Championship finals.

Germany...

Lothar Matthäus has played a total of 25 matches in World Cup Finals, a world record. He also shares another record (with Mexican goalkeeper, Antonio Carbajal), he has played in five World Cup Finals.

Striker Gerd Müller, nicknamed 'Der Bomber' scored an incredible 68 goals in 62 appearances for West Germany.

Played their very first international against Switzerland at Basle back in 1908, losing by five goals to three.

First game, ever, in the World Cup was a 5-2 win over Belgium in Italy back in 1938.

Player who has made the most international appearances for his country is Lothar Matthäus with 126 caps.

Best victory was an incredible 16 goal spree, without reply, against Tsarist Russia way back in 1912.

Worst moment during the early years must have been a six goal drubbing, without reply, by Austria back in 1931.

Holland...

Invented 'total football' during the 1970s; every outfield player was comfortable on the ball and was able to interchange and play in any position.

Have never lifted the World Cup.

Have reached the Final of the World Cup twice, once in 1974 and the second time in 1978, losing on both occasions to the host nation, West Germany and Argentina respectively.

Won the European Championship in 1988.

Greatest captain and player ever is Johan Cruyff; he scored 33 goals in 48 international appearances for his country.

Swept through the second round of the 1974 World Cup Finals scoring eight goals and conceding none. Their opponents had been Argentina, Brazil and East Germany.

Scored a goal in the 1974 World Cup Final before any of

Holland...

the opposing West German team had even touched the ball. English referee Jack Taylor awarded the penalty. Johan Cruyff had been brought down in the penalty area, and Neeskens converted the penalty?

First international was a friendly against Belgium in Antwerp back in 1905, which they won 4-1

First game in the World Cup was a 2-3 defeat by Switzerland in Italy back in 1934.

Ruud Krol won a record 83 international caps for Holland.

Player who has scored the most goals for his country is Dennis Bergkamp with a tally of 36.

Best victory was a nine-goal thrashing, without reply, of Finland back in 1912.

Worst defeat was by an amateur team, the England Amateurs of 1909 who found the net on nine occasions, only conceding a single goal themselves.

Were among Europe's minnows back in the 1950s when they lost 22 games out of 26 played.

Were eliminated from the European Championships in 1963 by tiny Luxembourg.

Hungary...

Took part in the first international match ever played on the Continent of Europe, a 5-0 defeat by Austria in a friendly in Vienna in 1902.

First World Cup match was a 4-2 defeat of Egypt in Italy '34.

Player who has been awarded the most caps is Jozef Bozsik with a round 100.

Truly great Ferenc Puskas is his country's highest goalscorer with a grand tally of 83.

Best victory is a 13-1 thrashing of France back in 1926.

Have been defeated by seven clear goals without reply on three occasions; the last time this happened was in 1941, inflicted by arch-rivals Germany.

Did not enter the first World Cup in 1930.

Have not qualified for the last stages of the World Cup on five occasions.

Have, in fact, not progressed beyond the qualifying round of the World Cup since 1986.

Were runners-up in the 1954 World Cup.

Came close to lifting the Jules Rimet trophy in 1954 when they lost to West Germany 3-2 in the final. Germany had actually lost to Hungary 8-3 earlier in the finals competition. Hungary appeared in the 1938 World Cup Final, losing 4-2.

Hungary...

Hold the record for going the most games, 29, as an international team, without defeat, between 14th May 1950 and 4th July 1954.

Were the best international football team in the world throughout the 1950s. Hungary dished out England's worst defeat ever, a 7-1 drubbing, in Budapest in 1954.

Were known as 'The Magnificent Magyars' during this decade; probably the best team never to have won the World cup.

Were the first country to defeat England at Wembley, 3-6 in 1953.

Laszio Kiss was the first player to be sent on as a substitute and net a hat-trick during the Spain '82 World Cup Finals.

Final tally of 10 goals, without reply by their opponents El Salvador, in this group three game was the recorded double figures World Cup Finals win.

Italy...

Are the most successful team, together with West Germany, in the history of the World Cup competition. They have reached five finals, equal with Brazil.

Are third in the list of countries who have scored the most World Cup goals, with a total of 105.

Did not enter the first World Cup in 1930 and have only failed to qualify once, 1958.

Nickname is the 'Azzurie', meaning - the 'Blues'

Have lost just one match in the World Cup Finals in open play since 1978, losing to France in 1986.

First international match was a friendly against France in Milan back in 1910. The hosts ran out winners by six goals to two.

Very first World Cup appearance was a seven to one drubbing of the USA in the 1934 World Cup Finals in Italy.

Italy...

Goalkeeper Dino Zoff was capped 112 by his country.

Sharpshooter with the most goals for his country is Luigi Riva having found the opposition's net 35 times.

Best victory is an 11-3 victory over Egypt back in 1928.

Worst defeat was by Hungary back in 1924, a seven to one goal thrashing.

Have lifted the World Cup three times, way back in 1934 and 1938, and more recently in 1982.

Have been knocked out of the World Cup Finals on penalties on three occasions since 1978, in 1990, 1994 and 1998.

Have only failed to progress past round one in the World Cup Finals on five occasions, in 1950, 1954, 1962, 1966 and 1974.

Won the play-off third place match of the 1990 World Cup Finals.

Was one of four countries, the others being Holland, Spain and Sweden, who failed in their bids to host the first World Cup in Uruguay and boycotted the event.

Kept 12 clean sheets up until World Cup 1974. Haiti was the unlikely team to end this run.

Northern Ireland...

First international was a 2-1 victory over England in Belfast back in 1923.

First World Cup Final match was played in Sweden in 1958, a 1-0 victory over Czechoslovakia.

Goalkeeping legend, Pat Jennings, played 119 times for his country.

Pat Jennings had the habit, during training, of sometimes not moving but shouting either "post" or "bar" when anyone took a shot at goal. On almost every occasion the ball either hit the bar or the post as stated.

Highest scoring victory is a 7-0 drubbing of Wales in 1930.

Striker, Joe Bambrick slotted-in an incredible six of the seven goal total against Wales in 1930 thus making him the record holder for having scored the most goals in a single match during a Home Championship.

Worst defeat was handed-out by England, a nine goal blitz with just two in reply, in 1930.

Top sharpshooter is Colin Clarke having found the net 13 times while sporting his country's colours.

Hold the record for having fielded the youngest player in the history of the World Cup Finals, midfielder Norman Whiteside. During the 1982 tournament in Spain he broke Pele's record by 195 days by taking the field at the tender age of 17 years and 42 days.

All-time footballing genius, George Best played a mere 37 games for his country, scoring a total of nine goals.

Northern Ireland...

Is the fourth oldest of all international football associations.

Concentrated solely on the Home International Competition each year until, in 1951, when they invited France to Belfast to play a friendly.

Reached the quarter-finals of the 1958 World Cup Final in Sweden when, led by their legendary captain Danny Blanchflower, they had already beaten Czechoslovakia and drawn with West Germany.

Beat their hosts, Spain by a Gerry Armstrong goal and reached the dizzy heights of the second round of the World Cup Finals of 1982.

Can boast of the only international manager to have scored the winning goal against England at Wembley when Terry O'Neil slotted home as Northern Ireland's player/manager and captain.

Manager, Billy Bingham, one-time coach of the Greek international team, masterminded Northern Ireland to two World Cup Finals.

Appointed an Englishman, and a one-time assistant to England coach Graham Taylor, ex-guardsman Laurie McMenemy as their national team manager in 1998.

Billy Bingham is the longest serving British international manager. He has occupied this hot seat for a grand total of 15 years, which includes an uninterrupted period of 13 years.

Keith Gillespie hit a long-range volley during a victory over Austria in a Euro '96 qualifier to register his first goal for his country.

Republic of Ireland...

First international was a 1-0 win over Bulgaria during the 1924 Olympic Games in Paris.

First game in the World Cup Finals was a 1-1 draw with England during Italia '90.

Player with the record number of appearances for his country is Paul McGrath with 83 caps.

Top goalscorer is Frank Stapleton with 20 goals to his credit.

Best ever win was a 8-0 victory over Malta in 1983.

Worst defeat was a 0-7 thrashing by Brazil in 1982.

Reached the World Cup Finals for the first time in 1990, led by their charismatic Englishman, 'Big' Jack Charlton.

Reached the quarter-finals of Italy '90 only to lose to the hosts 1-0.

Did not qualify for France '98.

Did not enter the first World Cup in 1930.

Did not qualify for the World Cup Finals between the years 1934 and 1986.

Did not lose a single match to England during the managerial reign of 'Big Jack'.

Republic of Ireland...

Record against England under Jack Charlton is one win and three draws. This inspired the Irish fans chant of, "You'll never beat the Irish".

Pre-Charlton high spot was reaching the quarter-finals of the European Championships in 1964, losing to Spain on this occasion.

Were the first nation to defeat England in England, 2-1 at Goodison Park back in 1949.

Failed to reach the finals of Euro '96 and Jack Charlton retired to spend more time with his fishing rods.

Romania...

First international was a 2-1 win over Yugoslavia in 1922.

First game in the World Cup was a 3-1 victory over Peru during the 1930 Finals in Uruguay.

Player with the most caps to his name is Georghe Hagi with a haul of 113.

Player who has slotted home the most goals for his country is also Georghe Hagi. He has a total of 32 goals to his name.

Captain, Georghe Hagi is nicknamed 'The Maradona of the Carpathians'.

Thrashed Finland 9-0 in 1973, Romania's best win, ever.

Hungary smashed nine goals past Romania without reply back in 1948.

Defeated Peru 3-1 in Montevideo during the 1930 World Cup. The game was played in front of the smallest crowd ever for a World Cup Finals game, a mere 300.

Have not qualified for the finals of the World Cup on seven occasions.

Have only reached the quarter-finals of the World Cup the once, in 1994. Romania have only gone beyond the first round on two other occasions, in 1990 and 1998.

Were knocked out of the 1990 World Cup Finals on penalties in a shoot-out with the Republic of Ireland.

Romania...

Suffered the same gut-wrenching fate in 1994 during their quarter-final match against Sweden. Georghe Hagi became the only international captain to see his side go out of two successive World Cups on penalties.

Players bleached their hair during France '98 to celebrate having progressed to the next round, all except their goalkeeper that is who was completely bald! Their main scalp had been the England team.

Went on in the second round to draw with Tunisia, losing their last game 1-0 to Croatia.

Scotland...

First international was a 0-0 draw with England in Glasgow way back in 1872. The Scottish team contained 11 Queens Park players. A crowd of 10,000 provided gate receipts of £38. This financed the travel expenses of the Scottish team for the return match in England.

First World Cup game was a 1-0 defeat by Switzerland back in 1954.

Most capped player, with 102 caps, is Kenny Dalglish.

Kenny Dalglish is, with Dennis Law, their country's leading goalscorers, with 30 apiece.

Best victory was a 9-0 drubbing of Wales back in 1878.

Worst defeat was a 7-0 thrashing by Uruguay without reply in 1954.

Hold the record for being the country who, having qualified for the most World Cup Finals (nine), have never progressed further than the first round.

Qualified for the finals of the World Cup for the first time in 1950.

Were prevented from going to the 1950 World Cup Finals by the Scottish FA because England had topped the Home Championships, which had been used to decide qualification. Injured pride at having finished only second had led to the Scottish FA's boycott.

Have only qualified for the European Championship Finals on two occasions, in 1992 and 1996.

Scotland...

New goalkeeper, Frank Haffey was beaten nine times (with only three in reply) at Wembley by the England team of 1961, giving rise to the popular joke of the period, "What's the time? Nearly ten past Haffey".

Happy-go-lucky Frank Haffey later emigrated to Australia and toured the cabaret circuit as a nightclub singer. He took to posing for the press in front of clocks with their hands at nine and three. Jimmy Greaves, who had joined in the goal feast that day, used these photos to assist in the propagation of the myth about Scottish goalkeepers.

Have won 40 games, lost 44, to the 'Auld Enemy', England, with 20 drawn.

'Wembley Wizards' of 1928 beat England 5-1.

Top internationals, Billy Bremner, Joe Harper, Pat McCluskey, Willie Young and Arthur Graham were banned for life in 1979 from representing their country after a night-out on-the-town celebrating a victory over Denmark in 1975.

Legendary manager, Jock Stein collapsed and died of a heart attack in November 1985 at Ninian Park after having led his country to the Finals of the 1986 World Cup. Alex Ferguson took over as caretaker manager during the World Cup tournament in Mexico.

Goalkeeper, Bob Wilson won two caps for his country against Portugal and Holland, both in 1971, and both were defeats.

Lost to the Czech Republic in March 1999, 2-1; the country's first home defeat in serious competition for an amazing 12 years.

Scotland...

Denis Law shares the record of 30 international goals with Kenny Dalglish but his were scored in only 55 matches. Law grabbed four on two occasions, against Northern Ireland in 1962 and Norway in 1963.

Ian St John netted nine goals for his country and was awarded 21 caps.

Scotland goalkeeper Andy Goram represented his country at football and cricket. In 1989 he won the first of his three cricket caps against the touring Australians.

Andy Goram pulled out of the Scotland squad for the 1998 World Cup Finals after a tabloid newspaper made allegations about his private life.

Scotland's Willie Johnston tested positive for drugs after the teams 1978 World Cup Finals game against Peru. The winger protested that he had taken pills for hay fever but few people believed him. He was ordered to pack his bags and was sent home immediately. He was later banned from international football for a year but never played for his country again.

Spain...

Did not enter for the World Cup in 1930, and 1938.

Best victory was a 13 goal thrashing of Bulgaria back 1933.

Emilio Buttragueno is top scorer with 26 goals.

First international was a 1-0 victory over Denmark during the 1920 Olympic Games held in Belgium.

Won the European Championship in 1964, running out 2-1 winners in the final over the then current holders of the title; the Soviet Union. Home advantage may have contributed to Spain's only major international success.

First World Cup game was a 3-1 win over Brazil in Italy 1934.

Did not qualify for the World Cup Finals on four occasions, in 1954, 1958, 1970 and 1974.

Won two international championships on the toss of a coin. Spain won the International Youth Championships in this manner in both 1952 and 1954 because on each occasion the final game ended in a draw.

Player who has been most honoured by his country is Andoni Zubizaretta with a tally of 112 caps.

Most crushing defeat was handed-out by Italy, 7-1 back in 1928.

Spain...

Were victorious in the 1992 Olympic Games, again with home advantage, lifting gold when they defeated Poland 3-2 in the final at Barcelona's Nou Camp Stadium.
Have never progressed further than the quarter-finals of the World Cup Finals. They achieved this on three occasions, 1934, 1886 and 1894.

Have got not further than the first round of the World Cup Finals on four occasions, progressing to the second round three times.

Pre-tournament form always seems to flatter to deceive. The Spanish team were defeated by Nigeria in the first match of France '98, then drew their second match in round one against Paraguay.

Went on to infuriate their supporters by winning their third match in style by drubbing Bulgaria 6-1.

Win in the third match of round one ended up as the record score of the competition but Spain's return to true form had arrived too late and they did not progress to the second round.

Uruguay...

Were the winners of the first World Cup ever held. Uruguay defeated arch-rivals Argentina 4-2 in 1930, home advantage may have helped Nasazzi and his team lift the trophy.

Were the first non-European side to lift the football Gold Medal when they won the final of the Olympic Games of both 1924 and 1928.

Played in front of the largest crowd ever. Almost 200,000 fans watched Uruguay defeat Brazil 2-1 in the last game of the 1950 World Cup.

Were the first South American team to lift the World Cup twice, in 1930 and 1950.

First ever international was a 2-3 defeat by Argentina in Montevideo way back in 1902.

First World Cup match was a 1-0 victory over Peru in Uruguay in 1930.

Rodolfo Rodiguez is his country's most capped player, with a tally of 78.

Have played Argentina 184 times since 1901; a record for two international teams.

Striker Hector Scarone has scored the most goals for his country, 29.

Most crushing win was a 9-0 thrashing of Bolivia back in 1927.

Uruguay...

Worst scoreline was a 6-1 defeat by Argentina in 1919. This result was duplicated by the same opposition some years later in 1955.

Lost by exactly the same score on two more occasions, in 1955 against Brazil and Denmark in 1986.

Did not qualify for France '98. In so doing they were the only past winners not represented in these World Cup Finals.

Had failed to qualify for the World Cup Finals on four other occasions, in 1958, 1978, 1982 and 1994.

Did not enter the World Cup competition in 1934 and 1938.

Finished in fourth place in the World Cups of 1954 and 1970.

Wales...

First international was a 4-0 drubbing by Scotland in 1876.

First World Cup appearance was in 1958 when they drew with Hungary 1-1 in Sweden.

Are the least successful in international competition of all the four home countries having qualified just twice for major tournaments.

Proudest hour must be when they reached the quarter-finals of the 1958 World Cup.

Had drawn all their group matches during the 1958 Finals before John Charles, Ivor Allchurch and company defeated the great Hungarians in a play-off.

Were finally knocked out at the 1958 World Cup quarter-final stage 1-0 by the Brazilians, who were to go on to reach the Final and lift the trophy.

Progressed to the two-legged quarter-final of the European Championship in 1976, missing out by two goals without reply in Zagreb and achieving a 1-1 draw once they got Yugoslavia back to Ninian Park. During the second leg Wales missed a penalty and had two goals ruled-out by the referee.

Player who has won the most caps is goalkeeper Neville Southall with 92. He had been a dustman before turning to football for a living.

Best victory is an eleven goal spree, without reply, over Ireland back in 1888.

Wales...

Worst drubbing was by Scotland way back in 1878, a 9-0 goal blitz without reply.

Ian Rush has scored 28 international goals and appeared 73 times for Wales.

Hold the record for having fielded the oldest international player ever when winger, Billy Meredith was awarded the last of his 48 caps in 1920, not far short of his 46th birthday.

Wizard of the dribble, Ryan Giggs was the youngest player to have represented his country, having won his first cap at the tender age of 17 years and 332 days, until Ryan Green pulled-on the all-red strip in a game against Malta in 1998 some 106 days younger.

Picked hard man Vinnie Jones at the late age of 29 for the first of his nine caps for his adopted country in 1994.

Vinnie Jones was sent off in a match against Georgia in 1995 and suspended for five matches.

The Welsh squad for the World Cup qualifier against Holland in 1996 voted Vinnie Jones captain, a decision that the manager, Bobby Gould honoured. Wales lost 7-1.

'Sparky', otherwise known as Mark Hughes has grabbed 16 goals in 65 matches for his country.

'Gentle Giant', John Charles, who could play at either centre-half or centre-forward at the top level, was never booked or sent off throughout his entire career.

Wales...

'Golden Boy' of Welsh football was Ivor Allchurch who won 68 caps and netted 23 goals for his country.

Manager Bobby Gould was in the hot seat when the Dutch handed out a 7-1 thrashing of the Welsh team in 1997 during a World Cup qualifier, the worst result for the national side since 1930.

Nathan Blake accused Bobby Gould of being a racist because of comments allegedly made by Gould to the player during a training session and the half-time talk during the Holland match of 1997. It appears that both parties have agreed that the entire affair was a misunderstanding.

Liverpool goal-scoring ace John Toshack scored a mere 13 goals for his country during 40 appearances in his country's colours.

THE

GREAT

PLAYERS

Tony Adams...

Made his Arsenal League debut in 1983.

**Won the PFA Young Player of the year award in 1987, as
well as being chosen by the fans as being Arsenal's Player
of the Year.**

Made his England debut against Spain in Madrid in February
1987, in doing so he became the first player born after the
World Cup victory in 1966 to represent England.

**Helped Arsenal win the 1987 League Cup with a 2-1 win
over Liverpool.**

Became Arsenal's youngest ever captain in 1988 when he
took over from Kenny Sansom.

Played for England in the 1988 European Championships.

Won his first League Championship in 1989, thanks to a
thrilling 2-0 victory away to Liverpool in the last game of the
season.

**Was voted by the fans as Arsenal's Player of the Year in
1990.**

Was jailed for drink-driving just before Christmas in 1990.

Won his second League Championship in 1991.

Guided Arsenal to a domestic cup double in 1993, beating
Sheffield Wednesday in both the League Cup and FA Cup
Finals. They won both of them 2-1 although the FA Cup did
take a replay after the original game ended in a 1-1 draw.

Tony Adams...

Led Arsenal to victory in the 1994 European Cup Winners' Cup Final with a 1-0 win over Italian club Parma.

Was voted Arsenal's Player of the Year for the third time by fans in 1994.

Suffered an unlucky defeat in the 1995 European Cup Winners' Cup Final when former Tottenham player Nayim lobbed Arsenal keeper David Seaman from the halfway line in the last minute to give Real Zaragoza an unbeatable 2-1 lead.

Starred for England in the 1996 European Championships, helping England reach the semi-finals before being knocked out on penalties by eventual winners Germany.

Admitted in 1996 that he was an alcoholic but has tackled the problem since then with the same grit and determination he shows on the field.

Guided Arsenal to their second League and FA Cup double in 1998.

Appeared for England in the 1998 World Cup finals in France, being knocked out in a penalty shoot-out by Argentina in the second round.

Has played almost 450 League games for Arsenal, his only club.

Played more than 50 times for England, scoring 4 international goals.

Osvaldo Ardiles...

Turned proffessional in 1969 with Huracan of Buenos Aires.

Starred for Argentina in the 1978 World Cup Finals, playing a key role in midfield as the hosts beat Holland 3-1 in the final.

Signed by Tottenham Hotspur manager Keith Burkinshaw for £300,000 immediately after the World Cup.

Played 238 League games for the London club, scoring 16 goals.

Won the FA Cup in 1981, beating Manchester City 3-2 in a replay after the original match ended 1-1.

The chorus of Tottenham's 1981 FA Cup song went: "Ossie's going to Wembley, his knees have gone all trembly."

Loaned out to French side Paris St. Germain during the Falklands conflict.

Broke his shin in only his fourth game back in England and was sidelined for 10 months.

Helped Spurs win the 1984 UEFA Cup after a penalty shoot-out with Belgian club Anderlecht.

Appeared in the 1987 FA Cup Final with Spurs, this time losing against Coventry City.

Loaned to Blackburn Rovers in March 1988 where he played five games.

Osvaldo Ardiles...

Joined QPR on a free transfer in the summer of 1988.

Became manager of Swindon Town in 1989.

Took over as manager of Newcastle United in 1991.

Replaced Terry Venables as manager at White Hart Lane under the chairmanship of Alan Sugar but failed to match up to the fans expectations.

In 1996 he became manager of Japanese J-League team Shimzu S-Pulse.

Roberto Baggio...

Nicknamed 'Il Codino Divino', (The Divine Ponytail).

Made his debut for the then Italian Serie B team Vicenza in 1982 at the age of 15.

Transferred to Fiorentina in 1985 after 36 games and 13 goals.

His move to Juventus in 1990 sparked off riots in the street by the Fiorentina fans that lasted for three days and needed the intervention of the police. He repaid the fee of £7.7 million by scoring 78 goals in 141 games.

In a match against Fiorentina in 1991, he was substituted after he refused to take a penalty against his old club.

1993 saw Juventus win the UEFA Cup. He topped 100 league goals and was voted FIFA World Footballer of the Year and European Footballer of the Year.

His penalty for Italy in the 1994 World Cup Final was one

Roberto Baggio...

that he would rather forget. With the score at 3-2 to Brazil in a penalty shoot-out Baggio stepped up knowing he had to score...and he skied it over the bar.

Won the Italian league in 1995, and then sensationally signed for AC Milan for £10 million after failing to agree a new contract with Juventus.

Even though he seemed to spend more time on the substitute's bench for AC Milan, they won the Italian league in 1996. Baggio became only the third player in Italian history to win a championship medal with different clubs in successive seasons.
His loss of form for AC Milan meant that he was dropped from the Italian squad for Euro 96.

He transferred to Bologna in 1997.

England's David Platt once said of him: "As footballers go, he's a genius."

Gordon Banks...

Was known as 'Banks of England' because he had the safest pair of hands in the country.

Won 73 England caps between 1963 and 1972, keeping an amazing 35 clean sheets.

Won more England caps than any other goalkeeper except Peter Shilton.

Started his playing career in 1955 with Chesterfield where he made 23 appearances before moving to Leicester City in 1959.

Made his England debut against Scotland at Wembley in 1963. Scotland won 2-1, their first victory in London for 12 years.

Appeared in two FA Cup Finals with Leicester City, 1961 and 1963, finishing on the losing side on both occasions.

Was transferred to Stoke City in 1967 for a British goalkeeping record fee of £65,000.

Gordon Banks...

Won the League Cup with
Leicester City in 1964 and
then with Stoke City in 1972.

**Was awarded the OBE in
1970 for services to football.**

Was the Footballer of the Year
in 1972.

**Played his last game for
England in 1972, a 1-0 victory over Scotland.**

Lost the sight of one eye in a car crash in 1972.

**Was responsible for what has been called the 'save of the
century' in the World Cup Finals in Mexico, 1970. When
Brazilian legend powered a header towards the top corner
of the goal and was preparing to celebrate, Banks flew
across the line and somehow scooped the ball away.**

Was replaced at Stoke City by a teenage Peter Shilton.

**Is Stoke City's most-capped player, earning 36 of his caps
whilst playing for the 'Potters'.**

Franco Baresi...

Had trials in 1974, along with his brother, with Italian side Internazionale when he was a teenager. He was rejected as being too weak and frail. A week later he joined AC Milan.

Made his League debut at 18 and a year later played a large part in helping AC Milan win the Italian Championship.

Suffered a blood disorder in 1980 which forced him to miss a large part of the season.

Experienced relegation when AC Milan were demoted following a betting scandal.

Was a member of Italy's World Cup squad for Spain 1982 but did not play.

Played against his elder brother, Giuseppe, a defender with arch rivals Inter Milan, more than 20 times.

Made his international debut in a 0-0 draw against Romania in Florence.

Steered AC Milan to European Cup and World Club titles in 1989 and 1990.

Played in the World Cup Finals in Italy 1990, captaining the side that beat England into third place.

Missed a penalty, along with Baggio, in the penalty shoot-out

Franco Baresi...

in the 1994 World Cup Final against Brazil.

Altogether he has won three European Cups. Six Seria A League titles, three European Super Cups and two World Club Cups.

Played over 600, games for AC Milan, his only club, scoring just 5 goals.

Played 81 times for Italy, scoring once, before retiring from international football in 1994.

John Barnes...

Was born in Jamaica in November 1963.

Made his debut for Watford in 1981, playing 233 League games for the club, scoring 65 goals in the process.

Made his international debut for England against Northern Ireland in May 1983.

Transferred to Liverpool for £900,000 in 1987.

Played 79 games for England, scoring 11 goals, although he has rarely shown his fantastic club form at international level.

In 1984, when aged just 20, he single-handedly beat the entire Brazilian defence and slotted the ball past the goalkeeper in front of a stunned crowd at the great Maracana Stadium in Rio.

Won two League titles with Liverpool, 1988 and 1990.

John Barnes...

Won the FA Cup twice with Liverpool, 1989 and 1992, as well as the Coca-Cola Cup in 1995.

Rumours doing the rounds suggest that when AC Milan bought Luther Blisset from Watford, they thought it was John Barnes they were buying!

His father was a centre-half who played for Jamaica.

Voted Player of the Year in 1988.

He was the first player ever to wear white boots in the FA Cup Final (when Liverpool lost 1-0 to Manchester United in 1996).

Transferred to Newcastle with ex-Liverpool colleague Ian Rush when Kenny Dalglish took over at St James Park.

Signed for Premier Division newcomers Charlton Athletic in 1998/99.

Peter Beardsley...

Made his League debut for Carlisle United in 1979, staying with them until 1982 and making 102 appearances, scoring 22 goals.

Moved briefly to Vancouver Whitecaps in Canada before being bought back to England by Manchester United, but failed to start a single match for them.

Moved to Newcastle United where he began to make a name for himself, scoring 61 League goals in 147 appearances.

Moved to Liverpool for £1.9 million in July 1987 where he helped them win two League titles, 1987/88 and 1989/90 and one FA Cup in 1989.

Made a shock move to Merseyside rivals Everton in 1991. He soon became one of just a few players to score for both clubs in Merseyside derbies.

Notched up 59 appearances for England, mainly as strike partner for goal-machine Gary Lineker. Peter himself scored nine international goals.

Moved back to Newcastle in 1993, once more dazzling the Geordies with his ball skills.

Was made youth team coach at Newcastle on the arrival of his ex-Liverpool colleague Kenny Dalglish.

Franz Beckenbauer...

Known as 'Der Kaiser'.

Germany's second highest capped figure with 103 appearances.

Effectively created the attacking sweeper role and mastered it like no other before or since.

Made his international debut in 1965 with a 2-1 World Cup qualifying win in Sweden.

Captained Bayern Munich to three European Cups in a row between 1974 and 1976.

Led West Germany to winning the World Cup in 1974.

European Footballer of the Year awards in 1972 and 1976.

Moved to the North American Soccer League during the 70s winning the NASL Soccer Bowl three times in 1977, 1978 and 1980.

Appointed national manager of West Germany in 1984.

Became the first man to captain and then manage a World Cup winning team when West Germany beat Argentina 1-0 in Rome in 1990.

After a short spell as coach of Olympique Marseille he returned as executive vice-president of Bayern in 1993.

In 1994 he took over as coach and guided Bayern to the league title.

David Beckham...

A product of Manchester United's famous youth policy, moving from London to join the Red Devils.

Made his league debut with Preston North End whilst on loan from Manchester United. He scored two goals in his five appearances.

Was voted the PFA Young Player of the Year in 1997.

Scored a fantastic goal on the opening day of the 1997-98 season, beating Wimbledon keeper Neil Sullivan from the half-way line.

Won the FA Cup in 1997 to add to his two Championship medals.

Was a firm favourite of England coach Glenn Hoddle prior to the 1998 World Cup Finals. He was the only player to have featured in all eight of the qualifying games.

Missed the first match of France '98 against Tunisia as Hoddle said he was worried about his temperament.

Soon won his place back in the starting line-up and scored a wonderful free-kick against Columbia to seal England's place in the next round.

Became only the fifth player ever to be sent off whilst playing for England when, in a fit of temper, he kicked Argentine midfield player Diego Simeone following a foul.

Is engaged to Posh Spice, Victoria Adams, and is the father of probably the world's most famous child, Brooklyn Joseph Beckham, born early in 1999.

Dennis Bergkamp...

Known as the 'Ice Man' at Arsenal because of the cool way he takes penalties.

Signed for the Ajax youth squad, he was promoted to the first team at 17. He appeared as a substitute in 1987 as Ajax beat Lokomotiv Leipzig 1-0 in Athens to win the European Cup Winners' Cup under the management of Cruyff.

Ajax won the UEFA Cup in 1992 where Bergkamp played a leading role.

In 185 matches for Ajax he scored 103 goals.

Played for Holland in the European Championship Finals.

In 1992 he transferred to Inter Milan of Italy who beat off bids from Barcelona and Juventus with a record fee of £8 million.

He didn't enjoy himself with the Italian club, often finding himself the butt of team jokes. (The players 'donkey of the week' competition was renamed 'Bergkamp of the week')

Dennis Bergkamp...

Despite everything he still won a UEFA Cup medal with Inter Milan.

Changed position within the Holland team in the World Cup Finals held in the USA in 1994, playing behind the main striker.

Following an incident aboard an aircraft in America in 1994, Bergkamp refused to fly ever again. He has stated that he will not play in any matches that he can't reach by coach or train.

Transferred to Arsenal in the summer of 1995 for a record club fee of £7.5 million.

Scored a hat-trick against Wales in a World Cup qualifier in 1997, helping Holland to the top of their group. Started to close in on the Dutch all-time scoring record held by Johan Neeskens in the 1970s.

During the 1997-1998 season he became the first player ever to win the top three goals in the BBC's *Match of the Day* 'Goal of the Month' competition.

George Best...

Quite simply the greatest footballer that British football has ever seen.

Joined Manchester United as an amateur at the age of 15, signing as a professional on his 17th birthday.

He went on to play 361 league games for United, taking them to league titles in 1965 and 1967 and to European Cup glory in 1968.

In 1964 he made his debut for Northern Ireland in a 3-2 win over Wales. The first of 37 international appearances in which he scored nine goals.

In 1968 he was named European Footballer of the Year.

Fined £100 and suspended for four weeks for bringing the game into disrepute after knocking the ball out of referee Jack Taylor's hands following the Manchester City Vs United League Cup semi-final in 1970.

On the 7th February 1970, in his first game back after suspension, he scored 6 of the 8 goals in an 8-2 win against Northampton in the FA Cup 5th round tie. He later said: "I was so embarrassed that I played the last 20 minutes at left-back."

In 1972 he announced he was quitting the game a week after he'd failed to show for a Northern Ireland match. He had flown to Spain for a holiday. This was to be the first of many such 'retirements'.

Made his last appearance for United in 1974 in a 3-0 defeat by QPR.

George Best...

He joined Stockport County on loan for three matches in the 1975-76 season, scoring two goals for them.

After a brief spell at Los Angeles Aztecs in 1976 he played for Irish side Cork Celtic.

Signed for Fulham in 1976 where he scored in his debut match after 71 seconds. A month later he became one of the first players to be shown a red card - for using foul language!

Played in all four countries of the British Isles in 10 days during 1977. Played for Northern Ireland in Belfast, for Fulham at home to Crystal Palace and then away to Cardiff and St. Mirren (this one a friendly).

After his spell at Craven Cottage, where he scored 8 goals in 42 appearances, he moved to Fort Lauderdale Strikers in the USA, then on to Hibernian in Scotland, before moving back to the States to play for San Jose Earthquakes.

He finished his playing career with Bournemouth in the 1983-84 season, making just 5 appearances for the English club.

He put his name to full commercial use, opening a chain of shops and endorsing everything from clothes to nightclubs.

Now works for Sky TV as a soccer pundit.

Danny Blanchflower...

Joined Irish League side Glentoran in 1945.

Transferred to Barnsley for £6,500 in 1945 where he made 65 appearances and scored two goals.

Made his international debut for Northern Ireland in October 1949 in a match against Scotland.

Moved to Aston Villa in 1959, making 148 appearances and scored 10 goals.

Transferred to Tottenham Hotspur in 1954 for £30,000.

Represented Great Britain against a Europe XI in 1955.

In 1957 he captained Northern Ireland in their shock victory over England at Wembley. It was the first time the Irish had ever won against England.

Despite the absence of Danny's brother Jackie, who had been seriously injured in the Munich air crash, he guided Northern Ireland to the quarter-finals of the 1958 World Cup in Sweden. Although this was Northern Ireland's greatest achievement, it ended rather badly with a 4-0 defeat at the hands of France.

Won the Footballer of the Year award in 1958...

... and then again in 1961 for captaining the Spurs side who became the first team this century to win the coveted League and FA Cup double.

Helped Spurs retain the FA Cup by captaining the side that beat Burnley 3-1 in the 1962 Final.

Danny Blanchflower...

Became the first captain of a British side to lift a major European trophy when Spurs beat Athletico Madrid 5-1 in the European Cup Winners' Cup Final in Rotterdam.

Won the last of his International caps against Poland in 1963, and, after a long battle against a knee injury finally retired from playing altogether in 1964.

He made 337 League appearances for Spurs, scoring 15 goals.

Became a much-respected football journalist after hanging up his boots.

Tried his hand briefly at management, first with Chelsea and then with Northern Ireland.

Has the distinction of being the first person ever to refuse to be the subject of television's *This Is Your Life*, running away when confronted by Eammon Andrews.

Died in London in 1993 after a long illness.

Liam Brady...

Made 253 League appearances for Arsenal between 1973 and 1980, scoring 43 goals.

Was affectionately known as 'Chippy' by team-mates and fans, not for his passing skills but for his love of Chips!

Was Arsenal's Player of the Year three times (1976, 1978 and 1979) and the PFA Player of the Year in 1979.

Played in the memorable 1979 FA Cup Final against Manchester United in which the Gunners eventually won 3-2.

Moved to Italian giants Juventus in 1980 for £514,000.

Won two League titles with Juventus and was much-loved by the passionate Italian fans.

Went on to play for Sampdoria, Inter Milan and Ascoli. Altogether he played 189 League games in Italy, scoring 24 goals.

Came back to England in 1987 to play for West Ham United, making 89 appearances, before retiring from playing in 1990.

Represented the Republic of Ireland on 72 occasions and scoring 9 international goals.

In 1991 he joined Scottish club Celtic as manager but life in Glasgow proved unsuccessful and he was soon dismissed.

Took over in the hot-seat at free-falling Brighton but this proved just as disastrous.

He returned to Arsenal to become the head of Youth Development.

Billy Bremner...

Made his debut for Leeds United in 1960 as a right-winger aged only 17. One of his team-mates on that day was Don Revie, a man almost twice his age and who later became Bremner's manager at the club.

Made his international debut in the 0-0 draw against Spain at Hampden Park in 1965.

Scored in the 2-1 defeat by Liverpool in the 1965 FA Cup Final.

Lost to Dinamo Zagreb in the final of the Inter-Cities Fairs Cup in 1967.

Played in the victorious side that beat Arsenal in the 1968 League Cup.

Proved a winner again six months later when he played in the side that beat Ferencvaros, also 2-0, in the Inter-Cities Fairs Cup.

Lead Leeds United to their first ever League Championship in 1969, scoring six goals in the process.

Won the Footballer of the Year award in 1970.

Lost to Chelsea in the FA Cup Final.

Beat holders Arsenal 1-0 in the 1972 FA Cup Final.

Won a second Championship medal with Leeds United, this time increasing his goal contribution to nine in the season.

Billy Bremner...

Scored less than 100 goals in total in his career, but whenever he did score, the goals usually turned out to be vital ones.

Was sent off in the 1974 Charity Shield game with Kevin Keegan. They became the first Britons to be sent off at the stadium and both players tore off their shirts as they trudged off the pitch. They later received five week bans.

Played in all three of Scotland's 1974 World Cup Finals games in West Germany, when they failed to qualify for the second round despite being undefeated.

Played for Scotland a total of 54 times and scored three international goals.

Had a 'goal' disallowed for offside in the 1975 European Champion's Cup Final in Paris, losing 2-0 to Bayern Munich.

Played his last game for Leeds United in 1976, after 586 League appearances and 90 goals.

Joined Hull City where he scored 6 goals in 61 appearances for the club.

Became player-manager at Doncaster Rovers in 1979, leaving in 1981.

In 1985 he returned to Elland Road and his beloved Leeds as manager but found the club in disarray. Despite reaching the FA Cup semi-final in 1987 he was sacked early the following season.

Died in December 1997, two days before his 55th birthday.

Trevor Brooking...

Joined The Hammers as an apprentice in 1965 and stayed with the blub for the rest of his career.

Won the FA Cup in 1975, beating Fulham 2-0 at Wembley.

Won the Second Division title with West Ham in 1981.

Scored the winning goal with his head, only the third headed goal of his career, in the 1980 FA Cup Final victory over Arsenal.

Played for England 47 times, scoring 5 international goals.

England only ever lost seven times when Brooking was in the team from 1974-82.

Finished his international career at the 1982 World Cup in Spain when England were knocked out in the 2nd round without actually losing a game.

Now works as a television and radio presenter with BBC's *Match of the Day* and *Radio Five Live*.

Steve Bruce...

Probably won of the best players of the modern game never to have been capped at international level.

Captained Manchester United to three Premiership titles in 1992/93, 1993/94 and 1995/96.

Also won two FA Cup winners' medals in 1990, beating Crystal Palace 1-0 after a replay, and in 1994 when United thrashed Chelsea 4-0.

Picked up more than 100 stitches in his career.

Made his League debut for Gillingham in 1979, playing over 200 League games for the Kent side, scoring 29 goals.

Moved to Norwich in 1984 and scored a goal on his debut - unfortunately it was an own goal!

Won a League Cup winners' medal in 1985, beating Sunderland 1-0.

Was bought by Alex Ferguson at Manchester United £800,000 in 1987.

Was soon in the thick of the action with his new club, breaking his nose in his debut game at Portsmouth.

Played a total of 309 games for United, scoring 36 goals, mainly from the penalty spot.

Joined Trevor Francis at Birmingham in 1996 where he played 72 League games and scored 2 goals.

Moved to Sheffield United in 1998, his first attempt at club management.

Eric Cantona...

As the sportswear adverts go, 1966 was a good year for English football, Eric Cantona was born!

Made his French League debut in Auxere in 1983.

Made his international debut for France against West Germany in 1987.

Moved to Marseille for £2 million after playing 81 games and scoring 23 goals for Auxerre.

He didn't settle at the club, playing just 22 games and scoring 5 goals. He went to play at Bordeaux, scoring 6 goals in just 11 games, before moving to Montpellier in 1989.

Helped Montpellier win the French Cup in 1990.

Was banned from the French national team for a year after insulting the manager Henri Michel.

Played for Marseille again, helping them to win the title in 1991, before going on to Nimes. He then quit the game after a shouting match with a disciplinary panel at the French FA.

Tempted by an offer to have trials with Sheffield Wednesday but was snapped up by Leeds United for £900,000.

He soon became a cult figure with the Elland Road crowd and helped Leeds win the Premiership in 1992.

Became a target of Manchester United and made a shock move to Old Trafford for £1.2 million at the end of the season. Surely this must be the bargain of the century!

Eric Cantona...

Was instrumental in helping United to their first League title since 1967 and in doing so he became the first man to win back-to-back English championships with different clubs.

Won the title again with United in 1994, making it four league titles for Cantona in four years (Marseille 1991, Leeds United 1992 and Manchester United 1993 and 1994)

Also won the FA Cup in 1994, helping Mnachester United to become only the fourth club this century to win the League and FA Cup double. He made it a personal 'treble' by being voted the Footballer of the Year in 1994.

Was involved in one of the most controversial moments in the history of English football when, in January 1995, he dived into the crowd at Selhurst Park and karate-kicked Crystal Palace 'fan' Matthew Simmons. He was fined £20,000 by Manchester United and £10,000 by the FA, together with an eight month ban. He was also ordered to complete 120 hours of community service by the courts.

On his return to the field in October 1995 he showed just how much he had changed. In the six months left of the season he was booked just once.

He scored the winning goal against Liverpool in the 1996 FA Cup Final in which he was captain and secured yet another League title.

Despite winning the Player of the Year award again he was left out of the French national squad for Euro '96.

In 1997 Manchester United won the League title again but were stunned when Cantona announced his retirement from the game in order to pursue an acting career.

Roberto Carlos...

Probably possess the most powerful left-foot in the world of football. Whilst playing for Inter Milan one shot was measured at a staggering 150 km/h.

The Brazilian left-back is also one of the world's most deadlist free-kick specialists. His 40-yard swerving shot against France at the 1997 Tournoi has been hailed by many people as one of the best free-kicks ever seen.

Made his League debut in 1991 for Brazilian club side Uniao Sao Joao.

Joined Brazilian team Palmeiras in 1993 before moving to Italy with Inter Milan for £4.5 million in 1995.

He scored the winning goal on his debut against Vicenza but failed to settle in Italy, moving to Real Madrid the following season.

He became the first Brazilian to play for Real Madrid.

Has played over 50 times for his country, scoring just a couple of goals.

John Charles...

Made his League debut for Leeds United in 1949.

Made his international debut for Wales in a match against Northern Ireland in March 1950. In doing so he became, at 18 years and 71 days, the youngest player to have played for Wales, a record which stood until a certain Ryan Giggs made his debut in 1991.

Scored 38 goals for Leeds United in the 1956/57 season, still a record for the club.

Moved from Leeds, after making 297 appearances and an astonishing 150 goals, to Italian giants in Juventus in 1957 for a British transfer record fee of £65,000.

Unlike many Brits who also went to Italy, he proved a great success, helping Juventus to three Italian Championships and two Italian Cups.

Moved back to Leeds briefly in 1962 after scoring 93 goals in 154 appearances.

Returned to Italy with Roma where he played 10 games and scored six goals.

Finished his career with Cardiff City in 1966.

Played 38 times for Wales, including the 1958 World Cup in Sweden where they lost 1-0 to the eventual winners Brazil.

Nicknamed the 'Gentle Giant', he was never booked or sent off in his career.

Holds an impressive record of scoring 270 goals in 538 appearances, an average of a goal every two games.

Bobby Charlton...

Signed as a proffesional with Manchester United in 1954 and in doing so became one of the 'Busby Babes'.

Scored twice on his club debut against Charlton Athletic.

Played in the 1954 FA Cup Final against Aston Villa as a 19-year old but unfortunately ended up on the losing side.

Survived the Munich air crash in 1958 which saw eight of his teammates lose their lives.

Played in the FA Cup Final of the same year, but once again ended up on the losing side as Bolton Wanderers triumphed 2-0.

Made his international debut in 1958 in a thrilling 4-0 victory over Scotland.

Third-time lucky in 1963 when he eventually won an FA Cup winners' medal as United beat Leicester City 3-1.

Won the League Championship in 1965 wih United.

Played a starring role in England's 1966 World Cup victory. Scored England's first goal of the tournament in the game against Mexico.

Won both the European Footballer of the Year and English Footballer of the Year in 1966.

Scored two goals as captain as United beat Benfica 4-1 at Wembley in the European Champions Cup Final in 1968.

Bobby Charlton...

Signed an eight-year contract with the club in 1968, the longest ever to be offered to a British footballer.

Won his last English cap in the 3-2 defeat by West Germany in the 1970 World Cup quarter-finals in Leon.

Altogether he played 106 times for England. His record of 49 England goals still stands.

Left Manchester United in 1973, having scored 247 goals in 754 appearances, a club record.

Joined Preston North End as player/manager, scoring 8 goals in 38 appearances.

Returned to Old Trafford as a Director.

Received a knighthood for his services to the game in 1994.

Is the nephew of Newcastle legend 'Wor' Jackie Milburn.

Jack Charlton...

Is the older brother of footballing legend Bobby.

Is known affectionately as 'The Giraffe'.

Made a record 629 appearances for Leeds United, his only club.

Scored 71 goals in his twenty year period at Elland Road.

Played a vital role in England's 1966 World Cup triumph.

Voted Footballer of the Year in 1967.

Played for England 35 times, scoring six goals.

Moved into management in 1973 when he retired from playing and had spells in the hot-seat at Middlesbrough, Sheffield Wednesday and Newcastle.

Took over as manager of the Republic of Ireland in 1986 and became the most successful manager in their history. He guided the minnows to their first major championship final in 1988 and two World Cup Finals, guiding the team to the quarter-finals in Italia 90, where they were beaten 1-0 by the hosts.

Under his guidance, the Republic of Ireland never lost a game to England.

After he failed to help the Republic qualify for Euro 96 he retired to spend more time fishing.

Is the nephew of Newcastle legend 'Wor' Jackie Milburn.

Ray Clemence...

Made his League debut for Scunthorpe in 1965 before moving to Liverpool in 1967.

In his spell at Liverpool he played between the sticks during the clubs most successful period.

He won three European Cups, five League titles, an FA Cup and a League Cup.

Played a total of 124 European club games, a record which stood until 1998.

He was awarded an MBE for his services to football.

Made 470 appearances for the Anfield club.

Transferred to Tottenham Hotspur in 1990 for £300,000 where he played more than 240 games.

Made 61 international appearances for England although this would have been more had he not been competing against another great keeper, Peter Shilton. England manager Ron Greenwood alternated the pair during his reign.

Is one of just six players to have played in five FA Cup Finals.

After finishing his career with Spurs in 1987 he worked in the media, offering expert advice on the Eurosport channel.

He took over as manager of lowly Barnet in 1996, a position he kept until he resigned to take up the job as England's goalkeeping coach under Glenn Hoddle.

Johan Cruyff...

Was enrolled by his mother in the Ajax youth section in 1959.

Signed professional terms with the club in 1963 when he was sixteen on the recommendation of the English coach Vic Buckingham and scored on his debut.

Made his international debut for Holland in 1966 and scored a last-minute equaliser in the 2-2 draw with Hungary.

Played in the 1969 European Cup Final with Ajax but lost 4-1 to Milan in Madrid.

In 1971 he won the European Cup Finals with Ajax, beating Greek side Panathinaikos 2-0 at Wembley.

Voted European Footballer of the Year in 1971.

Went on to win two more European Cup Finals with Ajax, beating Inter Milan 2-0 in 1972 and Juventus 1-0 the following year.

Moved to Barcelona for a world record fee of £922,000 in 1973 helping the club win the Spanish League in his first season.

Again won the European Footballer of the Year award in 1973.

In 1974 he captained Holland to the World Cup Final in Munich only to lose to the hosts 2-1. The 'Total Football' played by the Dutch side earned them countless admirers around the world.

Johan Cruyff...

He also won the European Footballer of the Year award for the third time in 1974, the first player to achieve such a distinction.

Retired from international football before the 1978 World Cup in Argentina, having played 48 times for the national side and scoring 33 goals.

Went to play soccer in America with Los Angeles Aztecs and Washington Diplomats.

In 1981 he returned to Europe to play for lowly Spanish side Levante before going back to Holland to play for Ajax and finally Feyenoord.

Took up the post of Technical Director at Ajax in 1984 and guided the club to victory in the 1987 European Cup Winners' Cup Final, beating Lokomotiv Leipzig 1-0.

Was appointed coach of Barcelona the following season.

Led Barcelona to four consecutive League titles between 1991 and 1994 and the European Cup for the first time in the club's history, beating Sampdoria 1-0 at Wembley in 1992.

Left Barcelona in 1996 after a record nine years in charge.

Suffered a heart attack in 1997 but recovered.

Kenny Dalglish...

Joined Celtic in 1967, just as the senior team were winning the European Champions Cup against Internazionale in Lisbon.

Made his international debut in 1991, coming on as a substitute against Belgium.

Played 204 games for Celtic, scoring 112 goals.

Won eight League titles, Six Scottish FA Cups and 4 League Cups with Celtic.

Replaced Kevin Keegan at Liverpool for a British record fee of £440,000 in 1977.

In 1978 scored the only goal of the game as Liverpool beat FC Bruges in the European Champions Cup at Wembley.

He was the Football Writers Player of the Year in 1979 and the PFA Footballer of the Year in 1983.

Played a record 102 times for Scotland, scoring 30 international goals. This is a record which he shares with Denis Law.

In 1985, on the eve of the Heysel Stadium tragedy, he was appointed manager of Liverpool in succession to Joe Fagan.

Made history in 1986 as he became the first player/manager to win the English League and FA Cup double.

Made his final appearance for Scotland in the 0-0 draw with Luxembourg in 1987.

Kenny Dalglish...

Made his final appearance as a Liverppol player in 1989, having scored 118 goals for the Anfield club. He was the first person to have scored 100 League goals in both England and Scotland.

Resigned as manager of Liverpool after a 4-4 draw with Everton in the FA Cup, largely as a result of stress following the tragedy at Hillsborough when 89 Liverpool fans died before the FA Cup semi-final against Nottingham Forest.

Won nine championships with the Reds and two FA Cup Finals, including three League titles in five seasons as manager.

Returned to football eight months later when he took over at Blackburn Rovers.

Steered the club, with the help of Jack Walker's millions, to their first League Championship for 81 years when he won the title in 1995. He became only the third manager to win the title with two different clubs.

Moved 'upstairs' as director of football before finally quitting the club before the start of the 1996 season.

Took over as manager of Newcastle United following Kevin Keegan's shock resignation and guided the Magpies to a Champions League place in 1997. Left the club under a cloud, stating he had been sacked and claimed unfair dismissal through the courts.

Once had said about him by Brian Clough – "He had a huge arse. It came down below his knees and that's where he got his strength from."

Dixie Dean...

Joined Tranmere Rovers in 1923 where he played 29 games and scored a fantastic 27 goals. He fractured his skull in one game but made a full recovery.

Joined Everton in 1925.

Made his international debut in 1927 as centre-forward against Scotland. He scored both goals as England triumphed 2-1, the first time England had won in Glasgow since 1904.

Went on to score 12 goals in his first five England appearances.

Scored 60 League goals in the 1927/28 season, ending with a hat-trick against Arsenal to beat the record set the previous season by Middlesbrough's George Camsell.

Also scored 22 goals in other games that season, bringing his tally to 82. A record which will surely never be beaten.

Helped, not surprisingly, Everton to the League title in 1927/28

Won another Championship medal in 1932.

Played his last game for England against Northern Ireland – having scored 18 goals in 16 appearances – as well as 47 goals in 18 other representative matches.

Scored a goal in the 3-0 win over Manchester City as Everton won the FA Cup Final in 1933.

Dixie Dean...

Finished playing with Everton at the end of the 1936/37 season, having scored 349 goals in 399 League appearances.

Scored his 200th League goal aged 23 years and 290 days old, amazingly exactly the same age as Jimmy Greaves was when he achieved this milestone some years later.

Moved to Notts County but only played nine games before moving to Ireland.

Helped Sligo Rovers reach the final of the Irish Cup.

Retired from playing football in 1939, having scored 379 League goals in 437 matches, including 34 hat-tricks, the most ever scored by a British player.

Absolutely hated his nickname of 'Dixie', preferring to be called by his real name of Bill.

Died, appropriately enough, at Goodison Park in 1980 after collapsing during a Derby game against Liverpool.

Alfredo Di Stefano...

Scored a hat-trick in 20 minutes for his first youth team, Los Cardales in 1940.

Left Los Cardales in 1942 after a row with the coach and joined his father's old club, River Plate.

Made his debut as a 17-year old playing against local rivals San Lorenzo.

Went on loan to Huracan where he scored the winning goal in a league game against River Plate.

Returned to River Plate in 1946 to head the attack nicknamed La Maquina (the Machine).

Won the South American Championship with Argentina in 1947. He represented Argentina 8 times and scored 5 international goals for his home country.

In 1949, following a strike by Argentina's footballers, was lured away to play in a pirate league in Colombia for Millonarios of Bogota.

Moved to Spain in 1953 to play for Real Madrid, where he stayed until 1964.

During his time with the Spanish giants he won five European Cups in successive seasons, scoring in each final, including a hat-trick in the 7-3 defeat of Eintracht Frankfurt at Hampden Park, Glasgow in 1960.

Also topped the Spanish league goal-scoring tables for five of the six seasons between 1954-59.

Alfredo Di Stefano...

Won the first of his 31 Spanish caps and scored 23 goals for his adopted country, adding to the caps he had already won for Argentina and the three he won for Colombia!

Has scored a record 49 goals in 58 European Cup matches.

Was kidnapped while on a tour of Venezuela with Real Madrid in 1963 but was released unharmed after three days.

Left Real Madrid to spend a season with Spanish side Español, before becoming coach for Elche.

Returned to Argentina in 1968 to coach Boca Juniors where he revived the sleeping giants into the force they once were.

Moved back to Spain in 1970 to take up a coaching position with Valencia and led them to their first League title in 24 years.

Ted Drake...

Made his League debut for Southampton in 1931, playing 72 times for the Saints, scoring 48 goals.

Played cricket for Hampshire.

Moved to Arsenal in 1934 and in his first season for the Gunners he scored a record 42 league goals.

In December 1935 he scored seven goals in a Division One game against Aston Villa. At the time he was suffering from a serious knee injury and was not playing to his full potential! He only had eight shots at goal that day, seven went in and one hit the bar!

He stopped playing at the start of the Second World War, having appeared for Arsenal in 168 League games, scoring 124 goals.

He earned five international caps with England, scoring a remarkable six goals.

Took over as manager of Chelsea in 1950 and set up one of the country's first youth teams. The players who progressed through to the first team became known as 'Drake's Ducklings'!

Guided Chelsea to their only Championship title in 1955.

Was assistant manager at Barcelona in 1970.

Became a full-time scout for Fulham until the mid-1980s.

Was also a member of the inaugural pools panel which decided the result of postponed games for the football pools companies.

Duncan Edwards...

Made his England representative debut, playing for the under-14s against Ireland at Oldham in 1950.

Signed for Manchester United in 1952.

Made his Manchester United debut in a 4-1 home defeat by Cardiff City on Easter Monday 1953. At 16 years and 185 days old he was the youngest player ever to play for the club.

After playing for England Youth, England Under-23, England B and the Football League he made his full debut in 1955. The match was a 7-2 defeat of Scotland and at 18 years and 183 days old he was the youngest player ever to represent England. This record stood until a certain Michael Owen broke onto the scene in February 1998.

Was the youngest member of the 'Busby Babes' Manchester United side to win the Championship in 1956.

Scored the opening goal in the 3-1 defeat of West Germany in Berlin in 1956 and earned himself the nickname 'Boom-Boom' for his shooting power.

Won the Championship again in 1957 and appeared at Wembley in the FA Cup Final. Unfortunately his side lost to Aston Villa.

Duncan Edwards...

Played his first European games in 1957 as United reached the semi-finals of the European Cup before losing to eventual winners Real Madrid.

Played a total of 175 League games for Manchester United, scoring 21 goals.

Considered by many to have been the most complete footballer of his generation. A powerful tackler, strong in the air and had wonderful ball control, he was seen by many as a future England captain.

Had said of him by Bobby Charlton "If I had to play for my life and could take one player with me it would be Duncan Edwards."

In 1958 he scored the first goal away at Arsenal in what has often been described as the best English League game ever. United were leading 3-0 at half-time before Arsenal pulled their socks up and drew level. United came back again and added two more to their tally, Arsenal got a fourth but ran out of time losing 5-4.

Secured a place in the 1958 European Cup quarter-final with a 3-3 draw away to Red Star in Belgrade. Unfortunately on their journey home, disaster struck when their plane crashed, wiping out most of the young side. Edwards died in hospital two weeks after the crash.

Eusebio...

Made his debut in 1958 with Mozambique's Laurenço Marques, a nursery club for Portugese giants Sporting Lisbon.

Travelled to Lisbon in 1961 but was 'kidnapped' on arrival by Benfica and hidden away in a fishing village on the Algarve until the two clubs settled their arguments.

Made his debut for Benfica in 1961.

Made his international debut just a short while later, with barely a dozen League games to his name. The match, against England at Wembley, was so successful for him that he was beginning to be talked about as a star of the future.

Helped win the Portugese Championship in 1961.

Scored two goals as Benfica beat Real Madrid 5-3 in the 1962 European Cup Final in Amsterdam. This was the first time Real Madrid had ever been beaten in a major European final.

Scored the consolation goal a year later when Benfica lost 2-1 against AC Milan in the final of the European Cup at Wembley.

Voted European Footballer of the Year in 1965.

Scored nine goals in the 1966 World Cup finals in England, including four in a match against North Korea. Despite also scoring in the semi-final defeat against England he left the pitch in tears.

Earned himself several nicknames throughout his career, including the 'new Pele', 'Black Panther' and 'Black Pearl'.

Eusebio...

Left Benfica in 1974, having won the Portugese League seven times, the Portugese Cup five times and the European Cup in 1962. He was also a runner-up in this competition in 1963, 1965 and 1968.

Played a total of 294 League games for Benfica, scoring an unbeatable 316 goals, many of them spectacular.

Moved to America to play in the newly formed NASL in 1974, playing at first for Boston Minutemen, then moving on to Torontos Metros before finishing with Las Vegas Quicksilver.

Returned to Benfica as coach in 1977.

A statue in his honour was unveiled outside Benfica's ground, Estadio da Luz, in 1992.

A film about his life was released called *Sua Majestade o Rei (His Majesty the King)*.

Giacinto Facchetti...

Joined the youth system of his local club CS Trevigliese in 1956 where he started as a centre-forward.

Signed professional terms in 1960 with Internazionale, his only club, where he was converted to full-back by coach Helenio Herrera.

Made his League debut in 1961 in a 2-0 away win over Roma.

Won the first of four Italian League titles in 1963.

Made his international debut in 1963 in a 1-0 win against Turkey in Istanbul.

Won the 1964 European Champions Cup against Real Madrid in Vienna, followed by the World Club Cup against Argentina's Independiente.

Giacinto Facchetti...

Won the same two trophies the following year.

Scored 10 goals, a record for an Italian full-back in the 1965/66 season. Altogether he scored an impressive 59 goals in 476 League games for Internazionale.

Captained Italy in his 25th international appearance.

Won the European Nations Final in Rome when Italy defeated Yugoslavia in 1968.

Captained Italy to runners-up in the 1970 World Cup, losing to Brazil in Mexico City.

Was dropped by the national coach in 1972 but returned to play in the 1974 World Cup Finals in West Germany in 1974.

Played his last game for Italy in the 2-0 defeat by England at Wembley in a World Cup qualifier in 1977. Italy still qualified but the injury prevented him from playing in the finals in Argentina or adding to his record total of 94 caps.

Tom Finney...

Signed for local side Preston North End in 1938 and didn't play for any other side.

Played in the 1941 wartime FA Cup Final before joining up and serving with the army in North Africa.

Made his League debut in 1946, eight years after signing for the club.

Played in a match against Scotland a month later although caps were not awarded for this match.

Won the first of his 76 international caps against Wales in 1947. Forty of his caps were as outside-right, 33 at outside-left and three as a centre-forward.

The flying winger, as he was known, spent much of his international career competing with Stanley Matthews for the title of 'Best right-winger in England'.

Played in England's first World Cup finals in 1950, ending up on the losing side in the shock 1-0 defeat by the USA.

Finished second in the League on goal-difference in 1953.

Appeared in the 1954 FA Cup Final but was beaten by 3-2 by West Bromwich Albion.

Appeared in the 1954 World Cup finals as England reached the quarter-final stages.

Became the first player to be made Footballer of the Year when he was awarded the honour in 1957.

Tom Finney...

Finished second in the League again in 1958, meaning that, despite being an excellent footballer, he never won a major club prize in his career.

Reached his third World Cup finals in Sweden in 1958, only to be beaten in a first-round play-off by the Soviet Union, a match which he missed through injury.

Played his 76th and final game for England against the Soviet Union in 1959. He had scored 30 international goals which, at the time, was a record.

Retired from playing in 1960 after 433 appearances for the club and scoring a record 187 League goals.

Nicknamed the 'Preston Plumber'

Was elected President of Preston North End in 1975.

Awarded a knighthood in the 1998 New Years Honours List for his services to football.

Just Fontaine...

Turned professional for French club Nice in 1953.

Won the French Cup in 1954.

Won the French League with Nice in 1956 before being transferred to Reims.

Made his international debut for France in 1956.

Did the French League and Cup double with Reims in 1958.

Led the attack for France in the 1958 World Cup finals in Sweden. He scored 13 goals in the tournament, a record which still stands, including a hat-trick against Paraguay and four against West Germany in the 6-3 win to secure third place.

Scored 27 international goals in just 20 appearances for France.

Suffered a broken leg in March 1960, an injury so severe it was feared he would never play again.

Broke the same leg again a year later.

Plunged French football fans into despair in 1962 when he announced his retirement following his failure to fully recover from his double leg fractures.

Became the first president of the French Professional Footballer's Union in 1963.

Was appointed director of the national team in 1967 but failed to hold the position for long.

Robbie Fowler...

Made his debut for Liverpool in 1993.

Scored five goals in a Coca-Cola Cup match against Fulham, it was only his fourth game for Liverpool.

Scored the fastest hat-trick in Premiership history when he netted three goals inside five minutes against Arsenal at Anfield in August 1994.

Won the PFA Young Player of the Year award in 1995 and 1996.

Scored 30 or more goals for the third season in a row in 1996/97.

Scored his first international goal in the 2-0 win over Mexico.

Missed out on the 1998 World Cup finals after suffering a serious ankle injury in a League game against Everton.

Was fined £1,000 in 1994 for baring his backside to Leicester City fans.

Revealed a vest showing support for striking Liverpool dockers during a Cup Winners' Cup match against Brann. UEFA later fined him £900 for a 'violation of the principles of sporting conduct.'

Received a letter of congratulations from FIFA General Secretary Sepp Blatter after he tried to get referee Gerald Ashby to overturn his decision to award a penalty when Arsenal keeper had apparently fouled him in the area.

Trevor Francis...

Made his debut for Birmingham City in 1970.

Scored more goals as a sixteen-year-old in the top flight than any other player before or since.

Notched up 15 goals in his first 15 games for The Blues.

Played a total of 280 League games for Birmingham, scoring 118 goals.

Transferred to Brian Clough's Nottingham Forest in February 1979 to become the first £1 million player.

He was also the first player to be transferred for more than £1 million on three separate occasions.

Scored the winning goal in the 1979 European Cup Final against Malmo.

Played for England on 52 occassions, scoring 12 international goals.

Transferred to Manchester City in 1981 where he made 26 appearances and scored 12 goals.

Moved to Italy in 1982, signing for Sampdoria at first and later for Atalanta. He scored 18 goals in the Italian League.

Tempted back to Britain by Graeme Souness at Glasgow giants Rangers where he played 18 times.

Trevor Francis...

Became player/manager of QPR in 1988 but fell out with the players over his style of man-management.

Reverted back to his playing career full-time with Sheffield Wednesday in 1989, before, once-again, taking over the player/manager title. He led the Yorkshire club to both the League Cup and FA Cup Finals in 1993 but was beaten in both games by Arsenal 2-1.

In 1996 he returned 'home' to Birmingham to become manager. His role is purely and simply to guide the club back to the top and out of the shadows of their neighbours Aston Villa. His relationship with Karren Brady has always been volatile, and at one point during the 1997/98 season he resigned after his son was subjected to verbal abuse by rival fans in the Director's lounge.

Hughie Gallacher...

Made his League debut for Queen of the South in 1920.

Moved to Airdrieonians a year later where he played 111 League games and scored 90 goals.

Moved to England with Newcastle United in 1925 and played 160 times for the Geordies, scoring 133 goals. He captained the side which won the League title in 1927.

Played for the Scottish side dubbed the 'Wembley Wizards' which thrashed England 5-1 in 1928. It was the last time Scotland had put three or more goals past the 'auld enemy'.

Scored four goals in the 7-3 victory against Northern Ireland in 1929, equalling the Scottish record.

With 23 goals for his country he is Scotland's third highest scorer, behind Kenny Dalglish and Denis Law. However his goals per game ratio is far superior after having played only 20 times for his country.

Transferred to Chelsea in 1930 for £10,000 but injury limited his appearances to just 132 in five years. He still, however, scored 72 goals in this spell.

Moved to Derby County in 1935 and scored an impressive 38 goals in 51 League games.

Spent the following three seasons with three different clubs, Notts County, Grimsby Town and Gateshead before retiring in 1939.

Committed suicide on a railway line in 1957.

Garrincha...

Was born Manoel Francisco dos Santos but became known by his nickname which means Little Bird.

Was born into poverty in Brazil and contracted polio as a child, leaving him with a badly twisted leg.

Made his League debut in 1947 with Pau Grande.

Inspired Brazil to victory in the 1958 World Cup Final, beating hosts Sweden 5-2.

Transferred to Botafogo in 1953.

Became only the second player to be sent-off in a World Cup semi-final in 1962 and was only allowed to play in the Final after a personal plea by the Brazilian President. He went on to collect a second winners' medal as Brazil beat Czechoslovakia 3-1.

Joined the Brazilian club side Corinthians in 1966 before moving briefly to Colombia to play at AJ Barranquilla. From here he returned to Brazil and Flamengo before finishing his career with Red Star Paris.

He played 51 times for Brazil, scoring 12 international goals.

Died prematurely in 1983 of alcoholic poisoning.

Paul Gascoigne...

Joined Newcastle United as an apprentice in 1983.

Made his first team debut in 1985, a month before he turned professional.

Made his England Under-21 debut in 1987.

Played 92 League games for the Geordies, scoring 21 goals.

Transferred to Tottenham Hotspur in July 1988 for £2 million.

Made his full England debut when he came on as a substitute in a game against Denmark in 1988.

Voted the Young Player of the Year in 1988.

Starred for England in the 1990 World Cup finals in Italy, helping England to a semi-final position before being beaten by Germany. Displayed tears of emotion when he was booked during this game, meaning that should England have gone on to win it he would have been suspended from the Final.

Won the BBC Sports Personality of the Year award in 1990.

Suffered a career-threatening cruciate ligament injury following a rash challenge on Nottingham Forest's Gary Charles in the opening minutes of the 1991 FA Cup Final. Spurs went on to win the game 2-1 after extra-time.

Moved to Italian side Lazio for £5.5 million in 1992, but only played 42 games in three seasons. Broke his leg in a freak training session.

Paul Gascoigne...

Returned to Britain in 1995 to play for Scottish Champions Rangers.

Won his first-ever League Championship in his first season at Rangers.

Completed the double by helping Rangers win the Scottish FA Cup, and in doing so became one of just a few players to win the Cup in both England and Scotland.

Completed a personal treble by being voted the Scottish Footballer of the Year in 1996.

Found himself in trouble with fans after his drunken antics on an England tour of the Far East in 1996.

Played a starring role for England in Euro '96, scoring the goal of the tournament against his Rangers team-mate and Scotland goalkeeper Andy Goram.

Played 87 League games for Rangers, scoring 35 goals and winning two championships.

Moved to Bryan Robson's Middlesbrough in 1998.

Left out of Glenn Hoddle's final World Cup squad.

After the break-up of his marriage and numerous off-field antics he seems to have grown-up and is desparately trying to impress new England coach Kevin Keegan and to add to his tally of 57 England caps and 10 international goals.

Ryan Giggs...

Made his Manchester United debut in a First Division match against Everton in March 1991.

Made his international debut against Germany in October of the same year and in doing so became the youngest player, 17 years and 332 days, to play for Wales.

Became, at 22, the youngest player to have played in two double-winning sides (1994 and 1996).

Has won four League titles, two FA Cups and a League Cup, all with Manchester United, his only club.

Although he plays for Wales he actually played football for England schoolboys in 1989. The name he used on this occassion was Ryan Wilson, the surname being that of his father, a former Welsh rugby league player.

David Ginola...

Made his League debut for Toulon in 1985 where he played 81 League games and scored 4 goals.

Moved on to Racing Paris 61 and Brest before signing for and Paris St. Germain in 1991.

Won the French League and French Cup (twice) whilst with them.

Was voted the French Player of the Year in 1994.

Suffered a low-point in his career when he gave the ball away in the last minute of a World Cup qualifying game against Bulgaria. They went on to score and knock France out of the competition.

Transferred to Kevin Keegan's Newcastle United for £2.5 million in 1995, playing 68 times for the Geordies, scoring 6 goals.

Fell out with new Newcastle manager Kenny Dalglish and was transferred to Tottenham Hotspur for £2 million in the summer of 1997.

Saved Spurs – almost single-handedly at times – from relegation but still wasn't considered good enough to join the 1998 World Cup squad.

International career looks like it will not progress further than the 15 appearances he has already won.

David Ginola...

Joined the BBC television team instead, offering his views on the televised games, and in doing so won a huge army of admiring female fans.

Was rumoured to be the first player to be sold when George Graham took over as manager at Tottenham in 1998 and indeed was substituted in George's first game in charge. Since then, however, he has played superbly and continues to impress the tough Scot.

Helped Tottenham win the Worthington Cup in 1999, beating Leicester City 1-0 at Wembley. This was the first trophy won by the London club for eight years.

Featured in a L'Oréal shampoo advert, a Renault car campaign and strutted the catwalk for fashion designer Cerruti.

Took over from Princess Diana as a campaigner against the use of Land Mines.

Has said publicly that he would like to become a lawyer (he is a former law student) when he retires from playing football.

Andy Goram...

Scotland's Number One goalkeeper played as a centre-forward until he left school.

Made his League debut for Oldham Athletic in 1981, playing a total of 195 League games.

Transferred to Edinburgh side Hibernian in 1987.

Scored a goal for Hibs against Greenock Morton, one of just a few keepers to achieve this feat. He launched a huge kick downfield which bounced over the head of the opposing keeper, David Wylie, and into the net.

Also played cricket for Scotland. In 1989 he won the first of his three Scottish cricket caps against the touring Australian side.

Became the most expensive goalkeeper in Scottish football when he moved from Hibs to Rangers in 1991 for £1 million.

Pulled out of the Scotland squad for the 1998 World Cup finals in France after allegations about his private life were made in a tabloid newspaper.

Andy Gray...

Made his League debut for Dundee United in 1973, making 62 League appearances and scoring 36 goals.

Moved to England in 1976 and played 113 league games for Aston Villa, scoring 54 goals for the Midlands club.

Made his international debut for Scotland in 1976.

Became the only player ever to have won the Young Footballer of the Year and the Footballer of the Year in the same season, 1977.

Became Britain's most expensive player when he moved to Wolverhampton Wanderers for £1,469,000 in 1979.

Scored the only goal of the game in the 1980 League Cup Final against Nottingham Forest at Wembley.

Moved to Everton in 1983 where he won the FA Cup against Watford, scoring a goal in the 2-0 win.

Completed the hat-trick of English club honours when he helped Everton win the 1984/85 League Championship.

Moved back to Aston Villa in 1985 but never found the form which had previously made him an idol of the fans. In this second spell at the club he scored just 5 goals in 54 appearances.

Made his final international appearance in 1985, playing 20 times for Scotland he scored just 7 goals, not quite what you would expect from such a prolific scorer.

Andy Gray...

Joined Notts County on loan for 4 games before transferring to West Bromwich Albion in the 1987/88 season. He played 32 League games for the 'Baggies', scoring 10 goals.

Returned to Scotland in 1988 when he joined Rangers. Playing just 13 league games, scoring 5 times.

Became assistant to manager Ron Atkinson at Aston Villa but left to work full-time for Sky Sports.

Has since gone on to win a hatful of media awards for his knowledge and passion of the game, including the Royal Television Society's Sports Broadcaster of the Year award and the Variety Club of Great Britain's Media Personality of the Year award, both in 1996, and the Cable TV Guide award for Best Sports Presenter in 1998.

Jimmy Greaves...

Joined Chelsea in 1957 and scored on his League debut.

Reached 100 League goals with Chelsea in just 133 appearances. At 21, he was the youngest player ever to have scored 100 League goals.

Played his first game for England against Peru in 1959 and again scored a goal in the 4-1 victory.

Scored 43 League goals for Chelsea in the 1960/61 season, setting a club record which still stands today. He also scored a post-war record of six hat-tricks.

Signed for Italian club AC Milan in June 1961, but, despite scoring nine goals in just 14 appearances (including a goal on his debut again), found the discipline of Italian soccer hard to live with.

He returned to England in December 1961, signing for Tottenham Hotspur. The transfer fee was set at £99,999 because Bill Nicholson, the Spurs manager, didn't want his new star saddled with the label of being the first £100,000 footballer!

Helped Spurs win the FA Cup in 1962 with a 3-1 win over Burnley.

Became the first Tottenham player to be sent off for 35 years in April 1963 during a European match against OFK Belgrade.

Scored twice in the 5-1 victory over Atlético Madrid in the 1963 European Cup Winners' Cup Final. It was the first European trophy to be won by an English club.

Jimmy Greaves...

Also scored 37 League goals for Tottenham in the 1962/63 season, meaning that he held the goal-scoring records at two London clubs at the same time.

Scored his 200th League goal aged 23 years and 290 days old, amazingly exactly the same age as Dixie Dean who had reached this figure with Everton some years earlier.

Was injured in the first round of the 1966 World Cup finals in the match against France and lost his place in the starting line-up to a certain Geoff Hurst. Unable to win back his place he became depressed and didn't turn up for the victory party at a London hotel after the Final.

Won the FA Cup again with Spurs in 1967, the opponents were Burnley and the score was 3-1, exactly the same as the 1962 encounter.

Won the last of his 57 international caps in a match against Austria in 1967. Altogether he scored 44 goals for England, including a record six hat-tricks.

Transferred to West Ham in 1970 as part of the £200,000 deal which took Martin Peters to Spurs. Once again he scored on his League debut for the Hammers.

Retired in 1971 aged only 31.

Admitted that he was an alcoholic but has dragged himself back in his battle against the booze.

Is now a much-loved and well-respected journalist and television presenter.

John Greig...

Moved from junior club Whitburn to join Glasgow giants Rangers in 1960.

Won the first of his 44 Scotland caps in the 1964 defeat of England at Hampden Park.

Voted Scottish Player of the Year in 1964.

Again won the Scottish Player of the Year award in 1966.

Lost after extra-time to Bayern Munich in the 1967 European Cup Winners' Cup Final in Nuremberg.

Became the only Rangers skipper to lift a European trophy when they beat Moscow Dynamo 4-3 to win the 1972 European Cup Winners' Cup Final in Barcelona's Nou Camp stadium.

Played for Scotland for the last time in 1976 in a match against Denmark. It was his first appearance for his country for five years.

Awarded the MBE for services to football in 1977.

Retired from playing in 1978 after 496 League appearances and took over as manager.

Won both Scottish Cups had an extended run in Europe in his first season in charge.

Resigned as manager in 1983, despite winning four trophies in five years, ending a 25 year association with the club.

Ruud Gullit...

Was discovered by Welsh coach Barry Hughes who signed him for Haarlem. Played 91 League games for the club and scored 32 goals.

Made his international debut on his 19th birthday in 1981 but ended up on the losing side as Switzerland won 2-1.

Joined Feyenoord in 1982 as a sweeper but converted to forward when he moved on to PSV Eindhoven in 1985.

Scored 46 goals in 68 League games in his new role and soon attracted the attentions of top clubs around Europe.

Moved to AC Milan for a world record fee of £6.5 million in 1987.

Was voted both the European and the World Footballer of the Year in 1987, only the third player, after Paolo Rossi and Michel Platini, to win such an accolade. He dedicated both these awards to the imprisoned Nelson Mandela.

Won the Italian League Championship with AC Milan in 1988, their first title for nine years.

Became the first captain to guide Holland to international success when they won the 1988 European Championships in Munich. He scored the first of their two goals in the Final against the Soviet Union.

Scored two goals as AC Milan beat Steaua Bucharest 4-0 in the 1989 European Champion's Cup Final at Barcelona's Nou Camp stadium.

Ruud Gullit...

Was voted the World Footballer of the Year for the second time in 1989.

Came back from a serious knee injury in 1990 to help AC Milan retain the European Champion's Cup with a 1-0 win over Benfica in Vienna.

Played a total of 117 League games for AC Milan, scoring 35 goals and winning three Seria A titles and two European Cup Finals before moving to Sampdoria in 1993.

Played his final game for Holland, his 65th cap, in 1993.

Finally left Italy in 1995 after unsuccessful spells at Sampdoria, AC Milan again and Sampdoria again and joined Chelsea under new manager Glenn Hoddle.

Was appointed player/manager at Stamford Bridge when Hoddle departed to become the new England coach in 1996.

Became the first non-British manager to win a club honour in England when he guided Chelsea to FA Cup Final success over Middlesbrough in 1997.

Was sacked by Chelsea chairman Ken Bates less than a year later for making excessive wage demands.

Took over as manager at Newcastle United following the sacking of Kenny Dalglish and immediately stated that he was going to bring 'Sexy Football' back to St James Park.

Georghe Hagi...

Made his debut for local team FC Constanta in 1980 and appeared in Romania's youth team in the same year.

At eighteen he became an established figure in the Sportul Studentesc side which he joined in 1983. He played 108 League games and scored 58 goals.

Made his full international debut in 1983 against Norway, still aged only 18.

Played for Romania in the 1984 European Championships but failed to win any of the group games.

Scored 20 goals from the midfield in the 1984/85 season, developing a reputation for his skill and accuracy with free-kicks and penalties.

Was top League scorer again in the following season, this time with 31 goals to his name.

Controversially moved to Steaua Bucharest in 1986 without a transfer fee, a move approved by the ruling Ceaucescu family, staunch supporters and directors of the club.

As a star player with Steaua Bucharest he earned the nickname the 'Maradonna of the Carpathians'.

Reached the second round of the 1990 World Cup finals in Italy, only to go out on penalties to the Republic of Ireland.

After 97 League games and 76 goals for Steaua Bucharest he moved to Spanish side Real Madrid in 1990.

Georghe Hagi...

Fell out with Madrid's other star players and was sold to Italian club Brescia in 1992. Here he joined the Romanian coach Mircea Lucescu and two other Romanian players.

Reached the quarter-finals of the 1994 World Cup in USA, only to be eliminated again on penalties, this time to Sweden. Hagi became the first international captain to see his side go out of two successive World Cups on penalties.

On returning to Europe after the World Cup in 1994 he was transferred to Barcelona. He then became the only Romanian player to have starred for both Spanish giants, Real Madrid and Barcelona.

Failed to impress the Barcelona manager Johan Cruyff and was sold to Turkish side Galatasaray in 1996.

Played in a disappointing European Championship campaign in Euro '96.

Played a record 113 times for his country and tops their goal-scoring chart with 32.

Helmut Haller...

Turned semi-professional with local club BC Augsburg in 1957.

Made his international debut for West Germany in a 1-1 draw with Denmark in Copenhagen, unfortunately he was injured and was substituted by Hans Cieslarczyk.

Transferred to Italian club Bologna in 1961.

Inspired Bologna to their first League Championship in more than 20 years after they beat Inter 1-0 in a title play-off in Rome after both clubs had finished level on points. His strike partnership with Dane Harald Nielsen proving successful for the club.

Played for West Germany in the 1966 World Cup Final, pouncing on a mistake by an England defender to shoot West Germany into a 1-0 lead. Unfortunately for him, England came back to win 4-2 after extra-time.

Left Bologna in 1968 after six seasons and joined Juventus.

Won the Italian League title in 1972 and 1973 with Juventus.

Played his 33rd and last international in the 2-1 victory over Morocco in the 1970 World Cup finals match. He was dropped immediately after this match.

Played for Juventus in the 1973 European Champion's Cup Final in Belgrade but lost 1-0 to Ajax.

Alan Hansen...

Made his League debut with Partick Thistle in 1974.

Won a First Division championship medal with the club in 1976.

Transferred to Liverpool at the end of the 1976/77 season for £100,000, a record fee received by Partick.

Quickly became the first name on the team-sheet at Anfield as he established himself in the team.

Was part of the Liverpool defence which conceded just 16 goals in 42 League games in 1978/79. This set a new record for the English game.

Won eight League Championships, three European Cups, two FA Cups and four League Cups with Liverpool.

Was not selected by Scotland's caretaker-manager Alex Ferguson for the Mexico World Cup, and without his defensive skills they were soon on the plane home.

Played a total of 26 times for Scotland.

Retired from playing in 1991 after 13 years at Anfield, making 434 League appearances and scoring 8 goals.

Now works on BBC television offering his opinion on everything football!

Said at the start of the 1995/96 season that Manchester United wouldn't win the title because "You don't win anything with kids" – By the end of the season they had won the double!

Johnny Haynes...

Joined Fulham as a schoolboy in 1950.

Turned professional with the club in 1952 after playing for England at Youth and Schoolboy levels.

Won the first of his 56 England caps against Northern Ireland, scoring in the 2-0 win. He became the first Englishman to be capped at all five international levels, Schoolboy, Youth, Under-23, 'B' and Full.

Succeeded Ronnie Clayton as England captain in 1960.

Became the first footballer to earn £100 a week following the abolition of the maximum wage in 1961.

Played a key role in England's midfield, partnered by future England manager Bobby Robson, as Walter Winterbottom's 4-4-2 system helped the national side win six sucessive games in 1961. Results of 5-2, 9-0, 4-2, 5-1, 9-3 (against Scotland) and 8-0 had the fans cheering from Land's End to Hadrian's Wall.

Johnny Haynes...

Captained England in the 1962 World Cup finals in Chile. After qualifying through the group stages the 3-1 quarter-final defeat by Brazil turned out to be his last game for England.

Suffered serious injuries in a car crash in August 1962 which sidelined him for a year.

Was the subject of a record-breaking bid by England's strongest team, Tottenham Hotspur, in 1963 but decided to stay loyal to Fulham.
Retired from English football in 1970, not having won a single honour in his eighteen years at Fulham.

Played a total of 56 times for England, 22 as captain, and scored 18 international goals.

Played an astonishing 594 League games for Fulham, scoring 145 goals.

Moved to South Africa in 1970 where he won a Championship medal with Durban City.

Glenn Hoddle...

Made his League debut in 1975 with Tottenham Hotspur.

Scored a fantastic goal on his England debut against Bulgaria in November 1979.

Won an FA Cup winners medal in 1981 when Spurs beat Manchester City 3-2 in a dramatic replay.

Won another in 1982 as Spurs became the first side this century to retain the trophy when they beat London neighbours QPR 1-0, again in a replay.

Helped Spurs win the UEFA Cup Final in 1984.

Joined French side Monaco and played under manager Arsen Wenger, later to become manager of Arsenal.

Became the first Englishman to win a French Championship medal when Monaco won the title in 1988.

Played his last game for England in 1988, achieving a total of 53 international caps and scoring 8 goals.

Returned to England in 1991 as player/manager of lowly Swindon Town.

Guided Swindon to the top-flight in 1993 for the first time in their history but left before the start of the season.

Took over as player manager at Chelsea and guided the London club to their first FA Cup Final for 24 years. Unfortunately for him and the Chelsea fans they were thrashed by 'double' winners Manchester United.

Glenn Hoddle...

Succeeded Terry Venables as England manager after Euro '96 and in doing so became, at 38, the youngest ever England manager since Walter Winterbottom.

His thoughtful, and sometimes controversial, methods helped England qualify for the 1998 World Cup finals in France, despite losing 1-0 to Italy in a qualifying match at Wembley; it was the first time England had lost a World Cup qualifier at home.

Steered England past the group stages in France but lost to Argentina on penalties in the next round.

Was sensationally sacked in 1999 after making some derogatory comments about disabled people.

Emlyn Hughes...

Made his League debut with Blackpool in 1964.

Transferred to Liverpool 1967, the season that saw Blackpool relegated.

Was nicknamed 'Crazy Horse'. He was told to impress the crowd by doing something crazy on the pitch by his manager – he attempted to tackle an opponent and failed so wrestled him to the ground!

Played his first game for England in 1970.

Won a League Championship and UEFA Cup winners' medal in 1973.

Won an FA Cup winners' medal after helping Liverpool beat Newcastle United 3-0 at Wembley in 1974.

Won a League Championship medal again in 1976, together with his second UEFA Cup winners' medal.

Was the first man to skipper Liverpool to a European Cup victory when they beat Borussia Moenchengladbach 3-1 in the thrilling 1977 final, just days after winning his third Championship medal.

Helped Liverpool become the first English club to retain the European Cup when they beat Club Brugge 1-0 in 1978.

Won a fourth League Championship medal in 1979.

Emlyn Hughes...

Has scored more goals against Liverpool than any player. Unfortunately they were all own goals when he was playing for them!

Played an incredible 474 League games, and scoring 35 goals, for the Anfield club before moving to Wolves in 1979.

Led Wolves to a 1-0 victory over Nottingham Forest in the 1980 League Cup Final, thus securing the only domestic honour he had never won with Liverpool.

Played his last game for England in 1980, scoring just once in his 62 international appearances.

Joined Rotherham in 1981, first as a player, then later as manager before leaving in 1983 when they were relegated to the Third Division.

Went on to captain a *Question of Sport* team on television.

Mark Hughes...

Made his League debut with Manchester United in 1983.

Made his international debut for Wales a year later.

Won the first of his FA Cup winners' medals in 1985 after a 1-0 defeat of Everton.

Played 89 League games in his first spell at Manchester United, scoring 37 League goals before transferring to Spanish giants Barcelona in 1986.

Because of the three-foreigners rule, and the arrival of Steve Archibald at the Nou Camp, Hughes was unable to hold down a regular spot in the first team. Playing in only 28 League games and scoring just 4 goals he was loaned to Bayern Munich in 1987.

Scored six goals in 18 appearances for the German side before moving back to Manchester United in 1989.

Won the PFA Player of the Year award in 1989.

Won his second FA Cup winners' medal when United beat Crystal Palace 1-0 in a replay after a thrilling 3-3 draw at Wembley in 1990.

Missed out on a Rumbelow's Cup winners' medal in 1991 when United were beaten 1-0 by Sheffield Wednesday.

Scored both goals in United's 2-1 win over Barcelona in the 1991 Cup Winners' Cup Final in Rotterdam.

Became the first player to have been voted the PFA Player of the Year twice when he won the award again in 1991.

Mark Hughes...

Won a Rumbelow's Cup winners' medal in 1992 after a 1-0 victory over Nottingham Forest at Wembley.

Won his first Championship medal in 1993 and his second a year later when Manchester United did the double, thrashing Chelsea 4-0 in the FA Cup Final.

Moved to Chelsea in 1995 after playing 256 League games in his second spell at Old Trafford, scoring 86 goals.

Became the first player to win four FA Cup winners' medals when Chelsea beat Middlesbrough 2-0 in the 1997 final.

Also joined a small band of just six other players to have played in five FA Cup finals.

Won a League Cup medal with Chelsea in 1998 and, despite not playing in the final itself, a European Cup Winners' Cup medal in the same season.

Moved to Southampton at the start of the 1998/99 season but failed to live up to former glories.

Geoff Hurst...

Was a talented schoolboy cricketer and had to decide which sport to persue.

Chose football, to the delight of millions of English fans, and signed for West Ham United under Ron Greenwood in 1959.

Scored a goal as West ham beat Preston North End 3-2 in the 1964 FA Cup Final.

Led West Ham's attack in the 2-0 victory over TSV 1860 Munich in the European Cup Winners' Cup Final played at Wembley.

Made his international debut for England against Scotland in 1966, having previously played at Youth and Under-23 levels.

Was in the England World Cup squad of 1966, replacing the injured Jimmy Greaves in the quarter-final match against Argentina and scored the winning goal.

Kept his place for the semi-final against Portugal, setting up one of Bobby Charlton's goals...

... and scoring a hat-trick in the final against West Germany.

Became the only player to have ever scored a hat-trick in a World Cup Final with his historic trio, a header, right-foot shot and a left-foot shot.

Became the last player to score six goals in a to flight League match when he bagged a double hat-trick for West Ham in a First Division game against Sunderland in 1968.

Geoff Hurst...

Played in the 1970 Mexico World Cup finals, this time losing to West Germany in the quarter-finals.

Is the joint-leading scorer, with Ian Rush, in the history of the League Cup with 46 goals.

Played 410 League games for West Ham in 13 seasons, scoring an impressive 180 goals.

Made his final appearance for England in 1972 in a match against West germany. He won 49 caps, scoring 24 international goals.

Transferred to Stoke City in 1972.

Played 108 League games for Stoke, scoring 30 goals, before moving to West Bromwich Albion in 1975.

Retired from playing a short while later.

Took over as manager of Chelsea in 1979 and presided, ironically, over the club's longest ever run without scoring a goal. In the last 9 games of the 1980/81 season the Chelsea players failed to find the net.

Sacked as Chelsea manager in 1981 and left football to enter the world of insurance selling.

Was inspirational in helping secure England's bid to host the European Championships in 1996 and in their bid for the 2006 World Cup.

Was awarded a knighthood in June 1998.

Jairzinho...

Was born Jair Ventura Filho on Christmas Day 1944.

Signed professional with Botafogo in 1959 as a 15-year old and deputised for the great Garrincha at outside-right.

Won a gold medal at the 1963 Pan American Games.

Played his first game for Brazil in 1964.

Played three games in the 1966 World Cup finals.

Became the first player to score in every round of a World Cup finals tournament in 1970. He scored two in the opening game against Czechoslovakia and one each against Romania, England, Peru, Uruguay and then one in the Final against Italy.

Broke his leg in 1971 and spent several months rehabilitating.

Moved to Europe in 1972 to play for French club Marseille but returned home within the year because of disciplinary problems.

Played in his third World Cup finals in 1974 but was knocked out by Holland in the second round.

Retired from international football shortly after the 1974 World Cup, having played 87 games and scoring 38 goals to make him Brazil's third top leading goalscorer, behind Pele and Zico.

Played with Cruzeiro in 1976, helping them win the South American Club Cup, although he did not play in the play-off through injury.

Kept links with Cruzeiro throughout the 80s and 90s and was able to recommend a talented 13-year old he had seen playing, his name was Ronaldo!

Pat Jennings...

Made his debut for Newry in Northern Ireland in 1961.

Moved to Watford in 1963 and played 48 games for the club.

Transferred to Tottenham Hotspur in 1964 as successor to Scotland keeper Bill Brown.

Made his international debut in 1964.

Won the 1967 FA Cup with Spurs, beating Burnley 3-1 at Wembley.

Scored a goal against Manchester United in the 1967 Charity Shield game. He launched a goal kickdown the field only to find it bounce over Alex Stepney's head and into the net.

Helped Spurs win the League Cup in 1971, beating Aston Villa 2-0.

Won the UEFA Cup in 1972, beating Wolves 3-2 on aggregate in the Final. It was the first and only time two English clubs have met in a European final.

Won the League Cup again in 1973, this time beating Norwich City 1-0.

Also collected the Footballer of the Year award in 1973.

Was surprisingly released by Spurs in 1977 after 472 League games and four trophies.

Was snapped up by London rivals Arsenal for a mere £45,000.

Pat Jennings...

Played in the 1978 FA Cup final for Arsenal against Ipswich Town but lost 1-0.

Returned to Wembley a year later in the classic 3-2 victory over Manchester United.

Appeared in his third consecutive FA Cup Final in 1980, this time losing 1-0 to unfancied West Ham and a rare headed goal by Trevor Brooking.

Played in the 1982 World Cup finals and helped Northern Ireland finish top in their group games. Lost to France 4-1 in the second round.

Earned in the region of £100,000 in his testimonial game played between Spurs and Arsenal in 1985.

Despite not having played senior club football for a year he still played between the sticks for his country, helping them secure a place in the 1986 World Cup finals.

Played his 119th and last game for Northern Ireland against Brazil on his 41st birthday during the 1986 World Cup tournament in Mexico. This remained a world record for international caps until Peter Shilton passed it in 1990.

Returned to football in 1993 as goalkeeping coach with Tottenham.

Jimmy Johnstone...

Made his Scotland debut against Wales in 1964 - the first of his 23 international caps.

Won his first League title at Celtic in 1966 under the management of legendary Jock Stein.

Won a unique four trophies in the 1966/67 season, the Scottish League, Scottish League Cup, Scottish FA Cup and the European Champions Cup Final, beating Internazionale 2-1 in Lisbon. This was the first European trophy won by a British club.

Played in the European Cup semi-final clash for Celtic against Leeds United. After winning 1-0 at Elland Road, the Scots, playing in front of a home crowd of 134,000 at Hampden Park, won the second-leg 2-1. They went on to face Feyenoord in the final but lost 2-1.

Reached his eighth consecutive Scottish League Cup Final with Celtic in 1972 but were surprisingly beaten 4-1 by lowly Partick Thistle, Johnstone was carried off injured midway through this match.

Won the Scottish FA Cup again in 1974, together with the League Championship again.

Won the last of his international caps in the 1-1 draw with Spain in the European Championship qualifier in 1975. Had he been able to overcome his fear of flying he would almost certainly have played more times for his country.

Won sixteen medals in total with Celtic, one European Cup, eight League titles, three Scottish FA Cups and four Scottish League Cups.

Kevin Keegan...

Was turned down by Jimmy Hill's Coventry City as not being good enough prior to turning professional with Scunthorpe United in 1968.

Played 124 League games for Scunthorpe, scoring 18 goals.

Moved to Liverpool for a bargain £35,000 in 1971 as an orthodox outside-right, becoming an overnight success at Anfield.

Made his international debut against Wales in Cardiff in November 1972 and helped England win 1-0.

Won his first League Championship in 1973, in the same year as he made his England debut in a 3-0 victory over Wales. His next two England games were also against Wales.

Won the League Championship again with Liverpool in 1976 and a few weeks later helped them win the UEFA Cup Final against Club Brugge.

Made his first appearance as England captain in 1976, ironically it was also against Wales. He wore the captain's armband a total of 31 times for his country.

Won the League for a third time with Liverpool in 1977 and inspired them to a 3-1 win over Borussia Mönchengladbach in Rome's Olympic stadium to win their first European Champions trophy.

Won the European Footballer of the year award in 1978.

Kevin Keegan...

Became, a year later, the only British player to win the European Footballer of the Year award twice, and only the second player, after Johan Cruyff, to win the award in consecutive seasons.

Transferred immediately after this final to Hamburg for £440,000 - having played 230 League games for Liverpool and scoring 68 goals.

Won the German League Championship in 1979.

Played in the 1980 European Champions Cup Final with Hamburg but lost 1-0 to Nottingham Forest in the Bernabéu stadium in Madrid.

Was on the verge of joining Italian giants Juventus in 1980 and only signed for Lawrie McMenemy at Southampton after his wife voiced concerns about being possible kidnap victims.

Played 68 League games for the Saints, scoring 37 goals.

Played in the 1982 World Cup finals in Spain, but was prevented from playing a major part due to a back injury. His only appearance was as a second-half substitute in England's last match, a 0-0 draw against Spain in the second round. It turned out to be the last of his 63 caps, during which time he had scored 21 international goals.

Moved to Newcastle United in 1982 for two seasons had proved a huge hit with the Geordie fans. He played 78 League games for the Toon, scoring a very respectable 48 goals. After his last game for the club he was whisked away by helicopter, still in his kit, after fears of crowd congestion by the local police.

Kevin Keegan...

Retired to Spain, playing golf after his spell at Newcastle, but was lured back eight years later as manager of the famous club.

Led Newcastle from the bottom of the old Second Division to safety in the last few months of the 1991/92 season, before guiding them to the top of the division a year later.

Guided Newcastle to second place in the Premiership in 1995/96, despite at one point having a 12-point lead over Manchester United.

Shocked the football world in January 1997 when he announced his resignation from the club. Thousands of Geordie fans were in mourning after he claimed to have been pushed out now, rather than waiting until the end of the season.

Returned to football in the summer of 1997 when he was appointed Director of Football at Mohamed Al Fayed's Second Division Fulham. He appointed former England colleague Ray Wilkins as team coach but sacked him at the end of the season, taking over full control of the footballing side of the club.

Was appointed part-time caretaker manager of England in 1999, following the sacking of Glenn Hoddle. His first match saw Manchester United's Paul Scholes score a hat-trick in the 3-1 win over Poland at Wembley in a Euro 2000 qualifying game.

Mario Kempes...

Turned professional in 1967 with his home town club Instituto de Cordoba.

Transferred to Rosario Central in 1970.

Made his international debut for Argentina in 1974 and starred in the World Cup finals in Germany.

Transferred to Spanish club Valencia in 1976.

Played again in the 1978 World Cup finals in his home country, the only foreign based player used by coach Cesar Luis Menotti.

Won the Golden Boot award for being top-scorer in these finals with six goals, including two in the Final helping the hosts to a 3-1 win over Holland.

Scored nine goals to help Valencia reach the 1980 European Cup Winners' Cup Final where they met Arsenal. After a boring 0-0 draw the game went to penalties, Valencia won the shoot-out but Kempes was the only player to miss from the spot!

Left Spain in 1981 to join River Plate in Argentina.

Played in his third World Cup finals in 1982 but failed to gel with the new Argentinian star Diego Maradonna. Retired from international football after this tournament, having played 51 times for his country and scoring 19 goals, making him Argentina's seventh highest goalscorer ever.

Briefly returned to Spain with Hercules before playing in Austria, first with Austria Vienna and then with Austria Salzburg.

Brian Kidd...

Made his League debut with local club Manchester United in 1966.

Played in the 1968 European Cup Final at Wembley against Portugese Champions Benfica on his 19th birthday. He became the youngest Brit to score in a major European final when he headed United's third goal, he had also set up their second and fourth goals in the 4-1 victory.

Won just two international caps for England, both in 1970, and scored one goal.

Played 203 League games for United, scoring 53 goals before transferring to Arsenal in 1974.

After 77 League games and 30 goals he moved back to Manchester in 1976, but this time to play for City.

Transferred to Everton in 1979, playing 40 League games and netting 11 goals.

Moved to Bolton in 1980 where he scored 14 League goals in 43 appearances for the club.

Moved to America in 1981 and had spells with Atlanta Chiefs, Fort Lauderdale Strikers and finally the Minnesota Kicks.

Became assistant to manager Alex Ferguson at Manchester United, playing a vital part in helping the club win the country's first ever double Double.

Moved to Blackburn Rovers in 1998/99 as manager.

Jürgen Klinsmann...

Started playing club football in 1982 with TB Gingen before moving to SC Geislingen and then Stuttgart Kickers.

Made his debut for the German national Youth team in 1982.

Played 61 League games for the Kickers, scoring 22 goals before transferring to V fB Stuttgart in 1984.

Was the club's second-highest goalscorer in his first season with 15 goals.

Made his debut for Germany at Under-21 level in 1984.

Scored 5 goals in a match in 1986, making him only the eleventh player to do so in the history of the Bundesliga.

Made his full international debut in 1987 in a 1-1 draw against Brazil.

Was the Bundesliga's top-scorer with 19 goals in 1988.

Played for West Germany in the 1988 European Championship finals, making a big impression.

Also collected a bronze medal at the Seoul Olympics, as the German team finished third.

Was voted German Footballer of the Year in 1988.

Helped Stutgart reach the final of the UEFA Cup Final but lost to Italian side Napoli.

Jürgen Klinsmann...

Played a total of 156 League games for V fB Stuttgart, and scored 79 goals before transferring to Inter Milan in 1989, scoring 13 goals for the Italian giants in his first season.

Helped Inter Milan win the League Championship in 1989, their first for nine years.

Was a key member of the German squad to win the 1970 World Cup Final in Italy.

Helped Inter Milan win the 1991 UEFA Cup.

Was a member of the German squad to be surprisingly beaten by Denmark in the 1992 European Championship Final.

Moved to Monaco in 1992 where he played 65 League games and scored 29 goals for the club.

Played for Germany in the 1994 World Cup finals in the USA, losing in the quarter-finals.

Was tempted to London by Tottenham Hotspur chairman Alan Sugar in 1994 and finished the season as Spurs top-scorer with 20 League goals in 41 appearances.

Was voted the English Footballer of the Year in 1995.

Captained the German national team for the first time against Spain in 1995.

Joined German club Bayern Munich in 1995, leaving Spurs under a cloud, with Alan Sugar claiming that he wouldn't even wash his car with a shirt Klinsmann had given him.

Jürgen Klinsmann...

Won the UEFA Cup with Bayern in 1996, scoring a record 15 goals in that years competition.

Finally won a League Championship medal in Germany in 1997 but left Bayern after 65 League games and 31 goals to return to Italy and a brief spell at Sampdoria.

Returned to England to captain Germany to triumph in Euro '96 and scored three goals in the tournament. Having scored in the 1988 and 1992 tournaments as well, he is the only player to have scored in three separate European Championships.

Alan Sugar made peace with the striker and he returned to White Hart Lane mid-way through the 1997/98 season. Despite only playing in the last 15 games, he scored 9 goals and finished top scorer with the club again. Without him Spurs would almost certainly have been relegated from the top flight.

Broke his jaw in a 1998 FA Cup match that saw Spurs get knocked out of the competition.

Played for Germany in the 1998 World Cup finals and scored 3 goals. His equaliser against Mexico was his eleventh goal in World Cup finals, only three other players, Gerd Müller, Just Fontaine and Pele have scored more.

Played 108 times for his country and scoring 47 international goals.

He is the joint top-scorer for Germany along with former strike-partner Rudi Voller, second only to the legendary Gerd Müller.

Brian Laudrup...

Is the son of former Danish international Finn Laudrup and younger brother of fellow international footballer Michael.

Began his career with Danish side Bronby in 1986, where he won two Danish Championships.

Moved to German side Bayer Uerdingen in 1989 where he played 34 League games and scored 6 goals.

Moved the following season to Germany's top side, Bayern Munich.

Travelled to Italy in 1992 to play for Fiorentina where he scored just 5 goals in 31 League games. Not surprisingly they were relegated to Serie B.

Was a member of the victorious Danish side to win the 1992 European Championships.

Joined AC Milan briefly on loan in 1993 before moving to Scottish club Rangers in 1994.

He won four consecutive Scottish titles with the Glasgow side as well as the Scottish FA Cup in 1996 and the Scottish League Cup in 1994. He played 115 league games, scoring 33 goals.

Starred alongside his brother in France 1998 as Denmark reached the quarter-finals of the World Cup for the first time, losing eventually to finalists Brazil 3-2.

Transferred to Chelsea on a free transfer under the Bosman ruling in July 1998, reportedly on a salary of £75,000 per week. He was unable to settle in the capital and returned to Denmark to play football.

Michael Laudrup...

Is the son of former Danish international Finn Laudrupp and older brother of fellow international footballer Brian.

Joined the youth section at Bronby in 1978.

Made his League debut in 1981 aged 17 for KB Copenhagen before moving back to play for Bronby.

Was voted Footballer of the Year in 1982.

Made his international debut on his 18th birthday in a 1982 game against Norway.

Was targeted by top European teams Liverpool, Ajax and Anderlecht but transferred to Italian giants Juventus in 1984. As they had too many foreigners he was loaned out to Lazio for two years where he made 60 League appearances and scored 9 goals.

Recalled by Juventus in 1985 he helped them win the World Club Cup.

Was voted Denmark's Footballer of the Year for the second time in 1985.

Played for Denmark in the 1986 World Cup finals in Mexico, and helping the team thrash Uruguay 6-1 in the Neza stadium the capital. After beating West Germany in another group game they crashed to a 5-1 second round defeat by Spain.

Grew tired of the discipline in Italian football and transferred to Barcelona in 1989.

Won his first Spanish title with Barcelona in 1991.

Michael Laudrup...

Did not play in the 1992 European Championships after falling out with coach Richard Moller-Nielsen over team selection and tactics.

Won three more Spanish titles in consecutive years at Barcelona, making it four in a row from 1991 to 1994.

Was left out of the Barcelona team who won the 1994 European Champions Cup Final and transferred to their great rivals Real Madrid.

Became the first Dane to play for both Spanish giants and the only player ever to have played for Barcelona in a 5-0 thrashing of Real Madrid and for Real Madrid in a 5-0 victory over Barcelona.

Made his peace with the national coach in 1994 and returns to international duty.

Helped Real Madrid win their first League title in five years in 1995, making it a very impressive personal five-in-a-row for him.

Captained Denmark in the European Championship finals in 1996 before moving on to play in the emerging J-League in japan with Vissel Kobe. This was expected to end his international career but he insisted he was still available to play for Denmark.

To prove his fitness at the top level he returned to Ajax Amsterdam in 1997.

Is the second most capped player in the history of Danish football, equal with Morten Olsen and just behind goalkeeper Peter Schmeichel. He is also the fifth highest goalscorer for Denmark with 37.

Denis Law...

Joined Huddersfield Town as a teenager in 1955.

Made his international debut for Scotland in 1958, scoring in a 3-0 win over Wales.

Transferred to Manchester City for a record British fee of £55,000 in 1960.

Made 44 League appearances for City and scored 21 goals.

Was sold in 1961 to Italian club Torino for a world record fee of £100,000, including a signing-on fee of £10,000. Despite scoring 10 League goals in 27 games he never settles in Italy and was bought by Manchester United manager Matt Busby a year later, increasing the world record to £115,000.

Scored four goals for Scotland against Northern Ireland in 1962.

Scored Manchester United's first goal in the 3-1 victory over Leicester City in the 1963 FA Cup Final.

Represented the Rest of the World in a Wembley game against England in 1963 and scored a goal.

Scored four goals again for Scotland, this time in a match against Norway. He is the only Scottish player to have scored four goals in a game on two occassions.

Was voted the European Footballer of the Year in 1964, only the second player, after Stanley Matthews, to win this award.

Denis Law...

Helped Manchester United win the 1964/65 League Championship.

Won another League title in 1967, despite suffering from recurring injuries throughout the season.

Scored a record five European hat-tricks for Manchester United in their various campaigns.

Did not play in the 1968 European Cup victory over Benfica due to a knee injury.

Played 309 League games for Manchester United, scoring 171 goals before crossing the city in 1973 to play for 'The Citizens' again.

In his last League game of his career in 1974 he scored a cheeky backheel goal which condemned his former club, United, to relegation to the Second Division. "I have seldom felt so depressed as I did that weekend," he said later.

Played his last international in 1974 in the World Cup finals against Zaire, it was his only appearance in the competition.

Scored an amazing 41 goals in the FA Cup, a record which stood until Ian Rush scored his 42nd in 1995.

Scored 30 international goals for Scotland, equal top-scorer with Kenny Dalglish, although he only played 55 times for his country, Kenny played 102 times.

Tommy Lawton...

Joined Burnley as an amateur in 1935 after scoring an unbelievable 570 goals in just three seasons as a schoolboy.

Made his League debut in 1936, just four days after his 17th birthday, and scored a hat-trick against Tottenham Hotspur. He was the youngest player to score a hat-trick in the English League.

Was sold to Everton in 1937 as replacement for the great Dixie Dean for £6,5000 a record for a teenager.

Finished the 1937/38 season as top scorer in the First Division with 28 League goals.

Finished top scorer again a year later with 34 goals, helping Everton win the League Championship.

Made his England debut against Wales in 1939 and scored a penalty to make him England's youngest-ever scorer at 19 years and 17 days old. Went on to score in the next five internationals he played in during that year.

Scored 24 goals in 23 wartime international games and was sold to Chelsea after the end of hostilities.

Scored 28 First Division goals for Chelsea in his first season, setting a new club record.

Became the first England player to score four goals in an international when he demolished Holland in November 1946.

Scored the quickest ever England goal in 1947, slotting one home against Portugal after just 17 seconds.

Tommy Lawton...

Joined Notts County, then in Division Three (South) for £20,000 in 1948, making him the most expensive footballer by far.

Won his last England cap in 1948 in the 0-0 draw against Denmark, finishing with 22 goals in 23 full internationals.

Led Notts County to promotion in 1950, scoring 31 goals in the process.

Became player/manager of Brentford in 1952.

Reverted back to being a player only when he signed for Arsenal in 1953, scoring 13 goals in 35 League games with the Gunners.

Finally retired from League football in 1955. He played a total of 390 League games and scored 231 goals for his various clubs and had not been booked throughout his entire career.

Became player/manager at non-League Kettering Town in 1956 before being tempted back to Notts County for a brief spell as manager in 1958. He was sacked a year later and retired completely from the game to run a public house.

Was awarded a testimonial game at Everton in 1972 which raised over £6,000 for him.

Died from pneumonia in 1997, aged 77.

Gary Lineker...

Signed for Leicester City in 1977.

Made his League debut on New Years Day, 1979.

Gained promotion from Division Two with Leicester City in 1980.

Won his first England cap in May 1984, coming on as a substitute in an away game against Scotland.

Scored his first international goal, at home against the Republic of Ireland in 1985.

Played 194 League games for Leicester, scoring 95 goals before being transferred to Everton for £1.1 million in 1985.

Scored the first of his five international hat-tricks in a World Cup qualifying game against Turkey in October 1985.

Scored the first goal in the 1986 FA Cup Final against Liverpool but still ended up losing 3-1 after extra-time.

Played 41 League games for Everton, scoring an impressive 30 goals.

Was voted Footballer of the Year in 1986.

Scored six World Cup finals goals in Mexico, the highest ever by any British player, to win the 1986 Golden Boot award.

Gary Lineker...

Was sold to Barcelona for £2.75 million in 1986, and a year later scored all four goals in a game against fierce rivals Real Madrid.

Scored all four England goals in a 4-2 win away to Spain in 1987.

Helped Barcelona win the Spanish Cup in 1988.

Won the European Cup Winners' Cup with Barcelona, beating Italian side Sampdoria 2-0 in the 1989 final in Berne.

Was sold to Tottenham Hotspur for £1.2 million in 1989 after 99 League games and 44 goals for the Spanish club.

Was First Division top scorer in 1990 for the third time with a third club – Leicester City, Everton and now Spurs.

Scored four goals as England reached the semi-final of the 1990 World Cup in Italy. His tally of ten World Cup Final goals is a record for an English player.

Played in the 1991 FA Cup Final for Spurs against Nottingham Forest, he missed a penalty and had a 'goal' disallowed but still finished up with a winners' medal.

Scored 67 League goals for Spurs in 105 games.

Again scored all four of England's goals in a game, this time away to Malaysia in 1991. In doing so he became the first English player to have twice scored four goals in a game.

Gary Lineker...

Played his last six England matches desparately trying to score his 49th international goal and break Bobby Charlton's record. He had a weak penalty against Brazil saved and was substituted by manager Graham Taylor in favour of Alan Smith in his last game against Sweden. It was his 80th international game.

Voted Footballer of the Year for the second time in 1992.

Signed for Japanese J-League team Grampus Eight but a persistent toe injury meant he played just 8 games for the club.

Was not booked once throughout his entire career.

On retiring from playing in 1996 he took up a media career.

Nat Lofthouse...

Played his first game for Bolton Wanderers in 1946.

Made his England debut in 1951, scoring twice in a 2-2 draw with Yugoslavia at Highbury.

Scored two goals in a game on 12 occassions for England but never managed a hat-trick.

Played a total of 33 international games, scoring 30 goals, he is England's joint fourth top scorer with Tom Finney. Only Bobby Charlton, Gary Lineker and Jimmy Greaves have scored more goals for England.

Won an FA Cup winners' medal in 1958 when he scored both goals in the 2-0 defeat of Manchester United. His second goal was probably the most controversial in the history of the competition: he charged both goalkeeper and ball into the back of the net!

In total played 505 matches in all competitions for the club, 452 in the League, and knocked in a phenomenal 285 goals, 255 in the League. He is by far the leading scorer for Bolton.

Retired from playing in 1960.

Ally McCoist...

Joined Perth side St Johnstone in 1978.

Made his senior team debut in 1979 and in his first season played fifteen games, six as substitute, all without scoring.

Improved greatly over the next couple of seasons, scoring 22 League goals in 57 appearances for the club.

Transferred to Sunderland for £300,000 in 1981 and scored his first goal for the club against Nottingham Forest's England goalkeeper, Peter Shilton. However, having found the net just eight times in 56 League games he was transferred back to Scotland and Rangers for £180,000 in 1983.

He scored in the first minute of his debut – against Celtic! – and immediately won over the Rangers fans who questioned the fact that he came from a largely pro-Catholic family.

Scored a hat-trick in the 1984 Scottish League Cup Final against old firm rivals Celtic.

Won another Scottish League Cup medal with Rangers in 1985.

Made his international debut in a game against Holland in 1986.

Won his first League Championship with Rangers in 1987, together with the Scottish League Cup.

Won the Scottish League Cup in 1988, followed by the League Cup and Championship in 1989.

Ally McCoist...

Won the League Championship in 1990, followed by the League Cup and another Championship title in 1991.

Voted Scotland's Player of the Year in 1992 and was awarded Europe's 'Golden Boot' award for being the leading goalscorer with 34 goals.

Won the Scottish League and Scottish FA Cup in 1992.

Won the Scottish League and League Cup in 1993.

Broke a leg in a 1993 World Cup qualifying game against Portugal and missed out on the chance to win a third medal with Rangers has they won the Scottish FA Cup that year.

Marked his comeback with a goal in the 2-1 victory over Hibs in the 1994 League Cup Final and secured yet another League title.

Won just the League title in 1995!

Became Rangers' all time record League scorer in January 1996 when he scored in a game against Raith Rovers. Played again for Scotland in 1996 after a 28-month absence from the national squad, scoring the winning goal against Greece.

Won another Championship medal with Rangers in 1996 and broke Scotland's post-war scoring record, passing the 264 mark in the season. Unfortunately he once again missed the chance to add to his medal collection when injury forced him to miss the Scottish FA Cup Final victory.

Scored Scotland's only goal in the European Championships in 1996.

Ally McCoist...

Won the Scottish League Cup Final in 1997.

Played a major part in helping Rangers equal Celtic's record of nine Scottish Championship titles in a row in 1997, and the tenth for McCoist since he joined the club.

Became the highest Scottish scorer in European football in August 1997. His two goals against GI Gotu, the Faroe island champions took him to twenty goals in Europe, two more than Celtic hero Willie Wallace.

Scored his 350th goal for Rangers in a Scottish Cup match against Dundee in March 1998.

Took over as team captain on BBC's *A Question of Sport*, whilst still playing.

Looks set for a media career when he finally decides to hang up his boots.

Danny McGrain...

Made his League debut for Celtic in 1967, the year that they had won every competition they had entered, including the European Cup.

Won seven Championship medals and five Scottish FA Cup medals during his twenty years at the club.

Played 657 League games for the 'Bhoys', scoring 8 goals.

Fractured his skull in 1972 in a clash with Falkirk's Doug Somner.

Made his international debut in 1973.

Appeared in the 1974 World Cup finals and, despite being undefeated, still didn't qualify for the second round.

Was diagnosed as suffering from diabetes in 1974 but continued playing.

Was voted Scotland's Player of the Year in 1977.

Suffered a serious ankle injury in 1977 which saw him sidelined for over a year.

Was appointed club captain in 1978 by the manager Jock Stein.

In 1980 he was appointed captain of Scotland, a position he held for ten games.

Played his 60th, and last, game for Scotland in 1982, without scoring a single international goal.

Dave Mackay...

Played in the Heart of Midlothian side which won their first Scottish Championship this century in 1958.

Made his Scotland debut in 1957.

Moved to Tottenham Hotspur and became the driving force behind the team that won the League and FA Cup double in 1961.

Broke his left leg twice within a year, which seriously threatened his career. However, he soon bounced back and led Spurs to a 2-1 victory over Chelsea in the 1967 FA Cup Final.

Played 268 League games for Spurs and scored 42 goals.

Moved to Derby County in 1968 and helped win promotion to the top flight.

Was voted the Footballer of the Year in 1969.

Moved to Swindon Town in 1971 where he played 26 League games, scoring just once.

Replaced Brian Clough as manager of Derby in 1974 and within a year he had won the League Championship with them. He was the most inexperienced post-war manager to win the League.

Steve McManaman...

Joined his local club Liverpool in 1990.

Shot to prominence in the 1992 FA Cup Final when he was a last minute replacement for the injured John Barnes. He tore into the Sunderland defence and set up Michael Thomas to score the first goal in the 2-0 win.

Made his England debut in November 1994, coming on as a substitute against Nigeria.

Was back at Wembley with Liverpool in 1995 in the League Cup Final against Bolton. He scored both Liverpool goals in the 2-1 victory and collected the Man of the Match award for his dazzling skills.

Played for England in the 1996 European Championships.

Made only one appearance in the 1998 World Cup finals in France.

Left Liverpool at the end of the 1998/99 season on a free transfer under the Bosman ruling to join Spanish giants Real Madrid on a staggering £75,000 per week.

Billy McNeill...

Signed professional terms with Celtic on his 17th birthday in 1957.

Made the first of more than 500 appearances for the club in 1959.

Won his first Scotland cap in the 9-3 defeat by England in 1961 and went on to play at least once a year for his country for the next 11 years.

Was voted Scotland's Player of the Year in 1965.

Helped Celtic win the Scottish FA Cup for the first time in 11 years.

Won the League Championship and League Cup in 1966.

Captained Celtic to success in the League, League Cup, Scottish FA Cup and the European Cup where they became the first British side to win the competition after a 2-1 victory over Italian giants Inter Milan.

Again won the League Championship and League Cup in 1968.

Won a Scottish treble of the Championship, League Cup and Scottish FA Cup in 1969.

Lost in the final of the 1970 European Cup, beaten 2-1 by Dutch club Feyenoord.

Made his final appearance for Scotland in 1972, a 1-0 defeat by England. He had won 29 caps in all.

Billy McNeill...

Won the Scottish FA Cup and League Championship in 1974. The League title was a record ninth consecutive title. In those nine seasons he played in 282 League games out of a possible 306, more than any other Celtic player.

Retired from playing in 1975 after winning both Scottish cups again. In all he had won an unprecedented haul of one European Cup, nine Championships, seven Scottish FA Cups, six Scottish League Cups plus numerous runners-up places.

Became manager of Manchester City in 1983.

Left to take up the manager's job at Aston Villa in 1986 but was sacked eight months later when Villa were relegated.

Went back briefly for two spells as manager at Celtic but neither was as successful as he or the crowd would have liked.

Sepp Maier...

Played in regional German Leagues until he turned professional with Bayern Munich in 1964.

Made his debut for West Germany in a 4-0 victory over the Republic of Ireland in Dublin on the eve of the World Cup finals in 1966 – for which he was West Germany's third choice keeper.

Helped Bayern Munich win the European Cup Winners' Cup in extra-time against Rangers in 1967.

Was first choice goalkeeper as West Germany won the European Championship in 1972.

Won his first League title with Bayern Munich in 1973, despite being ridiculed for his trademark long, baggy shorts.

Won the first of his three European Champions Cups with Bayern in 1974.

Played for West Germany in the 1974 World Cup Final in his home stadium in Munich. He became the first keeper ever to be beaten by a penalty in a World Cup Final when Holland's Johan Neeskens scored from the spot. He still went on to collect a winners' medal though.

Voted Footballer of the Year in West Germany in 1975.

Invested much of his football earnings into a centre specialising in what was his favourite sport – tennis in 1975.

Sepp Maier...

Won the World Club Cup against Cruzeiro of Brazil in 1976.

Kept goal for West Germany when they lost the Final of the 1976 European Championships to Czechoslovakia in a penalty shoot-out in Belgrade.

Voted West Germany's Footballer of the Year in 1977 and again in 1978.

Played 95 times for his country in an international career spanning 11 years.

Retired from playing because of injury. He had played 473 League matches, including a record run of 422 consecutive games.

Paolo Maldini...

Joined AC Milan's youth system under the coaching direction of his father, Cesare Maldini, a former captain of Milan, Italian national and future national team manager.

Made his League debut aged 16 in January 1985 in a 1-1 draw away to Udinese.

Won the Italian League title with AC Milan in 1988.

Made his international debut in a friendly game against Yugoslavia which finished 1-1 in Split.

Won the 1989 European Champions Cup in a 4-0 win over Steaua Bucharest in Barcelona.

Retained the European Champions Cup when he helped his club defeat Portugese champions Benfica 1-0.

Played for Italy in the 1990 World Cup finals, finishing in third place, after losing to Argentina in the semi-final.

Played in a record 17-month unbeaten League run for AC Milan. The run was finally broken by Parma who beat the with a goal by Faustino Asprilla.

Won the Seria A title again in 1992, 1993 and 1994, doing the double in the last of these three years by winning the Italian Cup as well.

Played an heroic role as Milan thrashed Spanish giants Barcelona 4-0 in the 1994 European Champions Cup Final in Athens.

Paolo Maldini...

Played for Italy in the 1994 World Cup Final in America, only to lose to Brazil on penalties.

Once again won the Italian League title in 1996.

Captained Italy in the 1996 European Championships in England.

Helped Italy secure a place in the 1998 World Cup finals by beating Russia in a play-off.

Captained the Italians to a quarter-final place in the tournament proper.

Has played more than 400 League games for AC Milan, his only club side to date.

Wilf Mannion...

Joined Middlesbrough in 1936.

Made his England debut in 1947, scoring a hat-trick against Northern Ireland.

Refused to play for Middlesbrough for six months in 1948 after a wages dispute.

Was a member of the England team that lost 1-0 to the USA in 1950 and said after the match, "Bloody ridiculous, can't we play them again?"

Played 26 times for England, scoring 11 goals and remains Middlesbrough's most capped player.

Played 368 League games for the Teesiders, scoring 110 goals.

Joined Hull City in 1954 but left after a few months after making allegations about illegal payments.

Diego Maradona...

Made his League debut as a 15-year old for Argentinos Juniors in 1976.

Made his international debut a year later in a friendly against Hungary.

Fell out with the national coach Cesar Menotti after he was left out of the squad which won the 1978 World Cup in front of their home crowd.

Moved to Boca Juniors in 1980 for £1 million, a record fee for a teenager. Played 40 League games for them and scored 28 goals.

Transferred to Barcelona in 1982 for another World record of £4.2 million.

Was put out of the game for four months after a reckless tackle by Bilbao's hardman defender Andoni Goicochea. He still managed to score 22 League goals in 36 appearances for the Spanish giants.

Moved for a third World record fee, this time of £6.9 million to Italian side Napoli in 1984.

Inspired Argentina to victory in the 1986 World Cup Final, unanimously being voted the Player of the Tournament, despite his 'Hand of God' goal against England in the quarter-final.

Led Napoli to their first-ever Italian League title in 1987 and for good measure helped them win the Italian Cup in the same season.

Won the 1988 UEFA Cup Final as Napoli beat Stuttgart.

Diego Maradona...

Appeared in his second successive World Cup Final in 1990, despite numerous injuries, and was unlucky as Argentina was defeated 1-0 by West Germany in Rome.

Failed a drug test in 1991 and was given a 15 month ban.

Made a somewhat disappointing comeback with Spanish side Seville in 1992 and was sacked.

Joined Newells Old Boys in Argentina in 1993 and regained his place back in the Argentina squad for the 1994 World Cup finals.

Tested positive for drugs again during the 1994 World Cup tournament and was banned for a further 15 months. Did not play again for his country, finishing on 90 caps and 33 international goals.

Had brief coaching jobs with Deportivo Mandiyu and Racing Avellaneda before returning to Boca Juniors as a player in 1995.

Retired from playing in 1996, only to make yet another comeback a year later with Boca.

Rodney Marsh...

Made his League debut with Fulham in 1962.

Headed the winning goal in a game against Leicester City in 1963 and ended up permanently deaf in one ear!

Moved to near neighbours Queens Park Rangers in 1966.

Scored a brilliant solo goal as he helped Third Division QPR beat top flight West Bromwich 3-2 to win the 1967 League Cup. At one stage QPR found themselves two goals down.

Scored an amazing 44 goals for QPR that year, with an astonishing 11 of those coming in the League Cup.

Made captain of QPR in 1970 and shaved his beard off to make himself look more dignified!

After 211 League games for QPR and 106 goals, he moved to Manchester City in 1972 for £200,000, making him the second most expensive footballer in British football.

Played 9 games for England between 1972 and 1973, scoring one international goal.

Helped City reach the League Cup Final in 1974 but lost 2-1 to Wolves thanks to a late goal. He refused to applaud the winners or collect his losers' medal.

After 118 League appearances and 36 goals for Manchester City he moved back to Fulham in 1976 to team up with George Best.

Enjoyed a lucrative business partnership with George Best after they finished playing football.

Lothar Matthäus...

Left school in 1977 and studied interior design and decorating before taking the plunge into the world of professional football.

Joined Borussia Mönchengladbach as a professional in 1978.

Made his national team debut as a substitute against Holland in the 1980 European Championships.

Scored for Borussia Mönchengladbach in their 1980 UEFA Cup Final defeat.

Played for West Germany in the 1982 World Cup finals held in Spain.

Joined Bayern Munich for a German record fee of £650,000.

Won three Championships and two German Cups as captain of Bayern Munich, playing 117 League goals for the club, scoring 57 goals.

Scored the winning goal against Morocco in the second round of the 1986 World Cup finals. Made it through to the Final where he faced Argentina, and Diego Maradonna, with a broken wrist. Ended up on the losing side.

Moved to Inter Milan in 1988 for £2.4 million.

Won the Italian League title with a record number of points (58), a figure which was not surpassed until the introduction of 3 points for a win in the 1994/95 season.

Captained West Germany to victory in the 1990 World Cup in Italy and was voted Player of the Tournament by the world's media.

Lothar Matthäus...

Subsequently picked up the German, European and World Footballer of the Year awards in 1990.

Scored a penalty in the 1991 UEFA Cup Final and picked up a winners' medal with the victorious Inter Milan.

Missed the 1992 European Championships – in which Germany lost to Denmark in the Final – because of a serious knee injury.

Returned to Bayern Munich from Inter Milan in 1992.

Regained his place back in the national side in 1993.

Represented his country at the 1994 World Cup in America.

Guided Bayern Munich to victory in the 1996 UEFA Cup Final.

Missed the 1996 European Championships, which Germany won, because of injury.

Won the German League Championship for a third time with Bayern Munich in 1997.

Played in the 1998 World Cup finals in France, making it a joint record of five appearances in the tournament shared with Mexican goalkeeper Antonio Carbajal (1950-66). He played in 25 World Cup finals games, more than any other player.

Played a record 125 times for the national side, scoring 22 goals.

Stanley Matthews...

Turned professional in 1932 with local club Stoke City, making his full League debut aged only 17.

Won promotion to the First Division with Stoke City in 1933 and stayed with them until after the Second World War. The 'Wizard of Dribble' as he became known as made 259 league appearances for the club, scoring 51 goals.

Made his England debut in 1935 in a 4-0 win over Wales in Cardiff.

Sold to Blackpool for £11,500 in 1946.

Played a key role in the 1948 victory over Italy in Turin, winning an impressive 4-0.

Voted Footballer of the Year in 1948, the first time the award had been made.

Took part in the 1953 FA Cup Final against Bolton. Losing 3-2 with just a few minutes to go he somehow inspired Blackpool to score twice to snatch a 4-3 victory. Despite team mate Stan Mortensen getting a hat-trick the game has gone down in history as 'The Matthews Final'. This was to be his only medal won on the football pitch.

Toured Mozambique on a summer tour in 1955 and mesmerised a ballboy called Eusebio, who was later to star for Benfica and Portugal.

Won the European Footballer of the Year award in 1956, again the first time this award had been made.

Was awarded a CBE in 1957.

Stanley Matthews...

Played the last of his 84 games for England in 1957 at the age of 41, in a World Cup qualifying match which saw Denmark lose at home in Copenhagen 4-1. He won a total of 54 official caps and scored 11 international goals.

Played 379 League games for Blackpool, scoring 17 goals before returning to Stoke City in 1961 for £2,800 as a 46-year old and guided them back into the First Division.

Won the player of the Year award for the second time in 1963.

He was awarded a knighthood for his services to soccer in 1965, and became the first and only footballer to be knighted while still playing.

Played for Stoke City against Fulham in February 1965 five days after his 50th birthday, (the only man over 50 to make an appearance in top flight football in England). It was to be his last game for the side.

A testimonial game was organised at Stoke's Victoria Ground in 1965 and stars such as Di Stefano, Puskas and yashin turned up to play tribute to the great man.

Joe Mercer...

Signed as a 16-year old for Everton in 1932.

Helped Everton win the First Division Championship in 1939.

Made his international debut against Scotland in 1939 and won four more caps that season.

Played in 25 non-cap internationals.

Returned to Everton in 1946 after serving as a physical training instructor in the army during the Second World War.

Transferred to Arsenal in 1946, despite a niggling knee injury which threatened to halt his career.

Captained Arsenal to the League Championship in 1948.

Led Arsenal to a 2-0 FA Cup victory over Liverpool in 1950.

Voted Footballer of the Year in 1950.

Played again in the FA Cup Final in 1952 when an injury-hit Arsenal battled hard against Newcastle before a late winner denied them glory.

Won his third League Championship in 1953.

Suffered a broken leg in 1954 which ended his playing career.

Took over as manager of Sheffield United in 1955.

Joe Mercer...

Became manager of Aston Villa in 1958, helping them secure promotion to the First Division and to victory in the League Cup.

Retired due to ill-health in 1964 but was later persuaded to come back as manager at Manchester City. To ease some of the burdens of day-to-day football club life he appointed Malcolm Allison as coach.

Won promotion to the First Division in 1967 and the following year won the First Division title.

Won the FA Cup in 1969 and in doing so had now won both the League and FA Cup both as player and as manager.

Guided Manchester City to victory in the 1970 European Cup Winners' Cup Final.

Retired, again, due to ill-health in 1972.

Tempted out of retirement (again) in 1974, this time to take over as caretaker manager of England following the sudden departure of Don Revie. He was in charge for seven matches, winning three, drawing three and losing only one.

Died at Goodison Park in 1990 on his 76th birthday.

Jackie Milburn...

Made his League debut for Newcastle United in 1946.

Became England's first ever hat-trick scorer in the World Cup, hitting three goals in the 4-1 defeat of Wales in the Home Championships, which doubled up as the World Cup qualifiers that year.

Won an FA Cup Final winners' medal in 1951 after a 2-0 victory over Blackpool. He scored in every round of the competition, including both of the goals in the Final.

Won the FA Cup again in 1952, this time helping to beat Arsenal 1-0.

In 1955 he won a third FA Cup winners' medal, scoring a goal after just 45 seconds to help Newcastle to a 3-1 win over Manchester City. This was the fastest goal scored in a Wembley final until Roberto Di Matteo scored after 42 seconds in 1997.

Scored more goals for Newcastle than anybody else before or since, despite never being able to head the ball. He scored 178 League goals in 354 appearances for the 'Magpies'.

Played 13 international games for England between 1949 and 1956, scoring 10 goals.

Is commemorated by a bronze statue in Newcastle city centre.

Took over from Alf Ramsey as manager of Ipswich in 1963 but soon found he wasn't cut out for the job.

Became a journalist in his home city of Newcastle.

The whole city mourned his death in 1988.

Is the uncle of England legends Bobby and Jackie Charlton.

Roger Milla...

Began his career in 1967 with Leopard of Douala before transferring to Tonnerre Yaoundé.

Made his international debut for Cameroon in 1972.

Was voted the African Footballer of the Year in 1976.

Moved to France in 1976 to join Valenciennes.

Transferred to Monaco where he helped win the 1980 French Cup.

Transferred to Corsican club Bastia in 1980 and won the French Cup with them in 1981.

Moved briefly to Saint-Etienne and then Montpellier.

Appeared in the 1982 World Cup finals in Spain with Cameroon. They were unlucky to be eliminated on goal difference in a group which included Poland, Peru and Italy.

Won the African Nations Cup with Cameroon in 1984, beating Nigeria 3-1 in the Final.

Finished runner-up in the African Nations Cup, losing to hosts Egypt on penalties in the Final.

Starred in the 1990 World Cup finals in Italy after being tempted out of retirement. He scored both Cameroon goals in their 2-1 win over Romania in the first round and then scored an extra-time winner against Colombia when extravagant goalkeeper Rene Higuita made a mistake. He celebrated his goals with a 'wiggle' around the corner flag that started off a fashion all over the world.

Roger Milla...

Was voted the African Player of the Year again in 1990, the first player to win the award twice.

Was tempted out of 'retirement' yet again in 1994 and became, at 42, the oldest player to appear in the World Cup finals. He also became the oldest player to score in the tournaments final stages when he netted Cameroon's consolation goal in the 6-1 thrashing by Russia. Before that goal the oldest player to score in a World Cup finals game was a 38-year old Roger Milla in Italy 1990!

Bobby Moore...

Signed for his local team West Ham United in 1958.

Won a record 18 Youth caps for England and went on to Play for the Under-23s before earning his first full cap in 1962.

Led West Ham to victory in the 1964 FA Cup Final with a 3-2 win over Preston North End, the Hammers scoring a goal in the last minute.

Voted Footballer of the Year in 1964.

Captained West Ham to a 2-0 victory over Munich 1860 at Wembley in the 1965 Cup Winners' Cup Final.

Became the first captain to lift three trophies at Wembley in consecutive years thanks to the victories in 1964 and 1965 and that certain other trophy he lifted in 1966!

Captained England to glory in the 1966 World Cup, becoming the first, and only, Englishman to lift the trophy after a nail-biting final which saw the team defeat West Germany 4-2 after extra-time.

Played in another cup final at Wembley in 1966, the two-legged League Cup Final. This time he was not a winner as the Hammers lost to West Bromwich Albion.

Falsely accused of stealing a bracelet while on a tour of Colombia with England in 1970.

During a league game in 1970 he attempted to clear the ball from oncoming strikers when he kicked it straight at the referee's head, knocking him unconscious. He immediately picked up the ref's whistle and blew it to stop play!

Bobby Moore...

Went on to captain England to the quarter-finals of the 1970 World Cup in Mexico where this time they were defeated by West Germany.

Played his 108th and last game for England in 1973, a record which would stand until Peter Shilton passed it in 1989. It was also the 90th time he had worn the captains armband, more than any other player.

Played 544 League games for West Ham, scoring 22 goals.

Transferred to Fulham in 1974.

Played in the 1975 FA Cup Final for Fulham but lost 2-0 to West Ham.

Played 124 League games for Fulham, scoring on just one occassion.

Retired from the English League in 1977 after a career total of 900 competitive games.

Played briefly in the USA first with San Antonio Thunder and then with Seattle Sounders.

Became manager of Southend United in 1984 before leaving the post two years later.

Went on to become a respected football analyst for a London radio station.

Died in 1993 after a long and courageous fight against cancer. He was just 53-years old .

Stan Mortensen...

Joined the RAF as a wireless operator at the start of the Second World War and was the only survivor when his bomber plane crashed in 1940.

After scoring dozens of goals during the war he was an England reserve in a match against Wales at Wembley in 1943. However, because Wales did not have a substitute of their own he took to the field for them!

Made his full international debut for England against Portugal in Lisbon in 1947 and promptly scored four goals.

Scored Blackpool's second goal in the 4-2 defeat by Manchester United in the 1948 FA Cup Final.

Represented England in their first ever World Cup finals, but was dumped out of the tournament by the unfancied USA who won 1-0.

Played again in an FA Cup Final, again losing it, this time 2-0 to Newcastle.

Played at Wembley in the 1953 FA Cup Final and, despite scoring a hat-trick in the 4-3 win over Bolton, the final has since been billed as the 'Matthews Final' in honour of his team mate Stanley Matthews.

Scored his 23rd, and last, international goal and won his 25th cap for England in the 6-3 defeat by Hungary in 1953.

Left Blackpool after scoring 197 League goals and 30 in the Cup and joined Hull.

Moved to Southport in 1957 before playing non-League football with Bath and then Lancaster.

Stan Mortensen...

Returned to Blackpool in 1967 to begin a two year stint as manager.

Made a freeman of Blackpool in 1989 after auctioning his medals to help raise money for the club during desperate times.

Died in 1991, just before his 70th birthday. More than 700 people attended his funeral in the town.

Alan Morton...

Joined Queens Park as an amateur in 1913 and earned himself the nickname 'The Wee Blue Devil' from an admiring English journalist.

Made his international debut for Scotland in 1920 in a 1-1 draw with Wales in Cardiff.

Earned his second cap in the 3-0 victory over Northern Ireland.

Turned professional in 1920 and became the first signing by Rangers' long-serving manager Will Struth.

Won his first Championship title with Rangers in 1921.

Played with the team known as the 'Wembley Wizards' as they beat England 5-1 in 1928. Three of the goals came from inch perfect crosses by Morton.

Played in the Scottish FA Cup Final in 1928 when a crowd of 118,000 saw Rangers thrash Celtic 4-0.

Won the last of his 31 caps as a 39-year old in a 3-1 win against France in 1932.

Won his second Scottish FA Cup medal as Rangers beat Partick Thistle in the 1932 Final.

Retired from playing in 1933, appearing 495 times for the club, scoring 115 goals. He had won the Championship nine times and Scottish FA Cup three times.

Became a director of the Ibrox club until he stepped down in 1968.

Died in Glasgow in 1971 at the age of 78.

Gerd Müller...

Joined Bayern Munich in 1964 from TSV Nordlingen at the insistence of club president Wilhelm Neudecker. The coach, Tschik Cajkovski, was not impressed, saying: "I can't put that little elephant in among my string of thoroughbreds." It's amazing to think he was so wrong!

Won the West German cup in 1966 with a 4-2 victory over Meideriecher SV.

Made his international debut in the 2-0 win over Turkey in Ankara in 1966.

Won the 1967 European Cup Winners' Cup with an extra-time victory over Rangers in Nuremberg.

Was voted Germany's Footballer of the Year.

Also finished top scorer in the German League with 28 goals, an accolade he was to collect again in 1968, 1970, 1972, 1973, 1974 (jointly) and 1978. Earning himself the nickname 'Der Bomber'.

Won the first of his five League Championships with Bayern Munich in 1969.

Was top scorer with 10 goals in the 1970 World Cup finals in Mexico, including two in the semi-final defeat by Italy.

Was voted European Footballer of the Year in 1970, the first time this award had been given to a German player.

Helped West Germany win the European Championships in 1972, scoring two goals in the 3-0 win over the USSR.

Gerd Müller...

Won the first of three successive European Champions Cups with Bayern Munich, scoring two goals in the 4-0 replay win over Spanish champions Atletico Madrid.

Scored the winning goal in the 1974 World Cup Final against Holland in his home club stadium in Munich. He retired from international football following this game, having scored an incredible 68 goals in 62 international matches, easily making him the country's leading goalscorer ever. He also holds the record for more World Cup finals goals – 14 – than any other player.

Helped West Germany to the Final of the 1976 European Championships, scoring one of their goals in the 2-2 draw with Czechoslovakia. (The Czechs went on to win 5-3 on penalties.) In scoring in this game he became the only man to have scored in two European Championship Finals, the other being in 1972.

Won the World Club Cup in 1976 as Bayern beat Cruzeiro of Brazil.

Quit Bayern in 1979 after playing 427 League games and scoring a record 365 Bundesliga goals.

Played for Fort Lauderdale Strikers in the newly formed NASL.

Returned to Germany in 1995 to take up a job on the coaching staff of Bayern Munich.

Johan Neeskens...

Made his League debut with Haarlem in 1968.

Played his first international game in 1970.

Moved to Ajax and helped them win the 1971 European Champions Cup with a 2-0 victory over Panathinaikos at Wembley.

Was the heart of the entertaining 'Total Football' developed by Ajax in the Seventies.

Won the Champions Cup again in 1972 with a 2-0 win over Inter Milan in Rotterdam.

Completed a hat-trick of Champions Cup wins by beating Juventus 1-0 in the final in Belgrade in 1973.

Scored the fastest ever goal in a World Cup Final when, in 1974, his Dutch team mate Johan Cruyff dribbled the ball into the West German penalty area straight from kick off and was brought down in the box. English referee Jack Taylor awarded a penalty, the first in a World Cup Final, and Neeskens put the ball past Sepp Maier. No German player had touched the ball and they were already losing! The joy was short-lived however as the host nation came back to win 2-1. Neeskens finished third top scorer in the tournament with four goals.

Moved to Barcelona in 1975, following his Ajax team mate Johan Cruyff.

Won the Spanish Cup in 1978, his only trophy in Spain.

Johan Neeskens...

Appeared in his second World Cup Final in 1978, when, once again, Holland lost to the host nation, this time Argentina beat them 3-1.

Helped Barcelona win the 1979 European Cup Winners' Cup, beating Fortuna Dusseldorf 4-3 after extra-time.

Played his 49th, and last, game for Holland in 1981, during which time he had scored 17 international goals.

Moved to the NASL in 1981, playing for New York Cosmos, before moving to Switzerland in an ill-fated attempt at a European comeback.

Gunter Netzer...

Joined Borussia Möenchengladbach in 1961 and became a key midfield player in Hennes Weisweiler's team.

Won his first international cap against Austria in 1965.

Won his first domestic honour when Borussia won the League Championship in 1970, and then again in 1971.

Partnered Franz Beckenbauer in midfield as West Germany won the 1972 European Nations Championship with a 3-0 win over the Soviet Union in the Final.

Won the Footballer of the Year award in 1972.

Won the West German Cup with Borussia in 1973.

Voted Footballer of the Year for a second consecutive year in 1973.

Appeared for West Germany in the 1-0 defeat by East Germany in the first round of the 1974 World Cup finals and lost his place to Wolfgang Overath. West Germany went on to win the tournament by beating Holland 2-1 in the Final.

Transferred to Spanish side Real Madrid in 1974.

Won the Spanish League and Cup double with Real Madrid in 1975.

Helped retain the Spanish title the following year.

Moved to Switzerland and Grasshoppers for a season in 1977 before returning to Germany and becoming General Manager of Hamburg.

Wolfgang Overath...

Turned professional with Köln in 1961.

Key member of the Köln side which won the first Bundesliga Championship.

Made his international debut for West Germany in 1963, coming on as a substitute in the 3-0 win over Turkey in Frankfurt.

Played in the 1966 World Cup Final but lost to England 4-2 after extra-time.

Starred in the 1970 World Cup finals in Mexico, scoring the only goal of the game against Uruguay to decide third place.

Was dropped from the national team in favour of Gunter Netzer after a disappointing 0-0 draw at home to Poland in a 1971 qualifying game for the European Championships.

Regained his place from Netzer in time to take part in the 2-1 World Cup Final victory over Holland in 1974. In doing so he became one of just a few players to have finished winner, runner-up and third in World Cup finals.

Retired from international football after the 1974 World Cup, having scored 17 goals in 81 games for West Germany.

Retired from club football in 1977 having played 409 League games and scored 83 goals for Köln, his only club.

Was honoured with selection for the World XI which played Brazil in a friendly in Rio de Janeiro in 1978.

Michael Owen...

Scored on his Liverpool debut against Wimbledon in May 1997.

Finished the 1997/98 season, his first full season, as joint top scorer in the Premiership with 18 League goals.

Was voted Young Player of the Year by both the PFA and the Football Writer's Association.

Scored on his debut in the League Cup and FA Cup.

Made his England debut at Wembley against Chile in February 1998 aged just 18 years and 59 days. He was the youngest player ever to play for England.

Scored his first international goal in his third game for England, against Morocco just three months later. He was 18 years and 166 days old and so became the youngest player to score for England, beating Tommy Lawton's record set in 1938.

Played for England in the 1998 World Cup finals and scored in his second game of the tournament against Romania. He then went on to score what was arguably the best goal of the finals against Argentina, before losing out to the South Americans on penalties.

Daniel Passarella...

Played for Argentinian sides Sarmiento and River Plate before moving to Italy to play for Fiorentina and Inter Milan.

Played 65 times for Argentina between 1976 and 1985, and became the first Argentinian captain to lead his side to success in the World Cup when he lifted the trophy on home soil in 1978.

Scored an impressive 20 goals for his country, despite the fact that he was a defender.

Retired from playing and returned to Argentina to coach River Plate.

Took over coaching the national team after the World Cup in 1994 and immediately insisted that he would not pick players with long hair!

Left the position of national coach after the quarter-final defeat by Holland in the 1998 World Cup finals.

Stuart Pearce...

Is an electrician by trade and began his career at non-League Wealdstone.

Made his professional debut for Coventry City in 1983 aged 21 and played 52 League games for the 'Sky Blues', scoring 4 goals.

Moved to Nottingham Forest in 1985 where he earned the nickname 'Psycho' for his uncompromising defensive skills.

Made his international debut in 1987.

Won the 1989 League Cup Final, beating Luton Town 3-1 at Wembley.

Helped retain the trophy by beating Oldham Athletic 1-0 the following year.

Missed a penalty in the 1990 World Cup finals shoot-out with West Germany in the semi-final.

Suffered relegation with Nottingham Forest in 1993, but helped them straight back up the following year.

Scored a penalty in the 1996 European Championship quarter-final shoot-out against Spain, and then again in the semi-final against Germany. (Unfortunately Gareth Southgate missed his!)

Was relegated again with Forest in 1997 and left to join Kenny Dalglish at Newcastle.

Played over 400 League games with Nottingham Forest, scoring 62 goals, many of them penalties.

Pele...

Full name is Edson Arantes do Nascimento.

Began playing football in 1950 with local club Bauru, where his father was a coach.

Transferred to Santos in 1956 and made his League debut at the age of 15.

Scored on his 1957 international debut against Argentina, still just 16 years old.

Played in the 1958 World Cup Final, scoring two goals as Brazil beat the hosts Sweden 5-2. He had already scored a hat-trick in the 5-2 semi-final thrashing of France.

Played in the 1962 World Cup finals but missed the Final win against Czechoslovakia because of an injury he sustained in the first round.

Won the World Club Cup with Santos in 1962, and again in 1963.

Scored his 1,000th senior goal in November 1969 when he slotted home a penalty for Santos against Vasco da Gama.

Inspired Brazil to their third World Cup Final success in

Pele...

1970, scoring the opening goal in the 4-1 thrashing of Italy.

Won the last of his record 111 international caps in 1971 having scored 97 goals. (Using stricter international definition the figures would read 92 caps and 77 goals.)

Retired from the game in 1974.
Tempted back eighteen months later to play for the New York Cosmos in the new NASL in America.

After helping Cosmos to their third title in 1977 he retired permanently from a career in which he had scored 1282 goals in 1363 matches.

Was awarded the FIFA Gold Medal Award for outstanding service to the worldwide game in 1982.

Was appointed Brazil's Minister for Sport in 1994.

Emmanuel Petit...

Made his League debut for Monaco in 1988.

Was voted the French Young Player of the Year in 1990.

Won the French Cup with Monaco in 1991 under the guidance of current Arsenal manager Arsen Wenger.

Helped Monaco win their first League title in almost a decade in 1997 before moving to Arsenal for £3.5 million. He had played 222 league games for the Monte-Carlo team, scoring just 4 goals.

Helped Arsenal win the League and FA Cup double 1998.

Played an impressive part in winning the 1998 World Cup Final with France, scoring the third goal in the shock 3-0 victory over Brazil in the Stade de France, Paris.

Has one of the worst discipline records in the Carling Premiership.

Martin Peters...

Made his West Ham debut in 1961.

Helped the 'Hammers' win the 1965 European Cup Winners' Cup Final at Wembley, beating German side Munich 1860 2-0. It was West Ham's first and only European trophy.

Made his England debut in 1966, going on to star in the victorious England squad that beat West Germany in the World Cup Final in July of that year. If German defender Weber hadn't scored a last-minute equaliser then he would have been immortalised as the man who scored England's World Cup winning goal, having scored to make it 2-1. However, the Germans did level the scores and Geoff Hurst took all the goal-scoring headlines.

Played 302 League games for West Ham, scoring 81 goals before transferring to Tottenham Hotspur in March 1970, a move which saw England colleague and member of the 1966 World Cup squad, Jimmy Greaves, go the other way.

Won the 1971 League Cup Final with a 2-0 win over Aston Villa.

Played a vital part in the 3-2 aggregate defeat of Wolves in the 1972 two-legged UEFA Cup Final. This was to be the first and

Martin Peters...

only time that two English teams faced each other in a final of a major European competition.

Won the League Cup final again in 1973, beating Norwich City 1-0.

Played his final game for England in 1974, notching up 20 goals in his 67 appearances.

Left Spurs in 1975, after 189 League games and 46 goals, to join Norwich where he played 207 League games and scored 44 goals.

He was awarded an MBE in the 1978 New Years Honours List.

He moved to Sheffield United as player/coach in 1980 but this proved unsuccessful and he quit the game to work in the insurance business.

Michel Platini...

Joined French club Nancy from his local side AS Joeuf in 1972.

Appeared for France in the 1976 Olympic Games in Montreal.

Played in the 1978 World Cup finals in Argentina, where he gave some indication of the great things to come.

Moved to St Etienne in 1979.

Helped France achieve fourth place in the 1982 World Cup finals in Spain. He was man of the match in the dramatic semi-final defeat by West Germany in Seville. (At one stage France led 3-1).

Transferred to Juventus immediately after the tournament for £1.2 million.

Was Italy's top scorer in 1983 and was voted European Footballer of the Year for the first time.

Scored a record nine goals as France won the 1984 European Championships on home territory. He scored the first goal from a free kick in the 2-0 defeat of Spain in the Final at the Parc de Princes in Paris.

Was once again Italy's top scorer in 1984 and for the second consecutive year won the European Footballer of the Year award.

Scored a penalty, the only goal of the game, in the 1985 European Champions Cup Final victory over Liverpool. Celebrations were, quite rightly, overshadowed by the Heysel tragedy.

Michel Platini...

Again finished up Italy's top scorer for the third year in a row and then went on to become the European Footballer of the Year for an unprecedented third consecutive year.

Shocked the football world in 1997 by announcing his retirement from the game while still comparatively young in order to concentrate on his growing commercial interests and television work.

He had scored 348 goals in 648 matches, including 41 international goals in 72 appearances for France.

Was persuaded to return to football in 1990 as national team manager and guided France to the finals of the 1992 European Championships. He left after the tournament to become joint head of the team set up to organise the 1998 World Cup finals being held in France.

Turned down the chance in 1996, to have the new World Cup stadium in Paris named after him. It became the Stade de France instead.

Was present at every game played during France 1998 except eight group matches.

David Platt...

Made his League debut for Crewe Alexandra in 1984.

Played 134 League games and scored 56 goals for the club before he was transferred to Aston Villa for £200,000 in 1988.

Made his England debut in 1989.

Volleyed home a spectacular shot in the last minute of extra-time against Belgium to put England through to the quarter-finals of the 1990 World Cup finals in Italy.

Voted the PFA Player of the Year in 1990.

Moved abroad to Italian side Bari for £5.5 million in 1991 after making 121 League appearances and scoring 50 goals for Aston Villa.

Played 29 League games for Bari, in which he scored 11 goals, he transferred to Juventus for £6.5 million in 1992.

David Platt...

Appeared in just 16 League games and scored 3 goals for the Turin side before he moved to yet another Italian club, Sampdoria, for £4.5 million in 1993. With the cost of his wages added on to the transfer loss, his goals for Juventus worked out at close to £1 million each!

Stayed at Sampdoria for two years, making 55 League appearances and scoring 17 goals before returning to England with Arsenal in 1995 for £4.8 million.

Finally won some trophies when he helped Arsenal to a League and FA Cup double in 1998, before finally hanging his boots at a relatively young age to take time out to travel the world to learn different coaching techniques.

Made 62 appearances for England, and scored 27 goals, impressive figures for a midfield player.

Returned briefly to Sampdoria in 1998 as coach but was unable to make any real impact on their dire position. He left soon after to continue his coaching education.

Ferenc Puskas...

Made his debut in 1943 for his father's old club, Kispest.

Played his first international for Hungary against Austria as an 18-year old in 1945. He was to go on and score an amazing 83 international goals in just 84 appearances for Hungary before he defected to Spain in 1956.

Transferred, with the entire Kispest club, to the new army side, Honved in 1948. Became top scorer with 50 goals in the League championship, earning him the nickname 'Galloping Major'.

Captained Hungary to victory against Yugoslavia in the final of the 1952 Olympic Games soccer tournament in Helsinki.

Scored two goals against England in the historic 6-3 victory at Wembley in 1953, condemning the hosts to their first defeat by a foreign team at Wembley.

Played, despite injury, in the 1954 World Cup Final which they lost 3-2 to West Germany in Berne, despite being 2-0 in front at one stage. It was their first defeat in four years.

Stayed in western Europe whilst the army team played a European Cup tie against Spanish side Bilbao at the start of the Hungarian Revolution in 1956.

Signed for his old Honved manager, Emil Oestreicher, now at Real Madrid in 1958. He was Spain's top League scorer for four seasons.

Ferenc Puskas...

Scored four goals for Madrid as they demolished Eintracht Frankfurt 7-3 in the 1960 European Cup Final at Hampden Park, Glasgow. He was the first man to score four goals in a European Cup Final. Altogether he scored 35 goals in 39 European cup games for the Spanish team.

Scored a hat-trick in the 1962 European Cup Final against Benfica, but still ended up losing 5-3 to the Portugese Champions.

Played for his adopted country Spain in the 1962 World Cup finals in Chile.

Retired from playing in 1966 and took up coaching.

Guided unfancied Panathinaikos of Greece to the 1971 European Cup Final, losing to Ajax 2-0 at Wembley.

Appointed, briefly, as caretaker manager of Hungary in 1993.

Fabrizio Ravanelli...

Made his League debut for Perugia in 1986, and went on to play 90 League games for them, scoring 41 goals.

Left here in 1989 to play a handful of games for Avellino in 1989, by this time he had already gone grey, despite still being only 21.

Joined Casertana in 1989 where he played 27 times in the League and scored 12 goals.

Transferred to Reggiana in 1990 before moving to Juventus in 1992.

In his four-year spell at the Turin club he scored 44 goals in 115 Serie A games. He also scored all five goals in the 5-1 win over CSKA Sofia in a 1994 UEFA Cup tie.

Made his international debut in March 1995, scoring in the 4-1 win over Estonia in Salerno.

Won a Championship medal with Juventus in 1995.

Scored his last goal for Juventus in the 1996 European Cup Final against Ajax which they won on penalties after a 1-1 draw.

Transferred to Bryan Robson's Middlesbrough for £7 million in 1996, on wages reported to have been as high as £42,000 per week.

Suffered two cup final defeats and relegation with Middlesbrough before leaving just over a year later for Marseille for £5.5 million.

Frank Rijkaard...

Turned professional in 1979 with Ajax Amsterdam under the management of legendary Johan Cruyff.

Made his international debut in the 1981 match against Switzerland, despite protests from Ajax that, at 18, he was too young.

Won the European Cup Winners' Cup with Ajax in 1987 and then appointed club captain following the sale of Marco Van Basten to Milan.

Fell out with Johan Cruyff at the start of the 1987/88 season and hardly played for the club.

Was sold to Sporting Lisbon in the spring of 1988, and then on to Milan in the summer.

Played for Holland in the centre of defence whilst all this was going on and won the 1988 European Championships by beating the Soviet Union 2-0 in the Final in Munich.

Played in midfield as Milan won the 1989 European Champions Cup in Barcelona, beating Steaua Bucharest 4-0 in Barcelona, the biggest winning margin for a final for fifteen years.

Won a second successive European Champions Cup in 1990 by beating Benfica 1-0 in Vienna.

Frank Rijkaard...

Played for Holland in the 1990 World Cup finals, but the team failed to live up to expectations. He is sent off in a game against Germany.

Played his last game for Milan in the 1-0 defeat by Marseille in the 1993 European Champions Cup Final in Munich.

Returned to Holland and spent two years with Ajax, playing his last game in the 1995 European Champions Cup Final, helping his team beat his former club 1-0 in Vienna. In doing so he became one of just a few players to have won the competition with two different clubs.

Retired from playing in 1995.

Luigi Riva...

Started his playing career in 1960 with Italian Third Division club Legnano.

Was signed by Cagliari in 1963.

Made his international debut in 1965 and went on to score a record 35 goals for the national side in just 42 appearances.

Guided Cagliari to win the League Championship in 1970, their first and, to date, only trophy.

Finished top League scorer in Italy in that and two other seasons, and became known as 'the Rumble of Thunder'.

Played a key role in steering Italy to the 1970 World Cup finals.

Scored twice against the Mexican hosts in the tournament and another against West Germany before losing 4-1 to eventual winners Brazil.

Suffered two broken legs which ended his career in 1974.

Roberto Rivelino...

Played for Brazilian club sides Corinthians and then Fluminense.

Made his international debut in 1965.

Shot to prominence in the 1970 World Cup finals in Mexico.

Scored a goal after just three seconds in a Brazilian league game in the 1970s. He hit the ball over the head of the opposition's keeper who was still kneeling down praying when the ball went in.

Starred in the 1974 World Cup finals, and impressed the watching world with his 'banana shot' free kick which curled past a ducking teammate and into the net in the game against East Germany.

Played for Brazil again in the 1978 World Cup finals in Argentina.

Retired from international football after the 1978 tournament, having played 94 games for the South Americans and scoring 26 goals.

413

Bryan Robson...

Joined West Bromwich Albion from amateur football in 1975. Made his senior debut at 18-years old.

Played his first international in 1980. Went on to play 90 times for England, making him the fifth most capped Englishman of all time. His 26 goals from midfield puts him in eighth position in the goal scoring charts for ther national team.

Joined his former manager at Manchester United in October 1981 for a British record fee of £1.5 million, having played 198 League games for WBA and scored 39 goals.

Played for England in the 1982 World Cup finals in Spain and scored after just 27 seconds of England's opening game against France.

Captained Manchester United to a 4-0 thrashing of relegated Brighton in the 1983 FA Cup Final replay. The first game had finished 2-2.

Led England to victory against Turkey in 1984 and became the first England captain to score a hat-trick for seventy-five years.

Led Manchester United to a 1-0 win over Everton in the 1985 FA Cup Final at Wembley.

Dislocated his shoulder in a friendly before the 1986 World Cup finals, then sustained the same injury in England's second game of the tournament. the team went on to lose to Argentina in the quarter-final.

Inspired United to win the 1990 FA Cup Final, beating Crystal Palace 1-0 in a replay after an initial 3-3 draw.

Bryan Robson...

Missed the later stages of 1990 World Cup finals in Italy due to another injury.

Led Manchester United to victory over Spanish giants Barcelona in the 1991 European Cup Winners' Cup Final.

Was club captain when Manchester United won their first Championship title for 25 years in 1993, but only played 5 league games that season due to injury problems.

Left United after 13 years and 345 League games to become player/manager of Middlesbrough in 1994.

Led them back into the top flight with promotion as Champions of the new First Division into the Premiership in 1995.

Joined coach Terry Venables on a part-time basis as part of the backroom staff for the national team.

Took Middlesbrough to both the League Cup and FA Cup Finals in 1997 but lost them both, to make matters worse, they were also relegated.

Lost a third Wembley Final in two years, when they were beaten 2-0 by Chelsea in the 1998 League Cup Final.

Gained promotion back to the Premiership in 1998 after finishing 2nd in the First Division.

Romario...

Joined Olario Juniors in 1983.

Scored four goals in a game against Vasco da Gama in 1985 and impressed the club so much they signed him.

Played for Brazil in the 1988 Seoul Olympics and scored seven goals. Finished second in the competition, losing to Russia in extra-time.

Moved to Dutch side PSV Eindhoven in 1989 after having scored 73 goals in 123 games for Vasco da Gama.

Represented Brazil in the 1990 World Cup finals in Italy but was limited to just 65 minutes of football after attacking the selection policies of manager Carlos Parreira who later banned him from the Brazilian team.

Suffered a broken leg in 1991 which kept him out of the game for much of the year.

Scored 125 goals for PSV and won three League Championships in five seasons.

Fell-out with his team mates at PSV and complained about the weather so much that he was transferred to Barcelona for £3 million in 1993.

Promptly scored a hat-trick in his first game for Johan Cruyff's side.

Was recalled back into the Brazilian squad that faced Uruguay in a vital World Cup qualifying game in 1993. Scored both goals in the 2-0 win to book a place to America.

Romario...

Helped Barcelona win the Spanish league title in 1994 but could do nothing to stop Milan thrashing them 4-0 in the European Cup Final in the same season.

Scored a total of five goals in the World Cup finals in 1994, including an 81st minute winner against Sweden in the semi-final that sent Brazil through to the Final where they beat Italy.

Returned to Brazil in 1995 to play for Flamengo.

Scored the winner for Brazil against England during Le Tournoi competition in France in 1997.

Was in the Brazilian squad for the World Cup finals in 1998 but was forced to pull out on the eve of the tournament through injury.

Ronaldo...

Made his League debut for Brazilian side Sao Cristovao in 1991 where he played 54 League games and scored 36 goals.

Moved to Cruzerio in 1993 where he scored almost a goal a game in his 60 League appearances for the club.

Made his international debut in 1993 and was picked to join the World Cup finals squad to go to America.

Travelled to the USA with the national squad but did not make an appearance in the tournament.

Transferred to Dutch side PSV Eindhoven in 1994 for a club record £5 million.

Scored 55 goals in just 56 League appearances for PSV.

Barcelona spent a world record £13 million in 1996 to lure

Ronaldo...

him to the Nou Camp stadium.

He scored 34 goals in 36 League games and won the Spanish Cup and European Cup Winners' Cup.

Moved to Italy and Inter Milan in 1997 for yet another world record fee, £18 million.

He won the European Player of the Year award and the FIFA World Player of the Year in 1997.

Signed a multi-million pound deal with sportswear giants Nike in 1997.
Won the 1998 UEFA Cup with Inter Milan, scoring in the Final against Lazio.

Became the first player to win the FIFA World Player of the Year two years running when he won it in 1998.

Scored four goals for Brazil in the 1998 World Cup finals, helping his country reach the Final against France. He was taken to hospital on the day of the match suffering from what was claimed to have been a stress-related epileptic fit.

Paolo Rossi...

Moved from Prato to the Juventus youth system in 1972.

After two knee operations Juventus released him on a free transfer to Como.

Signed for Serie B team Lanerossi Vicenza in 1976 and shot them to promotion with 21 goals in just 36 League games.

Made his international debut in 1977.

Starred for Italy in the 1978 World Cup finals, scoring in the games against France, Hungary and Austria.

Joined Serie A side Perugia for a world record £3.5 million in 1979.

Received a two-year suspension and the club were relegated to Serie B after being convicted in 1980 of alleged involvement in a betting scandal which rocked Italian football.

Bought by Juventus for £650,000 midway through his suspension.

Returned to the pitch in 1982 and, after just three games back, was recalled to the national team for the World Cup finals.

Was top scorer in the tournament with six goals, including a hat-trick against Brazil in the quarter-final and the opening goal in the Final victory over West Germany in Madrid.

Paolo Rossi...

Was voted European and World Footballer of the Year in 1982.

Helped Juventus win the 1984 Cup Winners' Cup Final with a 2-1 win over Porto.

Was a member of the winning Juventus team over Liverpool in the 1985 European Champions Cup, a match marred by the Heysel stadium tragedy.

Won the World Club Cup with Juventus in 1986.

Played his last international in 1986, finishing on 20 goals from 48 appearances for his country.

Retired at the age of 29 because of recurring knee trouble and moved to Spain to become a scout for the national team (Spain's team that is – not Italy's!)

Rummenigge...

Gave up his job as a bank clerk in 1974 when Bayern Munich paid Lippstadt £4,500 for their young star.

Collected his only European Champions Cup winners' medal in 1976 as Bayern beat French side St Etienne 1-0 in Glasgow. Went on to win the World Club Cup against Cruzeiro of Brazil later in the year.

Made his international debut in 1976 against Wales.

Scored twice for West Germany in the 6-0 win over Mexico in the 1978 World Cup finals in Argentina, followed by another goal in the 3-2 defeat by Austria.

Won the 1980 European Championship with West Germany, providing the corner from which Horst Hrubesch headed the injury-time winner in the Final against Belgium in Rome.

Won the European Footballer of the Year award in 1980, and again in 1981.

Netted twice against England at Wembley in a friendly match.

Captained West Germany in the 1982 World Cup finals, helping his country come from 3-1 down against France in the semi-final to draw 3-3 before winning on penalties. Lost to Italy in the Final.

Moved to Inter Milan for £2 million in 1984.

Finished as a runner-up again in the 1986 World Cup Final, being beaten 3-2 by Diego Maradona's Argentina.

Moved to Swiss side Servette Geneva in 1987 before retiring in 1989 to take up a career as a TV commentator.

Ian Rush...

Joined Chester in 1978 and made his debut as a 17-year old.

Transferred to Liverpool in 1980 for a bargain £300,000 when still only 19.

Played his first game for Wales in 1980.

Won his first medal, the 1981 League Cup, when he deputised for the injured Steve Heighway in the 2-1 replay win over West Ham United.

Won the League Championship and League Cup in 1982.

Won them both again in 1983.

Won a fourth League Cup in 1984, together with a third League Championships and the European Cup. Scored 47 goals in all competitions in this season, setting a new Liverpool record, and, not surprisingly, was voted Footballer of the Year.

Won his fourth league title with Liverpool in 1986, together with the FA Cup with a 3-1 win over Everton, scoring two of the goals.

Was a loser in the 1987 League Cup Final despite scoring Liverpool's goal in the 2-1 defeat by Arsenal. It was the first time Liverpool had lost a game after he had scored.

Moved to Juventus for £3.2 million in 1987.

Ian Rush...

Didn't settle in Italy, complaining that he had only scored seven League goals in a season because "It was like being in a foreign country out there."

Returned to Liverpool for £2.8 million in 1988.

Missed most of the 1988/89 season through illness but returned in time to come on as a substitute and score two FA Cup Final goals in the 3-2 victory over Everton.

Won his fifth League Championship in 1990.

Scored his fifth FA Cup Final goal in 1992 against Sunderland and picked up his third winners' medal. No other player has scored as many goals in FA Cup Finals.

Captained the Liverpool side to win the 1995 League Cup against Bolton Wanderers, for a record fifth time.

Finished his Liverpool career in 1996, being the club's highest scorer. Joined Leeds United but only scored three goals in the whole season.

Moved to Newcastle United in 1997 to team up with former Anfield boss Kenny Dalglish.

Has scored more FA Cup goals, 43, than any other player.

Is equal top scorer in the League Cup with 46, the same as England's 1966 World Cup hero Geoff Hurst.

Played 73 times for Wales, becoming the fourth most capped Welshman in history. His 28 goals tops the goal scoring charts for his country.

Ian St. John...

Began his career at Motherwell in 1959.

Scored 80 League goals for the Scottish club, including a hat-trick in just 2 and a half minutes – the fastest ever in Scottish football.

Played his first game for Scotland in 1959.

Signed for Liverpool in 1961 for £35,000, becoming the Anfield club's most expensive signing.

Scored 18 League goals in his first season for Liverpool, helping them win promotion as Second Division Champions.

Scored the winning goal against Leeds United in the 1965 FA Cup Final, helping Liverpool win the trophy for the first time.

Played a total of 419 games, 336 in the League and scored 118 goals, 95 in the League.

Played his 21st and last game for Scotland in 1965, scoring 9 international goals.

Moved to Coventry City in 1971 and then briefly on to Tranmere Rovers a year later.

Since retiring from playing football he has carved out a successful career as a television pundit.

Matthias Sammer...

Made his League debut for Dynamo Dresden in 1985.

Played his first international game in 1988.

Won two League titles with Dresden in 1989 and 1990.

Moved to VFB Stuttgart in 1990.

Became the first East German to play for the new united Germany national team in 1990.

Won the Bundesliga in 1992 with VFB.

Moved to Italy and Inter Milan in 1992 but after just 11 League games returned to Germany for the start of a highly successful spell with Borussia Dortmund.

Won the Bundesliga with Borussia in 1995 and was voted Germany's Player of the Year at the end of the campaign.

Retained both the League title and Player of the Year award the following year.

Also captained Borussia to their first ever European Cup Final victory when they beat Juventus 3-1 in 1996 in Munich.

Captained Germany to victory in the 1996 European Championships.

Was, in 1997, the fifth German, but the first from the former East Germany, to be voted European Footballer of the Year.

Missed most of the 1997/98 season through an ankle injury and was left out of the World Cup finals in France.

Peter Schmeichel...

Joined his local club Gladsaxe Hero in 1975.

Moved to Hvidovre in 1984.

Made his debut for Denmark Under -21s in 1984.

Transferred to Bronby in 1987.

Made his first full international appearance in the 5-0 win over Greece in 1987.

Won the Danish Championship with Bronby in 1988.

Kept goal for Denmark in the Olympic Games qualifying tournament.

Won the Danish Cup with Bronby in 1989.

Transferred to Manchester United in 1991 for £550,000 and made his debut in August in a 2-0 win over Notts County.

Appeared for Denmark in the 1992 European Championships and ended up a surprise winner in the Final against Germany.

Won his first English Championship title with Manchester United in 1993, their first title since 1967.

Won the Championship again in 1994, together with the FA Cup, thanks to a 4-0 thrashing of Chelsea.

Peter Schmeichel...

Was a runner-up in League in 1995, and finished up a Wembley loser when Everton beat United in the FA Cup Final.

Scored a goal in the 1995/96 UEFA Cup campaign for United. He came up for a corner and headed the goal past Rotor Volgograd's keeper, United still lost the tie and went out of the competition.

Was a member of the United side to win the League and FA Cup double in 1996, their second double in just three seasons.

Represented Denmark in the 1996 European Championships in England.

Won his fourth Championship in five years with United in 1997 and reached the semi-finals of the European Cup.

Helped Denmark reach the 1998 World Cup finals in France. Earning his 125th cap during the tournament. He is, by far, Denmark's most-capped player.

Announced his intention to quit Manchester United at the end of the 1998/99 season to go and play elsewhere in Europe. He blames the stress and tension of playing too much top class football is damaging the quality of his life!

Paul Scholes...

Joined local club Manchester United in 1994 and has not looked back since.

Won a League Championship title with United in 1996 and the FA Cup thanks to a victory over 1-0 victory over Liverpool, to complete a double.

Made his full England debut against Italy in Le Tournoi in June 1997. He scored one goal and laid on the other for strike partner Ian Wright as England won 2-0.

Picked up his second Championship title in 1997.

Scored England's first goal in the 4-0 win over Moldova in a World Cup qualifying game in September 1997.

Replaced Paul Gascoigne in the England squad to play in France, he scored a match-winning goal from the edge of the box against Tunisia.

Scored an impressive hat-trick in England's 3-1 win against Poland in a European Championships qualifying game in March 1999.

David Seaman...

Joined Leeds United in 1981 but failed to make the first team.

Transferred to Peterborough in 1982, where he played 91 League games.

Moved to Birmingham City in 1984 and played 75 League games for the Midlands club.

Joined London club Queens Park Rangers in 1986 and it was while at this club he made his England debut in 1989.

He also impressed Arsenal and, after paying £1.3 million, a record English fee for a keeper, he moved across London to join them in 1990.

Won the League Championship in his first season, conceding just 18 goals in the entire League campaign, the fewest for a First Division in over a decade.

Won both the FA Cup and League Cup in 1993, both against Sheffield Wednesday and both 2-1, although the FA Cup did take a replay.

Helped the Gunners win the European Cup Winners' Cup Final in 1994 with a 1-0 victory over Parma.

Was considered by some people to have been at fault when former Spurs player, Nayim, lobbed him from the halfway line in the last minute of the 1995 European Cup

David Seaman...

Winners' Cup Final to ensure a 2-1 defeat by Real Zaragoza.

Kept goal for England during the 1996 European Championships.

Won a second League title with Arsenal in 1988 and, thanks to a 2-0 win over Newcastle in the FA Cup Final, made this another double year for the Gunners.

Played heroically during the 1998 World Cup finals in France and even saved a penalty in the shoot-out against Argentina. (Unfortunately his opposite number, Carlos Roa, saved two!)

Uwe Seeler...

Joined his father's old club, Hamburg, as a 15-year old in 1952.

Made his first international appearance as a 17-year old. Coming on as a substitute for Termath in a match against France in 1954.

Made his first international start in the 3-1 defeat by England at Wembley a short time later.

Played in the 1958 World Cup finals, reaching the semi-final before being beaten by hosts Sweden.

Won his only German League Championship with Hamburg.

Was voted Germany's Footballer of the Year in 1960.

Reached the semi-final of the European Champions Cup in 1961 but lost to Barcelona.

Won the 1963 German Cup with Hamburg.

Uwe Seeler...

Was top scorer in the first ever unified Bundesliga in 1964 with 30 goals.

Was voted Germany's Footballer of the Year for the second time in 1964.

Captained West Germany in the 1966 World Cup Final defeat against England.

Captained Hamburg in the final of the 1968 European Cup Winners' Cup but were defeated 2-0 by AC Milan.

Scored a cheeky back-headed goal past England keeper Peter Bonetti in the quarter-final of the 1970 World Cup. This levelled the scores at 2-2 and enabled the Germans to push for a dramatic extra-time winner. This was the fourth World Cup finals he had scored in.

In total he played for West Germany 72 times, scoring 43 international goals.

Was voted Germany's Player of the Year for the third time in 1970.

Retired from playing in 1971, staying with Hamburg since 1952, rejecting numerous offers from Italian and Spanish clubs. He had played 239 league games for the club, scoring 137 goals.

Returned to Hamburg in 1996 to become club president.

Len Shackleton...

Was nicknamed the 'Clown Prince of Soccer' for his love of practical jokes.

Played for Bradford Park Avenue between 1940 and 1946.

Transferred to Newcastle for £13,000 in 1946, at the time making him the third most expensive player in English football.

Scored six goals on his debut for Newcastle in a 13-0 rout of Newport County. "And they were lucky to get nil," he was reported to have said afterwards.

Transferred to neighbouring Sunderland for £22,000 a year later, after playing 57 League games and scoring 26 goals for the Magpies.

Stayed with Sunderland for ten years before being forced to quit in 1958. He had made 320 League appearances for the club and scored 98 goals.

Became a journalist and is reported to have tipped Derby County to employing Brian Clough as a manager.

Alan Shearer...

Once had a schoolboy trial with Newcastle United as a goalkeeper, but was rejected as not being good enough.

Joined Southampton as a striker from minor soccer in his native North-East in 1986.

Made his League debut in March 1988 and promptly scored a hat-trick against Chelsea. At 17-years and 240 days he became the youngest First Division player to do do in his first full game.

Made his England Under-21 debut in 1991 and scored 13 goals in 11 international matches.

Made his full international debut in 1992 and scored a goal against France.

Was kept out of England's squad for the 1992 European Championships through a knee injury.

Joined Blackburn Rovers for £3.3 million, a British record fee, in 1992, having played 118 League games for the Saints and scoring 23 goals.

Hurt his knee again in a Boxing Day game in 1992 and did not play for eight months.

Finished the 1993/94 season with 31 League goals in 40 matches.

Helped Blackburn win their first Championship title for the first time since 1914 when he lifted the trophy in May 1995.

Alan Shearer...

Was voted the Player of the Year in 1995.

Scored 31 League goals in the 1995/96 season, becoming only the second player ever to pass the 30 goal mark in three consecutive seasons.

Starred for England in the 1996 European Championships, scoring two goals in the 4-1 thrashing of Holland and the quickest goal of the finals, after just two minutes, in the semi-final game against Germany. Prior to this he hadn't scored an international goal for 12 games, spanning 2 years.

He finished top scorer with five goals, two more than any other player.

Sold to Kevin Keegan at Newcastle immediately after the tournament. The fee of £15 million was almost double the current record for an English player.

Was made England captain by new national team manager Glenn Hoddle.

Scored 25 goals in 31 League games for the Magpies in 1997 to become the Premiership's top scorer again.

Suffered a horrific ankle injury at the start of the 1997/98 season but on his return scored a goal in his first full game back.

Peter Shilton...

Made his League debut for Leicester City in 1965 as a 16-year old.

Played in his one and only FA Cup Final, a 1-0 defeat by Manchester City in 1969.

Made his England debut between the sticks in 1971 in a game against East Germany.

Played 286 League games for Leicester City.

Joined Stoke City in 1974 as replacement for a certain Gordon Banks and spent three seasons with the club, playing 110 League games.

Transferred to Nottingham Forest in 1977, under the management of Brian Clough.

Won the League Championship in 1978.

Won the League Cup Final in 1979 with a 1-0 replay win over Liverpool.

Beat Malmo 1-0 to win the 1979 European Champions Cup.

Retained the title a year later by beating Kevin Keegan's Hamburg 1-0.

Played in the 1982 World Cup finals in Spain. England remained unbeaten in the competition and in five matches only conceded one goal.

Peter Shilton...

Moved from Nottingham Forest after 202 League games to Southampton in 1982 where he played a further 188 League games.

Played another all five England games in the 1986 World Cup finals in Mexico. England lost to Argentina in the quarter-final, thanks partly to the 'Hand of God' goal by Diego Maradona.

Moved to Derby County in 1987 and played 175 League games for the Rams.

Made his last appearance for England in 1990 in the World Cup third/fourth play-off match. He had played in 17 World Cup finals matches.

Played for England a record 125 times, a figure which would have been a lot higher had he not been alternating with Ray Clemence during Ron Greenwood's reign as England manager. He only conceded 80 goals for England, and kept a record 65 clean sheets.

Became player/manager of Plymouth Argyle in 1992 and played 34 times for the club. He was not considered to be as good a manager as he was a keeper though and was sacked three years later.

After brief on-loan spells with Bolton, where he played one League game, and West Ham where he was wanted as cover during an injury crisis involving their regular keepers but not used, he joined Leyton Orient for 10 games. During his time here he played his 1,000th League match on 22nd December 1996 in a 2-0 victory over Brighton.

Was released by Leyton Orient because he "couldn't kick the ball far enough," according to manager Pat Holland.

Socrates...

Made his international debut for Brazil in 1979.

Scored his first (and second) international goals in the 5-1 thrashing of Uruguay in Rio in 1979.

Captained his country in the 1982 World Cup finals in Spain, scoring his country's opening goal in the 2-1 victory over the Soviet Union.

Captained Brazil again in the 1986 World Cup finals in Mexico and again scored the South American's first goal, this time in the 1-0 win over Spain.

Like many of his compratriots, he was a heavy smoker, getting through three packets a day. He should have known better really, he was actually a qualified doctor!

Graeme Souness...

Having already played for Scotland Boys, he joined Tottenham Hotspur as an apprentice in 1969.

Turned professional with the club in 1970 but was limited to just one appearance as a sub in a 1971 UEFA Cup tie.

Joined Middlesbrough for £32,000 in 1973 and went on to play 176 League games for the club, scoring 22 goals.

Made his Scotland debut in a game against East Germany in 1974.

Transferred to Liverpool in 1978 for a record fee of £352,000.

Played 247 League games for the club, scoring 38 goals.

Won five League Championships, three European Cups and four League Cups in his time at Anfield.

Moved to Italian club Sampdoria in 1984 where he went on to win the Italian Cup.

Returned to Scotland as Ranger's first ever player/ manager in April 1986. Entrusted with vast amounts of money, he bought big signings from south of the border.

Won the last of his 54 Scottish caps in a 1986 World Cup finals game against West Germany. He had scored just 3 international goals.

Having won four League titles in Scotland and setting up a system which would guarantee success for years to come he was lured back to his beloved Liverpool after the shock resignation of Kenny Dalglish in 1991.

Graeme Souness...

Underwent extensive heart surgery in 1992, weeks before seeing his Liverpool side beat Sunderland 2-0 in the FA Cup Final.

Resigned as manager of Liverpool in January 1994.

Took over as boss of Turkish side Galatasaray in 1995 where he won the Turkish Cup.

Returned to England and took over as manager of Premiership side Southampton in 1996, becoming only their eleventh manager since the war.

Resigned in 1997 to take up an appointment with Italian club Torino. When the board failed to keep their promises he left to take over the manager's job at cash-strapped Portugese club Benfica.

Neville Southall...

After working as a dustman, he made his League debut for Bury in 1980.

After playing 39 League games for the club he was signed by Everton in 1981.

Was loaned out to Port Vale for nine games in the 1982/83 season.

Made his international debut in 1982.

Won the 1984 FA Cup with a 2-0 win over Watford, but missed out on the chance of a cup double by losing to Liverpool in the replay of the League Cup.

Finished as League Champions in 1985 and finished a magnificent season by beating Rapid Vienna 3-1 in the Final of the European Cup Winners' Cup. The only disappointment in this season was losing the FA Cup Final 1-0 to Manchester United.

Neville Southall...

Failed to win any trophies in 1986, finishing runners-up in the League and beaten 3-1 by Liverpool in the FA Cup Final.

Regained the top spot in the First Division with Everton in 1987.

Was beaten once again by Liverpool in the FA Cup Final in 1989, thanks mainly to Anfield legend Ian Rush. He came on as a substitute and scored twice to make it 3-2 to the Reds.
Had to wait until 1995 before playing in another Wembley final, this time Everton made no mistake against Manchester United and won 1-0. Despite being voted Man of the Match for his heroics he drove straight home to Wales after the match and missed the celebration party.

Played his 92nd and last game for Wales in 1997.

Moved to Stoke City in 1998 after losing his place in the Everton team.

Hristo Stoichkov...

Made his debut for Bulgarian team CSKA Sofia in 1984.

Banned for life by the Bulgarian Football Federation for becoming involved in a violent brawl during a domestic cup final between CSKA Sofia and Levski in 1985. However, because he was considered such an important player he was reinstated within six months.

Won his first international cap in 1987 in a match against Belgium.

Won the Bulgarian Footballer of the Year award in 1989.

Won three League titles with CSKA Sofia, playing in 119 League games and scoring a very respectable 81 goals.

Joined Barcelona for a Bulgarian record fee £2 million in 1990.

Was voted the Bulgarian Player of the Year for the second time in 1990.

Won Europe's Golden Boot award for 1990 after scoring 39 goals in the season, an award he shared with Real Madrid's Mexican star Hugo Sanchez.

Became Bulgaria's Player of the Year for a third consecutive year in 1991.

Helped Barcelona win the 1992 European Champions Cup 1-0 against Sampdoria at Wembley. He very nearly didn't play after falling out with coach Johan Cruyff over a transfer offer from Napoli.

Was runner-up to Roberto Baggio in the 1993 European Footballer of the Year award, a result he felt should have gone the other way.

Hristo Stoichkov...

Played for Bulgaria as they finished fourth in the 1994 World Cup finals in America. They had started badly, losing 3-0 to Nigeria but soon got their act together. He finished joint top scorer in the tournament with six goals.

Was finally awarded the European Footballer of the Year award in 1994.

Left Barcelona after four Spanish Championships and the European Cup. He had scored 104 goals but also collected 11 red cards.

Played for Italian side Parma for a year, scoring just 5 League goals in 24 appearances, before returning to Barcelona in 1996.

Captained Bulgaria in the 1996 European Championships but they were eliminated at the first round stage. He then boycotted the national team after falling out with the federation.

Came off the sub's bench in the 1997 European Cup Winners' Cup Final to help Barcelona beat Paris St.Germain 1-0.

Returned to his native Bulgaria in 1997 and rejoined his first club CSKA Sofia.

Made his peace with new national team coach Hristo Bonev in 1997 and helped Bulgaria qualify for the 1998 World Cup finals in France.

Has played 74 times for Bulgaria, scoring 35 international goals.

Frank Swift...

Made his debut in 1932, playing between the sticks for Manchester City, his one and only club.

Played in the FA Cup Final in 1934 and when the referee signalled the end of the game, and victory for City, the nervous 20-year old fainted on his goal-line.

Won the League Championship with City in 1937.

Was known as 'Big Swifty'.

Made his international debut with England in 1947 and went on to play for the national team 19 times in the next two years. He became the first goalkeeper to captain England.

Finally stopped playing altogether in 1949, after 338 League appearances for the club.

Became a respected coach and journalist.

Died whilst travelling with the Manchester United team in the Munich Air Crash in 1958.

John Toshack...

Made his League debut for Cardiff City in 1966.

Became part of the most successful Welsh side ever when Cardiff reached the semi-final of the European Cup Winners' Cup where they were unlucky to lose to Hamburger SV.

Made his Wales debut in 1969, and went on to play 40 international games, scoring 13 goals.

Played 162 League games for Cardiff City, scoring 75 goals.

Moved to Liverpool in 1970 to form a deadly strike partnership with Kevin Keegan. Together they helped the Anfield club win the FA Cup, the UEFA Cup and several Championships. He played 172 League games for Liverpool and scored 74 goals.

Returned to Wales in 1978 to become player/manager at Swansea City of the Fourth Division. He guided the Swans from the Fourth Division to sixth place in the First Division in his first four years at the club. Unfortunately, three years later he had led them back to the Third Division again!

Moved to Spain to take on the managers job at Real Madrid where he won the title in 1990.

Later had spells at Real Sociedad and Deportivo la Coruña.

In 1997 he moved to Turkey to take the helm at Besiktas.

Is always linked with the manager's job at Liverpool whenever there is a vacancy but, as yet, has not been tempted back to the club he had most success at.

Carlos Valderrama...

Joined his local club, Santa Marta, as a 16-year old in 1977.

Made his international debut in 1983.

Went on to play for Colombian club sides Millionarios and Atletico Nacional.

Starred for Colombia at the 1987 Copa America finals in Argentina.

Voted the South American Footballer of the Year in 1987.

Joined French club Montpellier in 1988.

Won the French Cup in 1990.

Led Colombia to the second round of the 1990 World Cup finals in Italy before losing to tournament outsiders Cameroons.

Moved to Spain and Valladolid after the tournament, teaming up with Colombian boss Pacho Maturana. But failed to find the form that made him such as star back home where he had become known as the 'South American Ruud Gullit', and not just for his silly Gullit-style haircut either!

Returned to Colombia in 1992 to join Atletico Junior of Barranquilla and then on to Nacional of Medellin.

Was part of the national team to thrash Argentina 5-0 in Buenos Aires in a World Cup qualifying game in 1993.

Carlos Valderrama...

Was voted South American Footballer of the Year for the second time in 1983.

Played for Colombia in the 1994 World Cup finals in America but the team failed to qualify beyond the first round. Days after returning home Colombian defender Andres Escobar was shot dead for scoring an own goal against the United States which sealed their fate.

Became the first Colombian player to reach a century of international appearances in a World Cup qualifying match in 1997.

Captained Colombia in the 1998 World Cup finals in France, but, once again, failed to make it beyond the first round. The 2-0 defeat by England was his last appearance in a World Cup match.

Has played 110 times for the national side, scoring 10 goals from his midfield position.

Marco Van Basten...

Signed by Ajax in 1980 after being spotted at the club's annual youth talent 'gala'.

Starred as a centre-forward for Holland at the World Youth Cup finals in 1983.

Scored 37 goals for Ajax in the 1985/86 season, earning him the 'Golden Boot' award for being top European marksman.

Captained Ajax to victory in the 1987 European Cup Winners' Cup Final against Lokomotiv Leipzig, scoring the winning goal.

Moved to Milan for £1.5 million after scoring 128 League goals for Ajax in just 133 appearances.

Won the Italian League Championship with AC Milan in 1988, their first title win in ten years, after teaming up with fellow Dutch striker Ruud Gullit.

Went on to star in the 1988 European Championships, scoring a wonderful long-range volley to secure the title with a 2-0 victory over the Soviet Union. In all he scored five goals in this tournament and finished top scorer. Three of his goals came against England, the last player to score a hat-trick against them.

Won the European Footballer of the Year award in 1988.

Scored twice as AC Milan beat Steaua Bucharest 4-0 in the 1989 European Champions Cup Final.

Was voted the European Footballer of the Year for the second time in 1989.

Marco Van Basten...

Became the first Dutchman to score five international goals in a match when he helped thrash Malta in 1990. (Bosman had achieved the feat in 1987 in a game against Cyprus but the match was declared void.)

Helped AC Milan win the 1990 European Champions Cup by beating Portugese side Benfica 1-0.

Played in the 1990 World Cup finals in Italy but were knocked out in the second round, losing 2-1 to eventual winners West Germany.

Helped secure a second League title with his club in 1992.

Missed a decisive penalty for Holland in the semi-final shoot-out of the 1992 European Championships against Denmark.

Retired from international football in 1992, making 58 appearances for his country, scoring 24 goals.

Became only the third player ever to have been voted the European Player of the Year award in 1992, joining Johan Cruyff and Michel Platini.

Won a third League title with Milan in 1993.

Played his final game in the 1-0 defeat by Marseille in the 1993 European Champions Cup Final in Munich. Persistant ankle injuries had cut short his brilliant career.

Ray Wilkins...

Signed for Chelsea as a 16-year old in 1973.

Became Chelsea's youngest ever captain when he wore the armband in 1975, aged just 18.

Made his England debut in 1976.

Moved to Manchester United in 1979 for a club record £825,000. He had played 179 League games for Chelsea, scoring 30 goals.

Scored an amazing goal as Manchester United beat relegated Brighton 4-0 in the 1983 FA Cup Final replay.

Played 160 League games for United, scoring 7 goals before moving to AC Milan in 1984 for another club record fee of £1.5 million.

After staying with the Italian giants for three years, and not winning a single trophy, he moved to Paris St Germain, only to be whisked away immediately by Graeme Souness

Ray Wilkins...

at Rangers.

Became the first Englishman to be sent off during a World Cup finals tournament when he threw the ball at the referee during England's 0-0 frustrating draw with Morocco.

He made just one more appearance for England after this dismissal, earning his 84th cap.

After playing 70 League games for Rangers, scoring just 2 goals, he moved back to London and played with QPR in 1989.

After playing 154 League games for the club he was tempted into management at Crystal Palace in 1994. After just one game as player/coach, a 6-1 thrashing at home by Liverpool, he returned to Loftus Road to take on the same role.

His first full season in charge was a nightmare as QPR were relegated in the 1995/96 season and he was forced to quit.

Became something of a footballing nomad from then on, appearing first for Scottish club Hibernian, before playing for three more clubs in the same season, Wycombe Wanderers, Millwall and Leyton Orient.

Joined his former England colleague Kevin Keegan at Fulham in 1997, taking over as team coach. However, two into one don't go and he was publicly sacked before the season had ended.

Bob Wilson...

Before becoming a professional footballer in 1964 he was a qualified schoolteacher.

Helped Arsenal win their first European trophy by beating Anderlecht 4-3 on aggregate to win the 1970 Fairs Cup.

Had a marvellous season in 1970/71, helping Arsenal to their first League and FA Cup double, first by pipping Leeds United to the League title, and then by beating Liverpool in the FA Cup Final.

Made just two appearances for Scotland, both in 1971, against Portugal and Holland, Scotland lost both matches.

Retired from playing in 1973.

Went on to become an anchorman for BBC football programmes such as *Football Focus*.

Moved to ITV in 1994 to become the station's main football presenter.

Is still the Arsenal goalkeeping coach.

Billy Wright...

Signed professional terms with Wolverhampton Wanderers, his only League club, in 1940, even though the current manager, Major Buckley, thought he was too small to make the grade.

Made his England debut in 1946 in a match against Scotland.

Captained Wolves in their 3-1 victory over Leicester City in the 1949 FA Cup Final.

Finished runner-up in the First Division with Wolves in 1950.

Played at wing-half and then centre-half in the 1950 World Cup finals in America, crashing out, unfortunately, against the host nation after a shock 1-0 defeat.

Voted Footballer of the Year in 1952.

Had the unfortunate honour of captaining England in their 6-3 defeat by Hungary in 1953, and then again in the 7-1 thrashing by the same country the following year.

Led Wolves to the club's first ever League title in 1954.

Played for England in the 1954 World Cup finals in Switzerland.

Finished runner-up in the First Division with Wolves in 1955.

Collected another League title with Wolves in 1958.

Played for England in the 1958 World Cup finals in Sweden.

Billy Wright...

Won his 100th England cap in 1959 in a game against Scotland, becoming the first man to pass the century mark for England.

Won his third League title with Wolves in 1959.

Retired at the start of the following season after being dropped in a friendly game by the manager Stan Cullis. He had played 491 League games for the club and scored 13 goals.

Went on to play his 105th and last international in 1959 in a game against the USA. He had missed just three of England's games since his first cap and had been captain on 90 occassions, 70 of which were in consecutive matches, a record which still stands.

Was awarded a CBE in 1959 for his services to football.

Took over as manager at Arsenal in 1962.

Parted company with the Gunners in 1966 and moved to television as a match analyst, before becoming a TV executive.

Became a director at Wolves in 1990.

Died in September 1994 at the age of 70.

Ian Wright...

Made his League debut with Crystal Palace in 1985.

Moved to Arsenal in September 1991 for £2.5 million, becoming the Gunners record buy and Palace's record sale.

Made his England debut in 1991.

Scored a hat-trick against Bolton in September 1997 to become Arsenal's most-prolific scorer in all competitions, beating Cliff Bastin's record of 178 goals.

Helped Arsenal win the domestic cup double in 1993, beating Sheffield Wednesday 2-1 in both the League Cup and FA Cup Finals.

Beat Parma 1-0 (for a change!) to win the European Cup Winners' Cup final in 1994, the club's first European trophy since 1970.

Went on to star in Arsenal's double winning season of 1997/98 before being surprisingly transferred to West Ham.

Was Arsenal's top scorer in each of the seasons he played for the club.

Was recalled to the national squad by Glenn Hoddle after being overlooked by Terry Venables, and helped England qualify for the 1998 World Cup finals in France. Unfortunately injury prevented him from taking part in the tournament.

Hosts his own television chat show on ITV.

Lev Yashin...

Joined Moscow Dynamo in 1946, originally as an ice hockey goaltender.

Made his first team debut in 1951.

Took over as first-choice keeper in 1953 after the regular goalkeeper, 'Tiger' Khomich, suffered a long-term injury.

Made his Soviet Union debut in 1954, helping defeat Sweden 3-2.

Won the Olympic Games gold medal in Melbourne in 1956.

Played in the 1954 World Cup finals with the Soviet Union.

Helped the Soviet team win the first European Championships in 1960 by beating Yugoslavia in the Final in Paris.

Played in the 1962 World Cup finals in Chile but lost against the hosts in the quarter-finals.

Became the only goalkeeper to win the European Footballer of the Year award in 1963.

Represented FIFA in a World XI at Wembley in a match to mark the centenary of the Football Association.

Played in the 1966 World Cup finals, helping the Soviet Union to a best-ever fourth place after losing to West Germany 2-1 in the semi final.

Lev Yashin...

Won the last of his 78 caps for the USSR in 1967.

Became, in 1968, the only footballer to be awarded the Soviet Union's ultimate honour, the Order of Lenin.

Was awarded with a farewell match in 1971, attended by world stars Pele, Eusebio, Bobby Charlton and Franz Beckenbauer. He was given the managers job at Dynamo the following day as a reward for his services to the country.

He had played an almost unbeatable 326 matches for Dynamo. Helping them to secure six League titles and two Soviet Cups.

Wore a distinctive all-black outfit for his games and was known, not surprisingly, as the 'Black Panther'.

Saved more than 150 penalties in his career.

Tragically died from cancer in 1990.

Zico...

Signed for Flamengo in 1968 but was considered to be too light. He was put on special diets and ordered to start weight training.

Made his international debut in 1975 playing against Uruguay. Scored with one of his famous free-kicks.

Became known in Brazil as 'the White Pele'.

Won the South American Footballer of the Year award in 1977.

Went to the World Cup finals in 1978 but fell out with the national team's coach, Claudio Coutinho, over team tactics.

Helped Flamengo win the1981 South American Club Cup Final against Cobreloa.

Played in the memorable 3-0 victory over Liverpool in the 1981 World Club Cup Final in Tokyo.

Was voted the South American Footballer of the Year for the second time in 1981.

Played in the 1982 World Cup finals but was knocked out by Italy in the second round.

Became South American Footballer of the Year for the third time in 1982.

Transferred to Italian club Udinese in 1982 but returned to Flamengo three years later.

Zico...

Was voted World Footballer of the Year in 1983.

Played in the 1986 World Cup finals in Mexico but, hampered by injury, never fulfilled his potential. He missed his penalty in the quarter-final shoot-out against France and brazil were eliminated.

Did not play for Brazil again after this tournament, finishing on a total of 88 international games, scoring 54 goals, only Pele has scored more goals for Brazil.

Retired from playing in 1992 and was appointed Brazil's Sports Minister.

Made a comeback for Kashima Antler in the newly formed Japanese J-League in 1993.

Returned to Brazil in 1997 and was appointed technical co-ordinator for the national team.

Zinedine Zidane...

Made his League debut in 1992 with Cannes.

Transferred to Bordeaux in 1994.

Was voted Best Young Footballer in France in 1994.

Made his international debut in August 1994 in a match against the Czech republic.

Played for Bordeaux in the 1996 UEFA Cup Final but ended up on the losing side. The club had qualified for the tournament that year through the much-maligned Inter-Toto Cup.

He moved to Juventus in 1996, going on to win the Italian League in his first season.

Collected a runner-up medal in the 1997 European Cup Final with Juventus after being beaten 3-1 by Borussia Dortmund.

Won the Italian League again in 1998.

Collected another runner-up medal in the 1998 European Cup Final, this time being beaten 1-0 by Real Madrid.

Captained France in the 1998 World Cup finals in his home country. He was banned for two games earlier in the tournament after getting himself sent off for stamping on a Saudi Arabian player in the first round. In the final he scored two headed goals in the 3-0 defeat of Brazil in the Final on 12 July 1998.

Dino Zoff...

Made his League debut with local club Udinese in 1961 and let in five goals! He played only 4 games for them in two years.

Transferred to Mantova in 1963 and went on to play between the sticks in 67 League matches.

Hit the big-time in 1967 with a transfer to Napoli.

Made his international debut in April 1968, playing in a 2-0 win over Bulgaria.

Kept his place in the national team as they went on to beat Yugoslavia in the 1968 European Championships in Italy.

Moved to Juventus in 1972 aged 30 and won seven League titles with the Turin giants.

Went 12 international games between 1973 and 1974 without conceding a goal. In total he played 1,143 minutes before Haiti's Emmanuel Sanon scored in Italy's first match of the 1994 World Cup finals.

Failed to qualify beyond the first round of the 1974 World Cup finals.

Won the 1977 UEFA Cup Final with Juventus.

Played in the 1978 World Cup finals in Argentina and secured fourth place.

Dino Zoff...

Captained Italy as they won the 1982 World Cup finals in Spain, beating West Germany 3-1 in the Final. Remarkably he was the second Juventus keeper to captain Italy to World Cup success. Gianpiero Combi had first achieved it in 1934.

Retired from playing in 1983 after a career spanning three decades.

Played a record 112 times for Italy and made almost 650 League appearances in his career.

Became Juventus coach in 1988.

Guided Juventus to success in the 1990 Italian Cup and then won the UEFA Cup Final a few weeks later, beating Fiorentina 3-0 on aggregate, despite being told earlier in the year that he would be sacked at the end of the season.

Joined Lazio in 1992 as first team coach before rising to become executive director of the club.

Andoni Zubizarreta...

Was discovered by Athletic Bilbao in 1981 while playing for regional club Alaves in the Basque region.

Played for the Spanish Under-21 team in 1984 when they lost to England in the Under-21 European Championships.

Made his full international debut in 1985, coming on as a substitute for Luis Arconada in a 3-1 victory over Finland.

Sold to Barcelona in 1986 for a then world record fee for goalkeepers of £1.2 million.

Played in the 1986 World Cup finals, losing to Belgium in a quarter-final penalty shoot-out.

Played in the 1990 World Cup finals, losing 2-1 to Yugoslavia in the second round.

Won the 1992 European Cup with a 1-0 extra-time win over Sampdoria at Wembley.

Became Spain's highest capped player in 1993 when he played in his 81st international in a World Cup qualifier against the Republic of Ireland in Dublin.

Played in the humiliating 4-0 defeat by AC Milan in the 1994 European Champions Cup Final.

Released by Barcelona on a free transfer in 1994 and signed for Valencia.

Played in his third World Cup finals in 1994, losing to Italy in the quarter-finals in America.

Helped Spain qualify for the 1998 World Cup finals in France, reaching a record 112 international caps for his country.

CLUB

CUP

RESULTS

FA Cup...

Year	Winner			Runner-up
1923	**Bolton Wanderers**	**2**	**0**	**West Ham Utd**
1924	Newcastle Utd	2	0	Aston Villa
1925	**Sheffield Utd**	**1**	**0**	**Cardiff City**
1926	Bolton Wanderers	1	0	Manchester City
1927	**Cardiff City**	**1**	**0**	**Arsenal**
1928	Blackburn Rovers	3	1	Huddersfield Town
1929	**Bolton Wanderers**	**2**	**0**	**Portsmouth**
1930	Arsenal	2	0	Huddersfield Town
1931	**WBA**	**2**	**1**	**Birmingham City**
1932	Newcastle Utd	2	1	Arsenal
1933	**Everton**	**3**	**0**	**Manchester City**
1934	Manchester City	2	1	Portsmouth
1935	**Sheffield Wed**	**4**	**2**	**WBA**
1936	Arsenal	1	0	Sheffield Utd
1937	**Sunderland**	**3**	**1**	**Preston North End**
1938	Preston North End	1	0	Huddersfield Town*
1939	**Portsmouth**	**4**	**1**	**Wolves**
1946	Derby County	4	1	Charlton Athletic*
1947	**Charlton Athletic**	**1**	**0**	**Burnley***
1948	Manchester Utd	4	2	Blackpool
1949	**Wolves**	**3**	**1**	**Leicester City**
1950	Arsenal	2	0	Liverpool
1951	**Newcastle Utd**	**2**	**0**	**Blackpool**
1952	Newcastle Utd	1	0	Arsenal
1953	**Blackpool**	**4**	**3**	**Bolton Wanderers**
1954	WBA	3	2	Preston North End

FA Cup...

Year	Winner			Runner-up
1955	**Newcastle Utd**	3	1	**Manchester City**
1956	Manchester City	3	1	Birmingham City
1957	**Aston Villa**	2	1	**Manchester Utd**
1958	Bolton Wanderers	2	0	Manchester Utd
1959	**Nottingham Forest**	2	1	**Luton Town**
1960	Wolves	3	0	Blackburn Rovers
1961	**Tottenham Hotspur**	2	0	**Leicester City**
1962	Tottenham Hotspur	3	1	Burnley
1963	**Manchester Utd**	3	1	**Leicester City**
1964	West Ham Utd	3	2	Preston North End
1965	**Liverpool**	2	1	**Leeds Utd***
1966	Everton	3	2	Sheffield Wednesday
1967	**Tottenham Hotspur**	2	1	**Chelsea**
1968	WBA	1	0	Everton*
1969	**Manchester City**	1	0	**Leicester City**
1970	Chelsea	2	2	Leeds Utd
	Chelsea	2	1	**Leeds Utd (r)**
1971	Arsenal	2	1	Liverpool*
1972	**Leeds Utd**	1	0	**Arsenal**
1973	Sunderland	1	0	Leeds Utd
1974	**Liverpool**	3	0	**Newcastle Utd**
1975	West Ham Utd	2	0	Fulham
1976	**Southampton**	1	0	**Manchester Utd**
1977	Manchester Utd	2	1	Liverpool
1978	**Ipswich Town**	1	0	**Arsenal**
1979	Arsenal	3	2	Manchester Utd

FA Cup...

Year	Winner			Runner-up
1980	**West Ham Utd**	**1**	**0**	**Arsenal**
1981	Tottenham Hotspur	1	1	Manchester City
	Tottenham Hotspur	**3**	**2**	**Manchester City (r)**
1982	Tottenham Hotspur	1	1	QPR
	Tottenham Hotspur	**1**	**0**	**QPR (r)**
1983	Manchester Utd	2	2	Brighton
	Manchester Utd	**4**	**0**	**Brighton (r)**
1984	Everton	2	0	Watford
1985	**Manchester Utd**	**1**	**0**	**Everton***
1986	Liverpool	3	1	Everton
1987	**Coventry City**	**3**	**2**	**Tottenham Hotspur***
1988	Wimbledon	1	0	Liverpool
1989	**Liverpool**	**3**	**2**	**Everton***
1990	Manchester Utd	3	3	Crystal Palace
	Manchester Utd	**1**	**0**	**Crystal Palace (r)**
1991	Tottenham Hotspur	2	1	Nottingham Forest*
1992	**Liverpool**	**2**	**0**	**Sunderland**
1993	Arsenal	1	1	Sheffield Wed
	Arsenal	**2**	**1**	**Sheffield Wed (r)**
1994	Manchester Utd	4	0	Chelsea
1995	**Everton**	**1**	**0**	**Manchester Utd**
1996	Manchester United	1	0	Everton
1997	**Chelsea**	**2**	**0**	**Middlesbrough**
1998	Arsenal	2	0	Newcastle United

* = after extra time. (r) = replay

League Cup...

1961	Aston Villa	0	2	Rotherham Utd (1st Leg)
	Aston Villa	3	2	Rotherham Utd (2nd Leg)*
1962	Norwich City	3	0	Rochdale (1st Leg)
	Norwich City	1	0	Rochdale (2nd Leg)
1963	Birmingham City	3	1	Aston Villa (1st Leg)
	Birmingham City	0	0	Aston Villa (2nd Leg)
1964	Leicester City	1	1	Stoke City (1st Leg)
	Leicester City	3	2	Stoke City (2nd Leg)
1965	Chelsea	3	2	Leicester City (1st Leg)
	Chelsea	0	0	Leicester City (2nd Leg)
1966	West Brom	1	2	West Ham Utd (1st Leg)
	West Brom	4	1	West Ham Utd (2nd Leg)
1967	QPR	3	2	West Brom
1968	Leeds Utd	1	0	Arsenal
1969	Swindon Town	3	1	Arsenal*
1970	Manchester City	2	1	West Brom*
1971	Tottenham Hotspur	2	0	Aston Villa
1972	Stoke City	2	1	Chelsea

League Cup...

1973	**Tottenham Hotspur**	**1**	**0**	**Norwich City**
1974	Wolves	2	1	Manchester City
1975	**Aston Villa**	**1**	**0**	**Norwich City**
1976	Manchester City	2	1	Newcastle Utd
1977	**Aston Villa**	**3**	**2**	**Everton***
1978	Nottingham Forest	1	0	Liverpool*
1979	**Nottingham Forest**	**3**	**2**	**Southampton**
1980	Wolves	1	0	Nottingham Forest
1981	**Liverpool**	**2**	**1**	**West Ham Utd***

Milk Cup

1982	Liverpool	3	1	Tottenham Hotspur*
1983	**Liverpool**	**2**	**1**	**Manchester Utd ***
1984	Liverpool	1	0	Everton*
1985	**Norwich City**	**1**	**0**	**Sunderland**
1986	Oxford Utd	3	0	QPR

Littlewoods Cup

1987	**Arsenal**	**2**	**1**	**Liverpool**
1988	Luton Town	3	2	Arsenal

League Cup...

1989	**Nottingham Forest**	**3**	**1**	**Luton Town**
1990	Nottingham Forest	1	0	Oldham Athletic

Rumbelows Cup

1991	**Sheffield Wed.**	**1**	**0**	**Manchester Utd**
1992	Manchester Utd	1	0	Nottingham Forest

Coca-Cola Cup

1993	**Arsenal**	**2**	**1**	**Sheffield Wed.**
1994	Aston Villa	3	1	Manchester Utd
1995	**Liverpool**	**2**	**1**	**Bolton Wanderers**
1996	Aston Villa	3	0	Leeds Utd
1997	**Leicester City**	**1**	**1**	**Middlesbrough**
	Leicester City	1	0	Middlesbrough (r)*
1998	**Chelsea**	**2**	**0**	**Middlesbrough**

Worthington Cup

1998	Tottenham Hotspur	1	0	Leicester City

Scottish FA Cup...

Year		Score		
1923	**Celtic**	1	0	Hibernian
1924	Airdrieonians	2	0	Hibernian
1925	**Celtic**	2	1	**Dundee**
1926	St. Mirren	2	0	Celtic
1927	**Celtic**	3	1	**East Fife**
1928	Rangers	4	0	Celtic
1929	**Kilmarnock**	2	0	**Rangers**
1930	Rangers	0	0	Partick Thistle
	Rangers	2	1	**Partick Thistle (r)**
1931	Celtic	2	2	Motherwell
	Celtic	4	2	**Motherwell (r)**
1932	Rangers	1	1	Kilmarnock
	Rangers	3	0	**Kilmarnock (r)**
1933	Celtic	1	0	Motherwell
1934	**Rangers**	5	0	**St. Mirren**
1935	Rangers	2	1	Hamilton Athletic
1936	**Rangers**	1	0	**Third Lanark**
1937	Celtic	2	1	Aberdeen
1938	**East Fife**	1	1	**Kilmarnock**
	East Fife	4	2	Kilmarnock (r)
1939	**Clyde**	4	0	**Motherwell**
1947	Aberdeen	2	1	Hibernian
1948	**Rangers**	1	1	**Morton**
	Rangers	1	0	Morton (r)
1949	**Rangers**	4	1	**Clyde**
1950	Rangers	3	0	East Fife
1951	**Celtic**	1	0	**Motherwell**
1952	Motherwell	4	0	Dundee
1953	**Rangers**	1	1	**Aberdeen**

Scottish FA Cup...

	Rangers	1	0	Aberdeen
1954	**Celtic**	**2**	**1**	**Aberdeen**
1955	Clyde	1	1	Celtic
	Clyde	**1**	**0**	**Celtic (r)**
1956	Hearts	3	1	Celtic
1957	**Falkirk**	**1**	**1**	**Kilmarnock**
	Falkirk	2	1	Kilmarnock (r)
1958	**Clyde**	**1**	**0**	**Hibernian**
1959	St. Mirren	3	1	Aberdeen
1960	**Rangers**	**2**	**0**	**Kilmarnock**
1961	Dunfermline Athletic	0	0	Celtic
	Dunfermline Athletic	**2**	**0**	**Celtic**
1962	Rangers	2	0	St. Mirren
1963	**Rangers**	**1**	**1**	**Celtic**
	Rangers	3	0	Celtic (r)
1964	**Rangers**	**3**	**1**	**Dundee**
1965	Celtic	3	2	Dunfermline Athletic
1966	**Rangers**	**0**	**0**	**Celtic**
	Rangers	1	0	Celtic (r)
1967	**Celtic**	**2**	**0**	**Aberdeen**
1968	Dunfermline Athletic	3	1	Hearts
1969	**Celtic**	**4**	**0**	**Rangers**
1970	Aberdeen	3	1	Celtic
1971	**Celtic**	**1**	**1**	**Rangers**
	Celtic	2	1	Rangers (r)
1972	**Celtic**	**6**	**1**	**Hibernian**
1973	Rangers	3	2	Celtic
1974	**Celtic**	**3**	**0**	**Dundee United**
1975	Celtic	3	1	Airdrieonians

Scottish FA Cup...

1976	**Rangers**	**3**	**1**	**Hearts**
1977	Celtic	1	0	Rangers
1978	**Rangers**	**2**	**1**	**Aberdeen**
1979	Rangers	0	0	Hibernian
	Rangers	**0**	**0**	**Hibernian (r)**
	Rangers	3	2	Hibernian (r)
1980	**Celtic**	**1**	**0**	**Rangers**
1981	Rangers	0	0	Dundee United
	Rangers	**4**	**1**	**Dundee United (r)**
1982	Aberdeen	4	1	Rangers*
1983	**Aberdeen**	**1**	**0**	**Rangers***
1984	Aberdeen	2	1	Celtic*
1985	**Celtic**	**2**	**1**	**Dundee United**
1986	Aberdeen	3	0	Hearts
1987	**St. Mirren**	**1**	**0**	**Dundee United***
1988	Celtic	2	1	Dundee United
1989	**Celtic**	**1**	**0**	**Rangers**
1990	Aberdeen	0	0	Celtic*
	Aberdeen won 9-8 on penalties			
1991	Motherwell	4	3	Dundee United*
1992	**Rangers**	**2**	**1**	**Airdrieonians**
1993	Rangers	2	1	Aberdeen
1994	**Dundee United**	**1**	**0**	**Rangers**
1995	Celtic	1	0	Airdrieonians
1996	**Rangers**	**5**	**1**	**Hearts**
1997	Kilmarnock	1	0	Falkirk
1998	**Hearts**	**2**	**1**	**Rangers**

* = after extra time. (r) = replay

Scottish League Cup...

1961	Rangers	2	0	Kilmarnock
1962	**Rangers**	**1**	**1**	**Hearts**
	Rangers	3	1	Hearts (r)
1963	**Hearts**	**1**	**0**	**Kilmarnock**
1964	Rangers	5	0	Morton
1965	**Rangers**	**2**	**1**	**Celtic**
1966	Celtic	2	1	Rangers
1967	**Celtic**	**1**	**0**	**Rangers**
1968	Celtic	5	3	Dundee
1969	**Celtic**	**6**	**2**	**Hibernian**
1970	Celtic	1	0	St. Johnstone
1971	**Rangers**	**1**	**0**	**Celtic**
1972	Partick Thistle	4	1	Celtic
1973	**Hibernian**	**2**	**1**	**Celtic**
1974	Dundee	1	0	Celtic
1975	**Celtic**	**6**	**3**	**Hibernian**
1976	Rangers	1	0	Celtic
1977	**Aberdeen**	**2**	**1**	**Celtic**

Scottish League Cup...

1978	Rangers	2	1	Celtic
1979	**Rangers**	**2**	**1**	**Aberdeen**
1980	Dundee United	0	0	Aberdeen
	Dundee United	**3**	**0**	**Aberdeen**
1981	Dundee United	3	0	Dundee
1982	**Rangers**	**2**	**1**	**Dundee United**
1983	Celtic	2	1	Rangers
1984	**Rangers**	**3**	**2**	**Celtic**
1985	Rangers	1	0	Dundee United
1986	**Aberdeen**	**3**	**0**	**Hibernian**
1987	Rangers	2	1	Celtic
1988	**Rangers**	**3**	**3**	**Aberdeen**

Rangers won 5-3 on penalties

1989	Rangers	3	2	Aberdeen
1990	**Aberdeen**	**2**	**1**	**Rangers**
1991	Rangers	2	1	Celtic
1992	**Hibernian**	**2**	**0**	**Dunfermline Athletic**
1993	Rangers	2	1	Aberdeen

Scottish League Cup...

1994	**Rangers**	**2**	**1**	**Hibernian**
1995	Raith Rovers	2	2	Celtic

Raith Rovers won 6-5 on penalties.

1996	**Aberdeen**	**2**	**0**	**Dundee**
1997	Rangers	4	3	Hearts
1998	**Celtic**	**3**	**0**	**Dundee United**